School Effectiveness for Whom?

School Effectiveness for Whom?
Challenges to the School Effectiveness and School Improvement Movements

Edited by Roger Slee and Gaby Weiner
with Sally Tomlinson

FALMER PRESS
Taylor & Francis Group

UK	Falmer Press, 1 Gunpowder Square, London
USA	Falmer Press, Taylor & Francis Inc., 1900 Frost Road, Suite 101, Bristol, PA 19007

First published in 1998

A catalogue record for this book is available from the British Library

Library of Congress Cataloging-in-Publication Data are available on request

ISBN 0 7507 0669 4 cased
ISBN 0 7507 0670 8 paper

Jacket design by Caroline Archer

Typeset in 10/12pt Times by
Graphicraft Typesetters Ltd., Hong Kong.

Printed in Great Britain by Biddles Ltd., Guildford and King's Lynn on paper which has a specified pH value on final paper manufacture of not less than 7.5 and is therefore 'acid free'.

Every effort has been made to contact copyright holders for their permission to reprint material in this book. The publishers would be grateful to hear from any copyright holder who is not here acknowledged and will undertake to rectify any errors or omissions in future editions of this book.

Contents

Contents

Chapter 1

Introduction: School Effectiveness for Whom?

Roger Slee and Gaby Weiner

Educational Failure and the Crisis of Schooling

Crisis in education? What crisis? Recent media reportage on schooling in Britain, and elsewhere, is characterized by panics over a litany of alleged failures in state schooling:

- falling standards of student achievement compared with the suggested performance of British students of past generations and against the performance of their international peers in Western Europe and Pacific-rim nations;
- the failure of urban comprehensive schools;
- teacher incompetence;
- 'out of control' student behaviour;
- inadequate teacher training in basic skills instruction in English and mathematics;
- irrelevant educational research in higher education.

Reflecting upon the 'despairing' and 'dismissive' national discussion of public schools in the United States, Mike Rose (1995) condemns the distorted reports of the failure of public education arguing that the dominance of such a discourse blinds us to the complex lives lived out in the classroom.

> It [the discourse of failure] pre-empts careful analysis of one of the nation's most significant democratic projects. And it engenders a mood of cynicism and retrenchment, preparing the public mind for extreme responses: increased layers of testing and control, denial of new resources — even the assertion that money doesn't affect a school's performance — and the curative effects of free market forces via vouchers and privatization. (Rose, 1995, p. 2)

The effective schooling research, in conjunction with its operational branch — the school improvement movement — has been adopted by policy-makers pursuant to the resolution of these alleged crises in state education (Mortimore, 1995; Barber, 1995 and 1996; Reynolds and Farrell, 1996). The academic voice of some sections of the school effectiveness research community are more tentative and considerate of the limitations of their research paradigm.

> An important conclusion that can be derived from research is that the margins for schools and classrooms are small. About 12 to 18 per cent of the variance in student outcomes can be explained by classroom and school factors . . . (Creemers, 1994, p. 20)

Reynolds (1992) and Creemers and Reynolds (1989) have been similarly cautious in his call for effectiveness researchers to resist superficial generalizing, and to problematize their work beyond producing endless lists of factors to be taken up as reform recipes by the school improvers. There is a problem that in different fora the strength of this plea lapses as he argues the case for 'high reliability organizations' in school and collapses effectiveness, improvement and inclusion together as a consistent set of educational goals (e.g. Reynolds, 1995; Reynolds and Ramasut, 1993). Geoff Whitty (1997) recently reminded us of Gerald Grace's well-founded, if cynical, observation that 'too often . . . the "bigger picture" is not entirely ignored but alluded to in . . . "contextual rhetoric" at the beginning of a book or paper and then forgotten' (p. 156).

As a number of the contributors to this book contend, the discourse of effective schooling and school improvement is narrow in its assessment of school effects (see Chapter 7, Lingard, Ladwig and Luke), reducing school learning to discrete assessable and comparable fragments of academic knowledge.

> But if our understanding of schooling and the conception we have of what's possible emerge primarily from these findings, then what we can imagine for public education will be terribly narrow and impoverished . . . If we think about education largely in relation to economic competitiveness, then we lose sight of the fact that school has to be about more than economy. If we determine success primarily in terms of test scores, then we ignore the social, moral and aesthetic dimensions of teaching and learning — and, as well, we'll miss those considerable intellectual achievements which aren't easily quantifiable. If we judge one school according to the success of another, we could well diminish the particular ways the first school serves its community. (Rose, 1995, pp. 2 and 3)

Such reductionism resonates with the neo-conservative discourse of performativity, efficiency and the highly contested notion of academic standards (see Ball, Chapter 6). In its apparent clarity and claims to common sense, that is that all schools should aim to be as effective as possible, school effectiveness is, in our view, epistemologically problematic and politically promiscuous and malleable (see Chapter 2, Hamilton; Slee, Chapter 8). The current dominance of school effectiveness research and school improvement discourses in education policy-making is a manifestation of this. The aim of this book, and here we move into new territory, is to issue a comprehensive challenge to the claims, and silences, of school effectiveness research with the aim of providing a more theoretically robust basis for understanding, evaluating and developing the work of schools and the experiences of teachers and students.

This book should not, then, be dismissed as the naiveté of the displaced and disgruntled Left ideologues. We will argue that schooling does have its troubles. However, we maintain that the analysis of the nature and location of these troubles by the school effectiveness research literature, and in turn those writing DfEE policy off the back of this research, is oversimplified, misleading and thereby educationally and politically dangerous (notwithstanding claims of honorable intent). This book is offered as a considered interruption to the dominance of the school effectiveness juggernaught as it rides roughshod over educational policy-making and research.

A History for Failure

Mass compulsory education was originally established as a system for the allocation to and preparation of children for their eventual work and social class destination. Whatever changes that have been made over the years, in the aspect of class selection, schooling has been remarkably successful (Hatcher, 1996). In their extended research into the operational distortions and brutality of the education market place Gewirtz, Ball and Bowe (1995) reflect upon the deep historic structure of class as articulated through and reinforced by schooling in the UK and its most recent manifestations, notwithstanding the deflective liberal discourse applied to the vicissitudes of the market.

> Our contextual analysis of choice and class goes to the heart of the ideology of the market and the claims of classlessness and neutrality. Choice emerges as a major new factor in maintaining and indeed reinforcing social-class divisions and inequalities. The point is not that choice and the market have moved us away from what was a smoothly functioning egalitarian system of schooling to one that is unfair. That is crude and unrealistic. There were significant processes of differentiation and choice prior to 1988 (within and between schools). Some skillful and resourceful parents were always able to 'work the system' or buy a private education or gain other forms of advantage for their children. But post-1988, the stratagems of competitive advantage are now ideologically endorsed and practically facilitated by open enrolment, the deregulation of recruitment and parental choice. Well-resourced choosers now have free reign to guarantee and reproduce, as best they can, their existing cultural, social and economic advantages in the new complex and blurred hierarchy of schools. Class selection is revalorized by the market. (Gewirtz, Ball and Bowe, 1995, p. 23)

Education in Britain and elsewhere has centrally been involved in the allocation of success and failure. Schooling has acted as the (credentialling) turnstile for higher education and the skilled and profession-based workforce. The requirements of the unskilled labour market, together with domestic family service for girls and a segregated system of special education have colluded with schools to disguise the extent of educational failure. Truancy amongst girls who were allowed to remain at home to service the home was not recognized as an educational problem (Abbott and Breckinridge, 1917). The segregation of the least intellectually able in special schools for the feeble-minded was another example of how failure was individually pathologized and not considered the responsibility of the school. Barton (1987) considers 'special educational needs' to be an institutional sleight of hand, a euphemism for the failure of schools. At the end of the twentieth century, the crisis in the unskilled youth labour market (Polk and Tait, 1992; Marginson, 1994) combined with changing familial expectations for girls (Spender, 1982; Weiner, 1995), the emergence of the community and comprehensive school (Pring and Walford, 1997; Simon, 1997), the increased surveillance of and provision for 'special needs' in regular schools (Tomlinson, 1982; Lewis, 1993; Slee, 1995), the retention, and exclusion, patterns of the schooling of black boys (Gillborn, 1995; Sewell, 1997), and the introduction of marketization and the highly scrutinized and reported competition between schools (Ball, 1994; Gewirtz, Ball and Bowe, 1995) have each exposed the continuing failure of the nineteenth-century artifact of a system of mass compulsory education.

The response to the increased exposure of schooling's failure has been the evocation of crisis and panic — moral, academic and cultural. We suggest that the crisis is manufactured (Berliner and Biddle, 1995). Rather than attempt the transformation of a fundamentally flawed and exclusionary system of education, a distraction from the main issues is created — the collapse of many traditional areas of (male) unskilled and skilled work, bourgeois panic about losing economic and social privilege, loss of empire and the ravages of post-colonialism (cultural restorationism), and so the list goes on. The sense of crisis has been addressed and exacerbated by the further condensation or reduction of what constitutes success to a narrowing band of academic qualifications (Pring, 1997; Lawton, 1997) and a polarization of the means by which qualifications are achieved. From this we derive the 'good' and the 'bad' school, the good and bad teacher, and axiomatically those high risk students (the 'fractious and unruly' working-class and underclass, students from non-English speaking backgrounds, 'special needs' students, and so the list goes on) who must be driven out of normal educational provision to protect the school's place on the published league table.

To what extent are the school effectiveness and school improvement movements implicated in this manufactured crisis? Why does this book set out to challenge educational initiatives which appear to have broadly consensual and common-sense goals? Who could quarrel with the aims of making schools better, more effective, more efficient? Why are we so uneasy about educational strategies which appear to respond to the wishes of politicians, parents — to a nation perceived to be at risk? As Reynolds points out, surely cutting-edge schools of a cutting-edge nation need to aim for 'high reliability', so that children in different schools can reliably expect to have exactly the same experiences and all achieve the highest of standards.

As will become clear in this book, such apparent common-sense philosophies and strategies mask some fundamental flaws. Effective schooling is essentially functionalist, veering away from difficult questions about the purpose of schooling and its relationship to the future beyond the crudest forms of human capital theory. Whitty (1997) is clear in his assessment of a flawed research interest:

> Certainly the more optimistic versions of work in this genre tend to exaggerate the extent to which local agency can challenge structural inequalities. Often it is not so much the specific claims that are significant, but rather the silences . . . Even today, some of the school effectiveness and school improvement literature glosses over the fact that one conclusion to be drawn from a reading of the pioneering Fifteen

Thousand Hours research (Rutter et al., 1979) is that, if all schools performed as well as the best schools, the stratification of achievement by social class would be even more stark than it is now. (p. 156)

Effective schools? Effective for whom? Effective for what? Who in fact gains from the school effectiveness research and school improvement industries? We maintain that while purporting to be inclusive and comprehensive, school effectiveness research is riddled with errors: it is excluding (of children with special needs, black boys, so-called clever girls), it is normative and regulatory (operating mainly within narrow sets of performance indicators), it is bureaucratic and disempowering. It focuses exclusively on the processes and internal constructs of schooling, apparently disconnected from education's social end — adulthood. School effectiveness seems to be neither interested nor very effective in preparing children for citizenship, parenthood or work (Ranson, 1997).

The readers of this book will observe thematic consistency and overlap throughout the chapters that follow. Let us précis some of these themes under the following headings.

School Effectiveness Research is Undermined by Epistemic and Methodological Reductionism

School effectiveness research bleaches context from its analytic frame. It is silent on the impact of the National Curriculum, the marketization of schooling, the press for selected entry and grant-maintained distortions of the relative performance of schools. There is a taken-for-granted set of assumptions about the purpose of schooling and what counts for the benchmarks for determining an effective education. The politics of identity and failure are irrelevant data for the school effectiveness researcher. Elliot's (1996, p. 204) conviction is that the outcome of the costly research and debate is a set of 'enduring truths' which are nothing but a set of platitudes. Nixon and his colleagues (1997) have argued that '. . . the "enduring truths" of school effectiveness research, have failed to recognize the impact of social and economic disadvantage upon learning', and argue against the normalizing project of school effectiveness for a localized community action research in order that schools 'reclaim their professional legitimacy and authority' (p. 122). School effectiveness research must square up to the challenge of power and method (Gitlin, 1994; Ladwig and Gore, 1994) as well as more rigorously addressing the challenges (see Brown, Chapter 4) to its claims to scientific status (Reynolds, 1995).

Political Opportunism and the Discourse of Performativity

The contributors to this book collectively form a picture of the school effectiveness and school improvement movement which is opportunistic and comfortable with a discourse of public policy which defines educational performance according to a narrow and fragmented set of test criteria. Students' achievements in pencil and paper limited and culturally specific tests are then used as the data for comparison and the compilation of published league tables. This discourse of performativity is characterized by 'incoherence and perversity' (Ball, 1996, p. 2). Ball illustrates this point by drawing our attention to the Conservative Government's celebration of increasing pass rates at GCSE level as testimony to their commitment to 'raising standards' and simultaneously condemning the data as evidence of 'declining standards'. The political appeal and utility of school effectiveness research and the school improvement movement is in its apparent statistical sophistication and provision of a 'ready reckoner' — a checklist of benchmarks against which to measure students' and schools' performances.

In proffering lists of factors characteristic to 'effective schools', schools are pathologized as good or bad schools. Teachers are adjudicated according to their adherence to disconnected criteria and school administrators are scored in relation to their personal embodiment of those attitudes and behaviours which support the effective schools model. This is entirely consistent with the extremely costly and punitive mode of operation of the educational inspection agency. We use the term 'agency' quite deliberately as inspection franchising is increasingly sub-contracted to the lowest bidders.

Effectiveness Models Favour the Privileged and Punish the Disadvantaged

A unifying theme throughout the ensuing chapters is the general failure of school effectiveness and school improvement discourses for disadvantaged students. This stems from the previously mentioned failure within this research genre to broaden its analysis to a contextualized analysis of school effects (see Chapter 7: Lingard, Ladwig and Luke). The liberal claim that ineffective or failing schools, by adopting the characteristics of those schools deemed successful, can also tread the path to success, is naive or disingenuous. Attempts to link school effectiveness research with the discourse of educational inclusion are challenged by this book (see Slee, Chapter 8, this volume). The normalizing project of school effectiveness obstructs the serious consideration of the politics of identity and difference in schools and the affirmation of the broader educational goals of social justice and democracy (Howe, 1997; Fraser, 1997).

The Structure of the Book

This book hosts an impressive collection of chapters from serious and highly regarded academics noted for their considered approaches to educational research and debate. We resist the current temptation of a form of educational populism, verging on journalese, which dominates educational writing and policy-making and corrals the discussion of schooling within narrowly prescribed parameters of 'raising stand-ards' and 'school effectiveness'. Organized into three sections: 1. Setting the Debates; 2. Theorizing the Debates; and 3. Experiencing the Impacts of School Effectiveness Research and the School Improvement Movement, this book opens with a series of compelling, passionate and rational assessments of the debates surrounding school effectiveness research and the application of its findings through the school improve-ment movement. In Setting the Debates, David Hamilton issues a provocative and comprehensive challenge to the foundations and scope of the 'truth claims' of school effectiveness research. Joe Rea and Gaby Weiner reflect upon the debates raised by Hamilton as they bear down upon their work in an inner-London school and de-partment of teacher education. Margaret Brown takes up the a number of methodo-logical issues within the school effectiveness research paradigm and exposes them to critical scrutiny. Particular attention is paid to the following of superficial inter-national comparisons.

In Section 2, Theorizing the Debates, Hugh Lauder, Ian Jamieson and Felicity Wikeley establish the conceptual confusion within the research programme, high-lighting its limits and capabilities to suggest a range of models for school develop-ment. In the chapters by Stephen Ball and by Bob Lingard, Jim Ladwig and Allan Luke the reader is invited to engage with a robust analysis of context and social theory to identify the politics of school effectiveness discourses and to consider different sets of questions for educational research into school effects. Roger Slee takes issue with the school effectiveness and school improvement claims for im-proving the academic and social outcomes of so-called 'special educational needs students' and suggests that this normalizing research genre and its subsequent set of policy imperatives will further disadvantage students who embody the risk of undermining schools' performances in the academic league tables.

The third section of the book, Experiencing the Impacts of School Effective-ness Research and the School Improvement Movement transports the reader into the field where the effects of the school effectiveness and improvement movements are directly felt. Gerald Grace brings questions of value and principle back to ques-tions of schools' educational and pastoral role and discusses notions of effective-ness in relation to Catholic education. Pat Mahoney and Ian Hextall draw on their extended research into the Teacher Training Agency in the UK to show how this funding agency has used dominant models of effectiveness to define and shape teacher effectiveness and school leadership in teacher training. Bob Spooner and Sally Tomlinson provide forceful local accounts of the damaging discourse of school failure and identify the paradoxical and damaging impacts of official interventions on children's educational experiences. Sheila Riddell, Sally Brown and Jill Duffield employ their research findings from Scottish schools to argue for the greater applica-tion of qualitative research methods in the evaluation of schooling and educational policy-making.

We stress that the point of this book is not to be negative. The point is to recognize the inevitability of the failure of school effectiveness research and the school improvement movement, even in its own terms of reference, and to sound a warning. This is not a self-serving academic text to increase the stocks of the authors in higher education effectiveness benchmarks; it is a serious challenge to the dangerously narrow platform of school effectiveness research upon which education policy is being mounted.

References

ABBOTT, E. and BRECKINRIDGE, S.P. (1917) *Truancy and the Non-attendance in the Chicago Schools: A Study of the Social Aspects of the Compulsory Education and Child Labour Legislation of Illinois*, Chicago: University of Chicago Press.

BALL, S.J. (1994) *Education Reform: A Critical and Poststructural Approach*, Buckingham: Open University Press.

BALL, S.J. (1996) 'Performativity and fragmentation in "postmodern schooling"', Paper presented to the Postmodernity and the Fragmentation of Welfare Conference, University of Teeside, 9–10th September.

BARBER, M. (1995) 'From characteristics to strategy', *Times Educational Supplement*, October 6: II [School Effectiveness Feature].

BARBER, M. (1996) *The Learning Game*, London: Victor Gollancz.

BARTON, L. (ed.) (1987) *The Politics of Special Educational Needs*, London: Falmer Press.

BERLINER, D. and BIDDLE, B. (1995) *The Manufactured Crisis*, Reading, MA: Addison-Wesley.

CREEMERS, B.P.M. and REYNOLDS, D. (1989) 'The future development of school effectiveness and school improvement', in CREEMERS, B.P.M., PETERS, T. and REYNOLDS, D. (eds) *School Effectiveness & School Improvement: Proceedings of the Second International Congress, Rotterdam, 1989*, Austerdam, Swets & Zeitlinger.

CREEMERS, B.P.M. (1994) 'The history, value and purpose of school effectiveness studies', in REYNOLDS, D., CREEMERS, B.P.M., NESSELRODT, P.S., STRINGFIELD, S. and TEDDLIE, C. (eds) *Advances in School Effectiveness Research and Practice*, Kidlington: Pergamon, Elsevier Science.

ELLIOTT, J. (1996) 'School effectiveness research and its critics: Alternative visions of schooling', *Cambridge Journal of Education*, **26**, 2, pp. 199–224.

FRASER, J.W. (1997) *Reading, Writing and Justice: School Reform As If Democracy Matters*, New York: SUNY Press.

GEWIRTZ, S., BALL, S.J. and BOWE, R. (1995) *Markets, Choice and Equity in Education*, Buckingham: Open University Press.

GILLBORN, D. (1995) *Racism and Antiracism in Real Schools*, Buckingham: Open University Press.

GITLIN, A. (1994) 'The shifting terrain of methodological debates', in GITLIN, A. (ed.) *Power and Method: Political Activism and Educational Research*, New York: Routledge.

HATCHER, R. (1996) 'The limitations of the new social democratic agenda', in HATCHER, R. and JONES, K. (eds) *Education After the Conservatives*, Stoke on Trent: Trentham Books.

HOWE, K.R. (1997) *Understanding Equal Educational Opportunity: Social Justice, Democracy and Schooling*, New York: Teachers College Press.

LADWIG, J.G. and GORE, J.M. (1994) 'Extending power and specifying method within the discourse of activist research', in GITLIN, A. (ed.) *Power and Method: Political Activism and Educational Research*, New York: Routledge.

LAWTON, D. (1997) 'Values and education: A curriculum for the 21st century', Paper presented at the Values and the Curriculum Conference, University of London, 10th–11th April.

LEWIS, J. (1993) 'Integration in Victorian schools: Radical social policy or old wine?', in SLEE, R. (ed.) *Is There a Desk With My Name On It? The Politics of Integration*, London: Falmer Press.

MARGINSON, S. (1994) *Education and Public Policy in Australia*, Cambridge: Cambridge University Press.

MORTIMORE, P. (1995) 'Mappers of the best way forward', *Times Educational Supplement*, October 6: III [School Effectiveness Feature].

NIXON, J., MARTIN, J., MCKEOWN, P. and RANSON, S. (1997) 'Confronting "failure": Towards a pedagogy of recognition'. *International Journal of Inclusive Education*, **1**, 2, pp. 121–41.

POLK, K. and TAIT, D. (1992) 'Changing youth labour markets and youth lifestyles', *Youth Studies*, **9**, 1, pp. 17–23.

PRING, R. (1997) 'Educating persons', in PRING, R. and WALFORD, G. (eds) *Affirming the Comprehensive Ideal*, London: Falmer Press.

PRING, R. and WALFORD, G. (eds) (1997) *Affirming the Comprehensive Ideal*, London: Falmer Press.

RANSON, S. (1997) 'For citizenship and the remaking of civil society', in PRING, R. and WALFORD, G. (eds) *Affirming the Comprehensive Ideal*, London: Falmer Press.

REYNOLDS, D. (1989) 'Concluding address', in CREEMERS, B.P.M., PETERS, T. and REYNOLDS, D. (eds) *School Effectiveness and School Improvement: Proceedings of the Second International Congress Rotterdam*, Lisse: Swets & Zeitlinger.

REYNOLDS, D. (1992) 'School effectiveness and school improvement: An updated review of the British literature', in REYNOLDS, D. and CUTTANCE, P. (eds) *School Effectiveness: Research, Policy and Practice*, London: Cassell.

REYNOLDS, D. (1995) 'Using school effectiveness knowledge for children with special needs — The problems and possibilities', in CLARK, C., DYSON, A. and MILLWARD, A. (eds) *Towards Inclusive Schools?*, London: David Fulton Publishers.

REYNOLDS, D. and FARRELL, S. (1996) *Worlds Apart? A Review of International Surveys of Educational Achievement Involving England*, London: OFSTED.

REYNOLDS, D. and RAMASUT, A. (1993) 'Developing effective whole school approaches to special educational needs: From school effectiveness theory to school development practice', in SLEE, R. (ed.) *Is There a Desk With My Name On It? The Politics of Integration*, London: Falmer Press.

ROSE, M. (1995) *Possible Lives — The Promise of Public Education in America*, New York: Penguin Books.

SEWELL, T. (1997) *Black Masculinities and Schooling: How Black Boys Survive Modern Schooling*, Stoke on Trent: Trentham Books.

SIMON, B. (1997) 'A seismic change: Process and interpretation', in PRING, R. and WALFORD, G. (eds) *Affirming the Comprehensive Ideal*, London: Falmer Press.

SLEE, R. (1995) *Changing Theories and Practices of Discipline*, London: Falmer Press.

SPENDER, D. (1982) *Invisible Women: The Schooling Scandal*, London: Writers and Readers.

TOMLINSON, S. (1982) *A Sociology of Special Education*, London: Routledge and Kegan Paul.

WEINER, G. (1995) *Feminisms in Education: An Introduction*, Buckingham: Open University Press.

WHITTY, G. (1997) 'Social theory and education policy: The legacy of Karl Mannheim', *British Journal of Sociology of Education*, **18**, 2, pp. 149–63.

Part One

Setting the Debates

Chapter 2

The Idols of the Market Place

David Hamilton

> There are also idols formed by the intercourse and association of men with each other, which I call Idols of the Market-place, on account of the commerce and consort of men there. For it is by discourse that men associate; and words are imposed according to the apprehension of the vulgar. And therefore the ill and unfit choice of words wonderfully obstructs the understanding. Nor do the definitions or explanations wherewithin some things learned men are wont to guard and defend themselves, by any means set the matter right. But words plainly force and overrule the understanding, and throw all into confusion, and lead men away into numberless empty controversies and idle fancies. (Francis Bacon, *Novum Organum*, 1620, aphorism 43)

The school effectiveness rationale, promulgated in the 1990s, is unwarranted. Its claims to be authoritative do not succeed; its prescriptions cannot be justified by appeals to the canons of science; it embraces an unconvincing rhetoric redolent of Bacon's idols of the market place. This chapter focuses upon these weaknesses. It constitutes a response to two aspects of the school effectiveness rationale. The first part — Peddling Feel-good Fictions (see also Hamilton, 1996) — addresses the logic of an argument which, in its turn, generates policy prescriptions cast in the form of 'key characteristics of effective schools'. And the second part of this chapter — Fordism by Fiat — examines the consequences of such a rationale, in this case focusing on the distributive assumption that effective schools are necessarily effective for all pupils.

Peddling Feel-good Fictions

Effective schooling has become an global industry. Its activities embrace four processes: research, development, marketing and sales. Research entails the construction of new prototypes; development entails the commodification of these prototypes; marketing entails the promotion of these commodities; and sales entails efforts to ensure that market returns exceed financial investment. The school effectiveness industry, therefore, stands at the intersection of educational research and social engineering.

There is another perspective on school effectiveness research. Its efforts cloak school practices in a progressive, social-darwinist, eugenic rationale. It is progressive because it seeks more efficient and effective ways of steering social progress. It is social-darwinist because it accepts survival of the fittest. And it is eugenic because it privileges the desirable and seeks to eliminate the negative.

But something else lurks beneath this liberal veneer. School effectiveness research underwrites, I suggest, a pathological view of public education in the late twentieth century. There is, it appears, a plague on all our houses. Teachers have been infected; schools have been contaminated; and classroom practices have become degenerative and dysfunctional. In short, schools have become sick institutions. They are a threat to the health of the economic order. Their decline must be countered with potent remedies. Emergency and invasive treatments are targeted. Schools need shock therapy administered by outside agencies. Terminal cases merit organ transplants (viz. new heads or governing bodies). And, above all, every school requires targeted inset therapy. Senior management teams deserve booster steroids to strengthen their macho leadership, while their remaining staff require regular implants of appraisal-administered HRT (Human Resource Technology) to attenuate their curriculum and classroom excesses.

From this last perspective, then, school effectiveness research hankers for prototypes — in the form of tablets, magic bullets or smart missiles — that are the high-tech analogues of the lobotomies and hysterectomies of the nineteenth century. It is no accident that David Reynolds (University of Newcastle-upon-Tyne), who co-authored a 'mission statement' on school effectiveness and school improvement in 1990, was moved five years later to caution against quackery: 'we need to avoid peddling simplistic school effectiveness snake oil as a cure-all' (*Times Educational Supplement*, 16th June, 1995, p. 19). For these reasons, school effectiveness research is technically and morally problematic. Its research findings and associated prescriptions cannot be taken on trust. They are no more than a cluster of assumptions, claims and propositions. They are arguments to be scrutinized, not prescriptions to be swallowed.

Key Characteristics of Effective Schools (Sammons, Hillman and Mortimore, 1995) illustrates these problems. It is a 'review of school effectiveness research', commissioned in 1994 by the Office for Standards in Education (OFSTED). The reviewers, based at the International School Effectiveness and Improvement Centre of the London University Institute of Education, saw their task as twofold. First, to summarize 'current knowledge' about school effectiveness; and secondly, to respond to OFSTED's request for 'an analysis of the key determinants of school effectiveness in secondary and primary schools' (p. 1). This task redefinition is noteworthy. The extension of OFSTED's remit — the attention to 'current knowledge' as well as 'key determinants' — suggests that the reviewers were reluctant to focus unilaterally on causality. There was, they imply, a 'need for caution' in interpreting 'findings concerning key determinants' (p. 1).

The redefinition also suggests that the sponsors and researchers did not share the same view of causality. OFSTED appears to espouse a straightforward, linear model of causality. In linear systems, a straightforward cause leads to a straightforward effect. In non-linear systems the outcome is so sensitive to initial conditions that a minuscule change in the situation at the beginning of the process may result in a large difference at the end. OFSTED assumes that, in cases of straightforward causality, outcomes can be linked directly and unambiguously to inputs. OFSTED believes, in effect, that it is possible to predict the final resting place of a set of billiard balls on the basis of the prior cue stroke. The Institute of Education reviewers, however, shared a more elaborate view of causality. They recognized that schooling cannot be reduced to the dynamics of the billiard table. If several balls are simultaneously impelled by separate cues, the play may remain straightforward; but it is much more difficult to distinguish the key determinants. Yet, if it is assumed that schools and classrooms are multivariate, non-linear, adaptive systems, their behaviour ceases even to be statistically straightforward. The Institute of Education reviewers candidly acknowledge such problems of interpretation and prediction. Yet, having voiced a series of 'caveats' (p. 2), they proceed to dilute or disregard them. The notion of key determinants is abandoned, to be immediately replaced by 'key factors' (p. 8).

Semantic sleight of hand continues. The key factors are packaged in an 'accessible [i.e. tabular] format' (p. 8). The preamble to this table of eleven factors denotes them as 'correlates *of* effectiveness' whereas the table itself is headed 'eleven factors *for* effective schools' (p. 8, emphasis added). Social engineering assumptions are smuggled back into the analysis. The factors, that is, provide a better understanding of possible 'mechanisms' of effectiveness (p. 8).

Once the factors have been identified, however, their aggregation presents further problems. The tacit OFSTED assumption seems to be that causal factors are independent, universal and additive; that is, they do not interfere with each other and are uninfluenced by their contexts. The OFSTED reviewers, in return, fully acknowledge that these conditions rarely apply in the multivariate world of education. Yet, as before, they appear disinclined to confront OFSTED's innocent assumptions. First, they aggregate results from different studies conducted at different times in different countries. And secondly, they aggregate factors into a summary table. The aspiration to simplify — in the interests of packaging and marketing — becomes self-defeating.

The reviewers run into difficulties because they conflate clarification (achieving 'better understanding') with simplification (the extraction of 'key determinants') (p. 1). They are careful to identify recurrent problems in school effectiveness research. They report, for instance, that previous reviews had commented that 'there is no consensus yet on just what constitutes an effective school' (p. 3). And they quote another author to the effect that 'defining the effectiveness of a particular school always requires choice among competing values' and that 'criteria of effectiveness will be the subject of political debate' (p. 3). Overall, the Institute of Education reviewers seem to accept that current school effectiveness debates are as liable to disagreement as any other area of human endeavour. But they make no effort to insert this caveat into their analysis. Clarification is about the honouring of complexity, not its obfuscation.

The conflation of simplification and clarification is also evident elsewhere in the reviewer's arguments. Effective schools, they suggest, are characterized by 'shared vision and goals' (Key Factor Two) which, in turn, are contingent upon notions of 'a sense of ownership', 'strong input from staff' and 'reciprocal relationships of support and respect' among pupils and staff (p. 12).

Elsewhere, however, the review projects a different model of collegiality. Key Factor One is 'professional leadership', a characteristic that, among other things, should 'usually' be 'firm and purposeful'. Under this last criterion, as a sub-heading, the reviewers go on to quote an American study which suggested that, 'in the early years of . . . an improvement drive' effectiveness is also enhanced by 'vigorous selection and *replacement of* teachers' (p. 9, emphasis added). Thus, it seems, school effectiveness depends on two kinds of reciprocity: 'strong' input *from* staff, and 'purposeful' output *of* staff. Such reciprocity is clearly asymmetrical. Its elaboration and retention serves a rhetorical purpose in the OFSTED review — as a feel-good fiction.

Key Characteristics of Effective Schools relates to a policy field where, the authors admit, reviews outnumber empirical studies (p. 1). The search for better understanding, it seems, is repeatedly overridden by the external demand for marketable prescriptions. Such imbalance arises because, as the reviewers also acknowledge, school effectiveness research suffers from a 'weak theoretical base' (p. 1). The associated demands of social engineering (and human resource management) outstrip the capacity of the research community to deliver the necessary technical wisdom. In these circumstances, research is shaped by the values or idols of the market place rather than steered by axioms and principles. It becomes product-oriented. It is expected to supply school management prototypes configured, in this case, as a package of 'key characteristics'. Sponsored by powerful quasi-governmental agencies, this package is placed on the global cash-and-carry market for educational panaceas. Bundled with a franchising deal and/or a complementary package of technical support, it is then disseminated around the world (e.g. east of Berlin, south of Rome and north of Euston).

I reject both the suppositions and conclusions of such research. I regard it as an ethnocentric psuedo-science that serves merely to mystify anxious administrators and marginalize uncertain practitioners. Its UK manifestations are shaped not so much by inclusive educational values that link democracy, sustainable growth, equal opportunities and social justice but, rather, by a hierarchical political discipline redolent of performance-based league tables and the spectre of performance-related funding.

The enduring lessons of the school effectiveness literature are to be found in its caveats, not its cure-alls. The OFSTED review should have given greater attention to the value suppositions as well as the empirical outcomes of such research; to its diversities as well as central tendencies; and to its exceptions as well as to its 'common features' (p. 7). By such means, the more enduring aspirations of the Institute of Education reviewers — a 'better understanding' of schooling — might indeed be obtained.

Fordism by Fiat

In this part of the chapter, my intention is to examine the effective schooling rationale as a managerialist, social engineering — or fordist — solution to a technical problem socially created by recent legislation in England and Wales.

The crucial development has been the breakdown of the post Second World War political consensus that education should be regarded as a site of human investment. The so-called 'new right' took a different position. Schooling could no longer be theorized as a site of public investment. Instead, it should be organized, managed and administered as a site of private consumption. Repositioned, schooling would be exposed to the freedoms of the market place and the discipline of performance indicators. In turn, British schooling would enjoy the same kind of profitable 'take-off' that British industry enjoyed following the weakening of similar constraints after Adam Smith published *The Wealth of Nations* in 1776. This, then, is the ideological impetus behind research into effective schooling. The rhetoric of effectiveness and productivity merely masks a political intent to re-introduce exclusive (i.e. discriminatory) educational practices. The OFSTED search for key characteristics, therefore, can also be seen as a search for key discriminators.

In the following year OFSTED's search for new access to the hidden gardens of education was extended by the publication of *Worlds Apart?* (Reynolds and Farrell, 1996), an OFSTED review of international surveys of educational achievement. OFSTED's espoused intent was to find new drive systems that could enhance the productivity of national school systems as well as their local units of production (viz. schools). But, as in the case of *Key Characteristics of Effective Schools* (Sammons et al., 1995), such drive systems — based on 'professional leadership', 'shared vision and goals' and 'purposeful teaching' (p. 8) — might also have other consequences.

Historically, the notion of drive systems stems from the work of Frederick Winslow Taylor, a time-served mechanical engineer who, while working for the Midvale and Bethlehem Steel Companies in the closing decades of the nineteenth century, devised new systems of industrial production that, in their turn, influenced the re-tooling of the Ford Motor Company just before the First World War (see, for example, Callahan, 1962; Braverman, 1974). Taylor's premise, as subsequently expressed in the introduction to *The Principles of Scientific Management* (1911) was that what 'Mr Roosevelt refers to as a lack of "national efficiency"' arises, among other things, from 'wastes [sic] of human effort' (p. 5).

Taylor's ideas about drive systems and scientific management found their expression in many forms. The reconciliation of human effort and national efficiency entered his overall philosophy rationale: 'the principle object of management should be to secure the maximum prosperity for the employer, coupled with the maximum prosperity for each employé [sic]' (1911, p. 9). And the same reconciliation suffused his efforts in the redesign of workshops and factories, the promulgation of piece rates, and the composition of new contracts of employment.

More than 60 years later, these Taylorist positions on wastage were taken up, in the context of schooling, by Reynolds and Farrell. The inefficiency of English schooling arises, they suggest, from its 'complex pedagogy', the associated 'lack of goal clarity' and the resultant 'dissipation of teacher effort' (1996, p. 58). The English classroom has 'the "constant" of the teacher for perhaps only 20 per cent of lesson time'. As a result children are 'thrown back [sic]', for much of their lesson time, onto 'their own internal resources' or those of their 'achievement differentiated group' (p. 57). The net result is that English schooling is diagnosed as suffering from 'schools of clearly *heterogeneous* quality' (p. 57). In other words, it does not conform to the commodification, centralization and intensification of production supposedly found among the UK's economic competitors. Hitherto, schools in England and Wales celebrated a diversity of practices that engaged with a rainbow curriculum. But now, it seems, they should be allowed to incorporate any pedagogic hue — as long as it is black.

Recent school effectiveness research, therefore, is bundled within a national efficiency package. It is about international rather than local and national league tables. It comes bundled with masters degrees in business administration (MBAs), the establishment of a centrally funded Centre for Research in Educational Marketing at Southampton University, the centralization of teacher training (e.g. at the Open University), and the segregated, management training of promoted teachers (sponsored and funded by the Teacher Training Agency). All of these innovations have been part of a new right-inspired and centrally funded exercise to transfer — by fiat — drive systems from one sector of the economy to another. By such means, schools are not only encouraged to conform to the qualitative correlates of school effectiveness, but also to devote themselves to raising their relative standing on quantitative indicators (e.g. examination scores). By this argument, school effectiveness research becomes embroiled in utilitarian — or greatest happiness of the greatest number — thinking. School effectiveness research is utilitarian because it builds upon aggregate measures (e.g. examination results, class sizes, attendance figures, costs per pupil). These, in turn, become surrogates — or 'proxy' measures (DES, 1991, p. 23) — of educational worth and economic potential.

Despite the plausibility of such arguments — as represented, for instance, by Taylor's claims about employer and employee prosperity — they suffer from a reconciliation problem. Aggregate measures apply to populations, not individuals. Thus two schools may have the same aggregate scores (e.g. pupil attendance), while differing sharply in the distribution of individual scores. This problem has also been noted with respect to classical utilitarian theory:

> The greatest happiness of the greatest possible number, introduces a distributive principle: each person is to count for one, and nobody for more than one. And questions of right and wrong turn upon the distribution, as well as the amount, of the pleasure to be produced. (Britton, 1969, p. 55)

Thus, attempts to reconcile school performance and the national good, however, suffer from two educational problems. First, they are open to zero sum (or transfer market) manipulation, when schools, for example, poach from their competitors. Such transfers occur within a closed system. The league-table standing of a school may rise, without necessarily having any impact on national productivity. Arguably, the procedure is also educationally counterproductive. It maintains national efficiency while disrupting the lives of individual pupils. Secondly, to resort to aggregate measures makes school effectiveness research vulnerable to the so-called 'ecological fallacy' (Robinson, 1950); that is, where aggregate measures are invalidly extrapolated to the performance of individuals. Here is an illustration of the ecological fallacy. Suppose it is discovered that 49 per cent of families in a given locality have three cars while 49 per cent of families in the same locality also receive free school meals. Superficially, then, there is a high correlation between car ownership and free meals. In fact, of course, such information says nothing about such an association, since the 49 per cent of families who own three cars may include none of the 49 per cent that receive free meals. So, the claim, for instance, that all individuals in high-rated schools are also, themselves, high-scoring is untenable. It is not only undermined by variations in the distribution of individual scores, but also by the fact that, by design or default, outlier scores (e.g. those of special needs pupils, see Lloyd, 1996) may have been eliminated from the calculation. Either way, illegitimate inferences may be made about the projected performance of individual pupils and teachers.

Put another way, school effectiveness research privileges the productivity of institutions over the performance (or change scores) of individuals. As a result, the promotion of school effectiveness may create tensions within the drive systems that operate within a school. For instance, different perspectives on 'purposeful teaching' may arise. Senior managers and governors, newly inducted into the mysteries of aggregate and institutional performance indicators, may come into conflict with teachers and parents whose attention falls preferentially upon individual performances that may not conform to the 'long-term vision' and 'agenda for action' of an institutional 'School Development Plan' (DES, 1989, p. 4). What, then, might this multi-level, within-school and structural tension mean for the 'unity of purpose', 'consistency of practice', 'collegiality and collaboration', and 'shared vision and goals' highlighted in the OFSTED tabulation of factors for effective schools (Sammons et al., 1995, p. 8)?

Conclusion

I believe, for reasons I have indicated, that OFSTED-sponsored school effectiveness research is approaching its epistemological sell-by date. In the words of Francis Bacon, its efforts have forced the debate and overruled the understanding. How long before educationists return to the issues raised nearly 80 years ago by John Adams, Director of the forerunner of the University of London's Institute of Education?

Adams discussed F.W. Taylor's *Principles of Scientific Management* (1911) shortly after its original appearance. He recognized its challenge to the diversification and advance of educational practice. He took his text from the writings of Taylor. 'We have before us, at a somewhat higher stage', he observed dryly, 'the science of pig-iron handling'. Yet, Adams' comments were carefully measured. The distributive difficulties prefigured in Taylor's innovations were apparent to him. As Taylor had shown, increased productivity could be achieved in steel plants and other cathedrals of mass production. But what other consequences arose from the reconfiguration of drive systems? Adams' conclusion, directed towards the fordism of his own time, is equally applicable to recent work on school effectiveness: 'perhaps the most important problem (he wrote) in the education theory of the future is the place the teacher is to occupy' (1912, p. 379).

David Hamilton

References

ADAMS, J. (1912) *The Evolution of Educational Theory*, London: Macmillan.

BRAVERMAN, H. (1974) *Labor and Monopoly Capitalism: The Degradation of Work in the Twentieth Century*, New York: Monthy Review Press.

BRITTON, K. (1969) *John Stuart Mill: Life and Philosophy* (2nd edn), New York: Dover.

CALLAHAN, R. (1962) *Education and the Cult of Efficiency*, Chicago: Chicago University Press.

DES (Department of Education and Science) (1989) *Planning for School Development* (Advice to Governors, Headteachers and Teachers), London: Her Majesty's Stationery Office.

DES (Department of Education and Science) (1991) *Development Planning: A Practical Guide* (Advice to Governors, Headteachers and Teachers), London: Her Majesty's Stationery Office.

HAMILTON, D. (1996) 'Peddling feel-good fictions', *Forum*, **38**, 2, pp. 54–6.

LLOYD, G. (ed.) (1996) *'Knitting Progress Unsatisfactory': Gender and Special Issues in Education*, Edinburgh: Moray House Institute of Education.

REYNOLDS, D. and FARRELL, S. (1996) *Worlds Apart? A Review of International Surveys of Educational Achievement Involving England*, London: Her Majesty's Stationery Office.

ROBINSON, W.S. (1950) 'Ecological correlation and the behaviour of individuals', *American Sociological Review*, **15**, pp. 351–7.

SAMMONS, P., HILLMAN, J. and MORTIMORE, P. (1995) *Key Characteristics of Effective Schools: A Review of School Effectiveness Research*, London: OFSTED.

TAYLOR, F.W. (1911) *The Principles of Scientific Management*, New York: Harper.

Chapter 3

Cultures of Blame and Redemption — When Empowerment Becomes Control: Practitioners' Views of the Effective Schools Movement

Joe Rea and Gaby Weiner

The Effective Schools Movement is currently a pervasive influence on education policy-makers and practitioners. Its claim that schools can act independently of local or socio-economic contexts mirrors the instrumental and technical nature of much of school management. The preoccupation with school effects has displaced many of the social issues once widely supported. From the position of practitioners working in the urban context, we argue that the Effective Schools Movement as a regulator in the education market is the antithesis of the empowerment it professes to offer.

We write as two teachers (one school-based and one university-based) who have become enmeshed in the new sets of social relations in education arising from recent government policy-making. This has ensured that Joe, who is headteacher of a large multi-ethnic primary school in an economically disadvantaged neighbourhood, is now responsible for financial management and is subject to the mechanisms of government testing, OFSTED inspections and league tables. Gaby works in a department of education in a university close to Joe's school. She is responsible for placing students in local schools, many of which are deemed as 'failing' by the inspectorate. She faces an increasingly regulatory framework in teacher training such that a national curriculum for teacher training is being proposed — to mirror the National Curriculum for schools. Both have been affected professionally by what seems to be a ritual condemnation of urban education by politicians, policy-makers and the media and are concerned, in particular, about the influence the Effective Schools Movement (ESM) has had on this situation.

In this chapter we examine the impact of school effectiveness discourses on our lives and the lives of our respective institutions. In particular we focus on the relationship of school effectiveness research to policy-making and regulation, social justice and equal opportunities, empowerment and educational values, and the changing roles and perspectives of teachers. We conclude that while school effectiveness research may have something important to offer to teachers and schools, the discourse of regulation and blame which is currently used by its advocates and in government policy, can only detract from any higher order aims or aspirations.

The Effective Schools Movement and Policy-making

Though sharply contested by others in this volume, the research outcomes of the ESM — principally that schools can act independently of local or socio-economic contexts — are understandably popular with policy-makers. Such findings are helpful politically because they enable any inadequacies in the school system to be passed on: to teachers and teacher trainers in the case of 'progressive' teaching methods; and to the poor leadership of headteachers in the case of 'failing schools'. The school effectiveness findings are being used simultaneously to describe education, especially urban education, in pathological terms and to propose superficial solutions for the so-called under-performance of inner-city schools. In other words, the attraction of school effectiveness research lies in its political convenience rather than its intellectual integrity.

This is at first surprising since among advocates of school effectiveness (characterized by the work of Reynolds, 1994; Sammons, Hillman and Mortimore, 1995; Nuttall, Goldstein, Prosser and Rasbash, 1989) there is an awareness that claims may have been overstated regarding the efficacy of research findings. Barber (1996) remarks that:

> I am conscious, at this point in the argument, of moving from summarising what is essentially a set of research findings to making proposals for the future which are inevitably controversial. I recognise that they [ESM principles] are open to question and indeed will admit to sensing more doubt myself than might be apparent from the written style. (p. 12)

Why is it that despite this scepticism, school effectiveness research is so powerful and attractive a discourse for policy-makers of the New Right and New Labour alike? We need to consider why school effectiveness currently frames the language of school practice and management, why it is accepted and indeed welcomed seemingly uncritically by many teachers, and why it currently forms the basis of much professional development nationally.

These questions can be explored by consideration of the ESM's position in the education market. The ESM has gained considerable political influence precisely because of its emphasis on 'school effects'. In blaming individual schools for below-average performance, the reasons for the creation of the educational market and the introduction of competition between schools, are restated and reinforced. Not only has a culture of blame been created, it has also been used as a rationale for the allocation or non-allocation of resources. Good school effects, it is claimed by some, do not have a price tag: a bad school costs as much as a good one.

This rationale, then, formed the basis of the New Right's education reform programme of the 1980s and 1990s. Urban schools were more deeply affected than their suburban and rural counterparts, by the abolition of the larger, metropolitan, elected education authorities in 1988, and by the decrease of funding for the poorest areas, previously targeted as in need of extra, not less, funding for example by the creation of Education Priority Areas in the 1970s.

Additionally, urban schooling and, by implication, the teachers working in urban schools, have been used as scapegoats for Britain's economic decline. Hence, the culture of blame has been widened to include failings at an international level. A recent government publication (OFSTED, 1996) reported that, according to international league tables of academic performance, British children do not compare well their peers in other countries. This is a theme echoed by Barber (1996) whose book *The Learning Game* offers as a future educational 'vision' the wish 'to match the Asian tiger economies in terms of performance while maintaining and renewing our liberal traditions' (Barber, 1996, p. 9). By quoting ESM research, Barber emphasizes the role of educational research in developing political strategies around how failing schools can be 'saved'. We suggest that data gathering and interpretation used in this way should be regarded as policy study rather than research; and that university departments or centres advocating ESM should be recognized formally as 'think-tanks' for policy-makers, rather than as independent research centres.

Such 'shame and blame' discourses generated by successive governments have compelled teachers to operate within a culture of guilt (Hargreaves, 1994). As a consequence, the 'revivalist' undertones of ESM appear deeply attractive to them, offering salvation with a litany of redemptive recipes. Thus 'a culture of redemption' has emerged for late twentieth-century British teachers, similar to that promoted by early twentieth-century educational discourses in the US which aimed 'to save the child for society and to rescue society through the child' (Popkewitz, 1997, p. 92).

> In an important sense, the discourses of professionalization and pedagogy combined . . . competence, achievement and salvation. Professionalism constructed the deliverance of the 'soul' (the child to be rescued) through a revisioning and visioning of the dispositions and capacities of the teacher who administers children. (Popkewitz, 1997, p. 96)

By substituting 'teacher' for 'child', the current culture of redemption aims to save the teacher for society and to rescue society through the teacher. Competence, achievement, deliverance and salvation are promised to present-day teachers who are 'named and blamed' for the failings of decades of inadequate education recipes and policies.

Yet, the range of reasons given for British economic decline in the twentieth century have been many and various, including, for example, loss of empire, the flight of capital to the so-called 'tiger economies', the amorality of market-led policy and an increasingly de-skilled and low paid workforce (Hobsbawm, 1969). To suggest that the poor performance of a minority of the teaching force is a main cause is clearly untenable, but this is one perspective that is currently receiving wide support.

The reforms of the late 1980s and early 1990s have clearly needed the compliance of teachers if they (both reforms and teachers) are to be effective (Hatcher, 1994; Ball, 1990). This can be achieved through new management regimes produced simultaneously by increased central state regulation and the imposition of a quasi-education market. ESM research, which draws on earlier empirical enquiry into social class and educational achievement, appears to accord well with current educational management regimes which have their origins in the theoretical and practical translation of industrial and commercial organizational management techniques to educational contexts. This dual perspective — of school effectiveness and educational management — thus facilitates the exposure and comparison of 'school effects' through the utilization of industrial metaphors such as input/output, process variables and, importantly, 'value added'.

The emphasis on school 'effects' and differences masks the social justice issues of concern to those teaching in urban contexts. Hamilton (in this volume) argues that the ESM is:

> ... shaped not so much by inclusive educational values that link democracy, sustainable growth, equal opportunities and social justice but rather by a divisive political discipline redolent of performance based league tables and performance related funding.

ESM, Value-added and Equal Opportunities

It is suggested that ESM principles are underpinned by concerns for increased equality. Sammons, Mortimore and Hillman (1996), for example, have challenged Hamilton's interpretation on the grounds that their conception of 'value added' is a valid and equity-based critique of the use of both raw league tables and misleading information about inner-city schools. The argument reflects the controversial nature of the term 'equality of opportunity', and the social and political arguments that surround it. It may be helpful to look at some definitions to illustrate differences in perception.

Wood (1987) suggests that definitions of equal opportunities fall broadly into four categories. These are:

1   Equalizing life chances
2   Open competition for scarce opportunities
3   Equal cultivation of different capacities
4   Level of educational attainment independent of social origins

With regard to the first definition, schools might attempt to ensure that all children have the same educational experiences: yet life chances are affected also by other factors such as poor living conditions, parents' un/employment and individual children's cognitive and/or physiological characteristics. The second definition involving open competition revolves around whether factors acquired accidentally such as ability, intelligence, aptitude or talent should be used as a basis for allocating reward or, rather, whether educational equality should be seen as a right or entitlement. The third definition is exemplified by the use, in the 1940s and 1950s, of 'intelligence' testing to allocate children to different forms of secondary schooling as a means of increasing individual potential. Yet, entrants to grammar schools formed the only group having increased economic and social mobility and advantage. The fourth and perhaps the most attractive definition — that which separates attainment from social class — has been frustratingly difficult to attain. Attempts by public policy-making in the 1970s to operationalize this interpretation were viewed as failing because they produced deprivation and deficit models, responsive only to targeted, compensatory and expensive educational programmes (Coleman et al., 1996; Jenks et al., 1972).

Sammons et al. (1996) argue that school effectiveness research was a response to the pessimistic interpretation of compensatory education by researchers in the USA and UK (as above) rather than a consequence of more recent market-driven education reform. The second of Wood's definitions — open competition for scarce resources — appears highly suited to market perspectives, though constitutes a narrow view of equality of opportunity. Apple (1993) points out that educators should not collude in allowing this limited vision of equality to become part of the social and educational agenda. Rather, he argues, attention should be refocused on important curricular questions of inclusivity and critical awareness.

The narrow view of equality espoused by the education market in the UK has recently been highlighted by Gerwitz, Ball and Bowe (1995) who have identified two conceptions of equality. The first follows Gray's (1993) observation that accepting marketization involves acceptance of the unpredictable dispersion of rewards, only partly connected with individual merit or achievement. Gerwitz et al. (1995) ask whether within these terms, the new education market is improving the chances of access to a better quality of education for those deemed 'deserving', that is the 'respectable, thrifty and industrious' working class.

The second concept examines need-based definitions of equity embedded in left-leaning arguments for choice. Crump's (1994) defence of choice in education as programmes of choice built upon 'genuine democratic community interests' have potential to be more equitable than more bureaucratically led systems. Such conceptions of choice may well make state schools more responsive to the needs of low income, minority, single-parent and other excluded groups. Whilst acknowledging that need-based conceptions of equality do not form part of the current British education market system, Gerwitz et al. (1995) question whether, indeed, the market could offer a more equitable distribution of resources. Their research findings lead them to conclude that expectations flowing from both conceptions of equality remain unrealized by market mechanisms which allow resources to accrue to children with least need, thereby contributing to growing, not declining, inequality of access. Equality targeted principally at the 'deserving' has also not been realized because success in the market place seems to be a function of 'parental skill, [and] social and material advantage' rather than family or individual motivation.

Within the current educational climate the notion of 'value added' seems merely to have added another pathology to descriptions of urban education and to have adopted a narrowed remit for education — of programmes, targets, outputs and tests. Pupils are objectified as 'intake variables' by a cultural deficit model which appears to collude with schools' perceptions of 'low' or 'high quality' of intake. Thus certain schools are 'excused' for poor assessment scores but only in the case of some working-class children.

Solutions to low student performance are sought through 'school improvement' projects and although school improvement and effective schools strategies rest on different research paradigms (see Reynolds, 1994), merging the two traditions has become a priority (Gray et al., 1996). This shift in the ESM's ambitions has been necessary since the performative characteristics of the 'effective school' must be seen to underpin and inform the 'improving school'. So are political and academic reputations made and sustained!

ESM and Regulation

The influence of the ESM has been strengthened through its association with the Office of Standards in Education (OFSTED). OFSTED has become a key player in educational market regulation because of its power to determine what constitutes a successful school. Through 'contracted' inspections, OFSTED has been able to utilize effectiveness research to underpin its inspectoral and regulatory role. In fact, two of the earliest reviews of research commissioned by OFSTED concerned school effectiveness (Sammons et al., 1995; Reynolds and Farrell, 1996). OFSTED's stated aim for such reviews is that they provide an overview of research in order to make research findings more accessible to teachers and trainee teachers. While more recently, research reviews have been commissioned on social factors affecting schooling (i.e. gender and ethnicity), the ESM still remains the *de facto* research arm of current and would-be policy-makers and politicians. As such it exercises considerable control over, and regulation of, education and has extended its influence to the funding of professional development. For example, the current funding allocation for in-service training is dependent on schools using an 'effectiveness' rationale for school-based projects (see Mahony and Hextall in this volume).

As we have seen, although advocates of school effectiveness have cautioned against using the effectiveness findings simplistically (see, for example, Reynolds and Cuttance, 1992), it is our experience that practitioners often welcome them uncritically, as much needed solutions to an apparently grid-locked downward spiral of blame. Significantly, the doubts about and complexities surrounding school effectiveness research voiced by Reynolds and Barber are not presented in the OFSTED summaries which, instead, adopt a sales-pitch discourse by offering self-study DIY packages of information and value-added strategies.

ESM and the Changing Role of Teachers

The educational reforms have reconstituted the role of the teacher away from that of (semi-) professional towards that of a technician by fundamentally changing conditions of employment and professionalism (Grace, 1992). Because of the mass of new legislation and statutory duties, all of which require surveillance and inspection, this new role has brought with it considerable work overload, much added stress but little feeling of empowerment. To cope with all these pressures, it has become overwhelmingly compelling for teachers to be 'born again' by embracing ESM principles. So, it is argued, being part of the ESM makes teachers feel better. Unfortunately this 'feel good' factor is based on what Elliott (1996) describes as a set of platitudes, side-lining and silencing vital social justice issues.

ESM and Empowerment

Professional development within the ESM is framed by a discourse of 'empowerment'. Yet, in a recent examination of this notion and the way it has been used in research, Troyna (1994) notes how the discourse has been transformed in the ideological shift from 'welfarism' to 'neo-liberalism' which has permeated government policy since 1979. Ironically, as regulation becomes sharper, the concept of empowerment is used with increasing intensity, as are its variants — enfranchisement, entitlement, consultation, involvement, partnership, participation, and choice. Troyna argues that the re-articulation of the discourse of empowerment has become the basis for framing social and educational policy. So for example, the creation of diversity in education supposedly gives parents power through choice. Yet Gerwitz and her colleagues found that the concept of 'choice' itself is contentious and in fact is exercised differentially according to the social class of parents (Gerwitz et al., 1995).

The discourse of empowerment has been used to good effect, as exemplified by 'The Empowered School' written by ESM advocates David Hargreaves and David Hopkins. Here the authors refer to the empowering qualities of 'management arrangements' and describe the empowered school as one which:

> . . . is neither the unwilling victim of externally driven changes nor the innovator who reacts unthinkingly to every fad or whim. It is the school which responds to the challenge of change by recreating its own vision, by redefining management to support change and by releasing the energy and confidence to put its ideas into practice. (Hargreaves and Hopkins, 1991, p. viii)

Based on a government-sponsored study, their work offers through 'development planning' a way to bring together the initiatives of government, LEAs and schools as part of a new partnership. The seemingly genuine wish to empower teaching professionals masks the range of macro- and micro-political features of managerialism in schools which mitigate against such empowerment.

It seems that whether reference is made to 'management arrangements' or 'key characteristics', the message remains the same. If prescriptions are adhered to, the promise is that the individual or institution will be 'empowered' to change. The change required, however, is not necessarily part of any one institutional agenda and is a reflection largely of wider political rather than educational interests. Change thus becomes bureaucratic and managerial, administered through development plans, programmes, targets, outputs and measures of success and failure, with agendas predetermined by what are seen as measures of success — usually SATs and examination results. These success measures are then tied to funding, more for success and less in the case of failure, which in turn helps to regulate and replenish the education market. It is in this context that school effectiveness has become a control mechanism of individuals and institutions rather than, as is claimed, a source of liberation.

ESM and Educational Values

We have argued that the ESM's credibility can best be explained through its place as a regulator in the education market. The question remains as to whether it would have any credibility in a different situation. What if anything might teachers and schools utilize from school effectiveness research? In common with other critics, Elliott (1996) has argued that the 'list' of factors promoting school effectiveness (see, for example, Sammons et al., 1995) seems at first glance to state the obvious — that effective schools are . . . effective. Similarly, in a review of the literature regarding 'effective teaching', Silcock (1993) questions as dubious 'the search for principles beyond those we already assume as necessary for a job where one person has to make knowledge available to another'. The kind of generalizations offered make easy assumptions that any institution can be adjudged against the effectiveness 'list' whatever its stance towards ESM.

However, a closer look at ESM headings or indicators of effectiveness reveal more than mere platitudes. They describe a belief in a particular kind of education concerned not with promoting overall improvement in teaching and learning but rather, as Elliott (1996) points out, having a particular ideology — that of the grammar school tradition — to be imposed on all children.

Impact of the ESM on Urban Education Practitioners

One problem for policy analysis is how to disentangle the direct impact of the ESM on urban educational contexts from that of other aspects of New Right policy. For example, the creation of the National Curriculum in 1988, and 1993 legislation to expand and extend previous forms of school inspection, the creation of league tables and in the context of university teacher education, the rolling set of inspections instigated by the Teacher Training Agency (formed in 1994), have each heightened anxiety and created massive increase in workloads of staff at a time of diminished resources. ESM advocates clearly cannot be held responsible for all of these. Yet the discourses of the ESM which emphasize specific 'school effects' have long been used to underpin government policy rationale, and to export responsibility for success or failure, say in examinations and assessment, to individual institutions and individual children. This flies in the face of widespread evidence, both in the UK and abroad, which shows that socio-economic and other factors are hugely important (Gray et al., 1995).

If we attempt, then, to isolate the specific impact of school effectiveness discourses on our respective institutions, we can note the following:

- The inevitable low position of institutions such as ours in any league tables, not as a consequence of poor teaching, poor management or low expectations but because of the way in which 'success' and 'failure' is measured.
- The consequent demoralization and powerlessness of staff, and to some extent pupils and students, because they *can never be good enough*, especially if they are compared with more elite and better resourced institutions in their locality and elsewhere.
- The increasing demarcation between so-called 'good' and 'bad' schools, often identified by inspectors but based on school effectiveness criteria. This is exacerbated by the drift of pupils with 'discerning' (middle-class) parents away from the inner-city to 'better' schools.
- Increasing devaluation and/or lack of acknowledgement of the *extra* level of skills needed by staff teaching in poorer urban contexts, and the lack of support for the specific professional development needs of such staff.
- Concentration of current staff development resources on the generic requirements of school effectiveness, rather than on professional needs as articulated in specific contexts or at individual levels.
- Increased demands of a bureaucratic and regulatory system which takes up time that could be used for reflection on, and improvement to, teaching and learning.
- An imposed shift of values from professional to market-led, which has rendered most individual staff, schools and university education departments incapable of both framing educational values according to the needs of the community or challenging the dominant shift in educational values where they fail to meet such community needs.
- An apparent pathologization of all practices and outcomes that constitute the lived experience and values of those studying and teaching in poorer urban areas, in particular, those of the inner city.

Since, clearly, teachers as professionals will always want to seek improvement or become more effective, it has become hugely difficult for both of us to be seen to have doubts about the ESM, particularly as we work in contexts pathologized by school effectiveness discourses. As practitioners in urban school and university contexts, where measures of 'ineffectiveness' have become the weapons of ambitious politicians and policy-makers, it has been imperative for us to ensure that our respective institutions are 'seen' to be effective. This begs the question 'effective for what?' The response demanded of us relies on both meeting the narrow conditions favoured by advocates of school effectiveness, and acknowledging that educational objectives have been fundamentally changed by the New Right and more recently by New Labour. Yet this cannot remain our sole response since it has resulted in massively escalating stress and demoralization among staff, governors, pupils and students.

If education policy-making during the 1970s was influenced by issues surrounding social and educational equality, this has now given way to the notion that the country's competitive edge is dependent on specific outcomes of state education and, in particular, on the competence of its education professionals. As shown earlier, rather than involved with broader concepts of education regarding citizenship, ethics and personal development, improvement in effectiveness seems to rely on strict adherence to government discourses of education identified primarily in terms of students' acquisition of qualifications. Whilst the concept of 'value added' may acknowledge progress made in urban schools, it does little to increase the life chances of the children it inscribes. The concept is patronizing in its communication to urban communities (students, pupils, parents, teachers) that DESPITE being working class with the odds stacked against them, they can still, with effort and hard work, do 'quite well'. In other words, the liberal myth of achievement advocated by value-addedness, conceals the material conditions needed for educational success.

To adhere uncritically to effectiveness principles is to ignore key issues concerning the success of our respective institutions. As the principal determinants of institutional success, outcome measures cannot be regarded as neutral. Rather they assume that the main task of the educational institution is to lever as many pupils/students as possible through a given, targeted, and often narrow assessment system. And they render marginal the 'other' goals of education and schooling such as the development of self-esteem, citizenship, political awareness, social responsibility, and life-long learning.

'Good practice' is another term which has been colonized by the ESM despite the fact that most professionals aspire to improvement of practice as a main goal. This colonization has meant that 'good practice' has now come to be seen as a set of 'techniques' to be used instrumentally, imposed rather than constructed, negotiated or developed by those immediately involved. However, such techniques and the use of sophisticated statistical analysis which characterizes school effectiveness studies are no substitute for micro-political analyses and certainly tells us little about how individuals and groups use power to achieve their goals in institutions (Hoyle, 1986; Ball, 1987). Institutional micro-politics tend to be viewed by school effectiveness researchers as a challenge or block to effectiveness rather than the dynamic upon which educational institutions work. The importance of teachers' lives and how they influence practice is thus rendered invisible. However, our experience as practitioners has taught us that it is people and events and not only systems, that shape institutions and ensure their success.

Concluding Remarks

For us, therefore, the fundamental weakness of the ESM analysis is that it ignores the 'context' in which educational events happen. Rather, urban poverty, social class, race, gender and so on, become variables that need to be 'controlled for', to be put aside so that 'real' factors can be scrutinized. By using the market concept of 'value added' to resolve questions of effectiveness, the ESM has thus both rendered equality issues invisible, and ensured that key factors which continue to sustain inequality of opportunity in our educational system remain sidelined and neglected. However we also suggest that certain aspects of school effectiveness could be of immense use to institutions such as our own. For example, we need to regain the notion of 'value added' as a diagnostic tool by which teachers and educational institutions are able to identify and improve weaknesses and build on strengths — rather than as a means of pathologizing urban education.

The current market model of education is one that is likely to be sustained in the UK for the foreseeable future. As practitioners working within the education market, we acknowledge the notion of 'value added' as certainly more sophisticated than any strict adherence to raw scores and league tables. However, it is essential that value-added measures and strategies for curriculum and pedagogical improvement and change acknowledge the achievements of the best practitioners, not in order to 'score over' their less skilled colleagues, but to help improve practice and teacher morale at a wider level.

References

APPLE, M. (1993) *Official Knowledge: Democratic Education in a Conservative Age*, New York: Routledge.

APPLE, M. (1996) *Cultural Politics and Education*, Buckingham: Open University Press.

BALL, S.J. (1987) *The Micro-Politics of the School: Towards a Theory of School Organization*, London: Methuen.

BALL, S.J. (1990) *Politics and Policy Making in Education: Explorations in Policy Sociology*, London: Routledge.

BARBER, M. (1996) *The Learning Game: Arguments for an Education Revolution*, London: Victor Gollancz.

BARBER, M. and DANN, R. (eds) (1996) *Raising Educational Standards in the Inner Cities*, London: Cassell.

COLEMAN, J.S., CAMPBELL, E.Q., HOBSEN, C.J., McPORTLAND, J., MOOD, A.M., WEINFIELD, F.D. and YORK, R.I. (1966) *Equality of Educational Opportunity*, Washington D.C.: US Government Printing Office.

CRUMP, S.J. (1994) *Public School Choice: A Pragmatist Perspective*, Sydney: Dept of Social Policy Studies in Education, University of Sydney.

ELLIOTT, J. (1996) 'School effectiveness research and its critics: Alternative visions of schooling', *Cambridge Journal of Education*, **26**, 2. pp. 199–224.

GERWITZ, S., BALL, S.J. and BOWE, R. (1995) *Markets, Choice and Equity in Education*, Buckingham: Open University Press.

GIPPS, C. and MURPHY, P. (1995) *A Fair Test?* Buckingham: Open University Press.

GRACE, G. (1992) 'The state and teachers: Problems in teacher supply retention and morale', in GRACE, G. and LAWN, M. (eds) *Teacher Supply and Teacher Quality*, Clevedon: Multilingual Matters Ltd.

GRAY, J. (1993) *Beyond the New Right: Markets, Government and the Common Environment*, London: Routledge.

GRAY, J. and WILCOX, B. (1995) *Good School, Bad School*, Buckingham: Open University Press.

GRAY, J., REYNOLDS, D., FITZGIBBON, C. and JESSON, D. (1996) *Merging Traditions: The Future of Research on School Effectiveness and School Improvement*, London: Cassell.

HARGREAVES, A. (1994) *Changing Teachers, Changing Times*, London: Cassell.

Joe Rea and Gaby Weiner

HARGREAVES, D. and HOPKINS, D. (1991) *The Empowered School*, London: Cassell.
HATCHER, R. (1994) 'Market relationships and the management of teachers', *British Journal of Sociology of Education*, **15**, 1, pp. 41–61.
HOYLE, E. (1986) *The Politics of School Management*, London: Hodder & Stoughton.
JENKS, C.S., SMITH, M., ACKLAND, H., BANE, M.J., COHEN, D., GINTIS, H., HEYNS, B. and MICHOLSON, S. (1972) *Inequality: A Reassessment of the Effect of Family and Schooling in America*, New York: Basic Books.
NUTTALL, D., GOLDSTEIN, H., PROSSER, J. and RASBASH, J. (1989) 'Differential school effectiveness', *International Journal of Educational Research*, **13**, 7, pp. 769–76.
POPKEWITZ, T. (1997) 'Educational sciences and the normalizations of the teacher and the child: Some historical notes on current USA pedagogical forms', in NILSSON, I. and LUNDAHL, L. (eds) *Teachers, Curriculum and Policy: Critical Perspectives in Educational Research*, Umeå, Sweden: Department of Education, Umeå University.
REYNOLDS, D. (1994) 'School effectiveness and quality in education', in RIBBINS, P. and BURRIDGE, E. (eds) *Improving Education: Promoting Quality in Schools*, London: Cassell.
REYNOLDS, D. and CUTTANCE, P. (1992) *School Effectiveness Research, Policy & Practice*, London: Cassell.
REYNOLDS, D. and FARRELL, S. (1996) *Worlds Apart: A Review of International Surveys of Educational Achievement Involving England*, London: Ofsted, HMSO.
SAMMONS, P., HILLMAN, J. and MORTIMORE, P. (1995) *Key Characteristics of Effective Schools: A Review of School Effectiveness Research*, London, Institute of Education/OFSTED.
SAMMONS, P., MORTIMORE, P. and HILLMAN, J. (1996) 'Key characteristics of effective schools: A response to Peddling Feel-good Fictions', *Forum*, **38**, 3, pp. 88–90.
SILCOCK, P. (1993) 'Can we teach effective teaching?' *Educational Review*, **45**, 1.
TROYNA, B. (1994) ' "Blind faith?" Empowerment and educational research', Paper presented at the annual conference, International Sociology of Education, University of Warwick.
WOOD, R. (1987) Assessment and Equal Opportunities: text of public lecture, University of London Institute of Education, 11 November.

Chapter 4

The Tyranny of the International Horse Race

Margaret Brown

International Comparisons, National Policy and the Media

There is a close analogy between the concept of the effectiveness of an individual school, and the concept of the effectiveness of the national education system.

The publication of league tables in relation to examination results, whether national or local, can improve the effectiveness of an individual school, by stimulating a useful process of analysis and action which leads to a genuine raising of educational standards. Alternatively, pressure to move up the league tables can trigger teacher stress and short-term anti-educational solutions, like rejection of poor attenders or low-attaining pupils by their nearest schools, or changing to an examination board that sets less challenging questions and gives higher grades for a given level of performance. Hard-working teachers may become disillusioned deciding with some justification that league table results do not provide a valid evaluation of their own effectiveness. Similarly, the publication of international league tables can all too easily be used by politicians and others to put additional pressure on an already overburdened education system, and to justify short-term policies which may not address genuine weaknesses.

The argument will be made in this chapter that, as with school league tables, the information in international league tables is often too technically flawed to serve as an accurate measure of national effectiveness. The remainder of the chapter is devoted mainly to the scrutiny of how performance is viewed in mathematics, since mathematics is both the subject thought to be most susceptible to international comparisons, and the one where the political response has been the most frequent and far-reaching.

Examples of the manipulation of international comparisons for political ends can be seen in recent events. In 1994, 45 countries took part in TIMSS (the Third International Mathematics and Science Study), the largest ever international comparative survey of attainment in mathematics and science. The results for the 13-year-old sample were known by May 1996, but the testing agencies and government officials in each country were required to maintain confidentiality until mid-November, when there would be synchronized press conferences in each participating country. The delay before this official announcement was protracted in order to ensure that the poor results of the United States, pledged to become first in the world by the year 2000 following the publication of *A Nation at Risk* (National Commission for Excellence in Education, 1983), did not affect the outcome of the American presidential elections due to take place in the first week in November.

This demonstrates the link between education and national politics, as does the fact that the only country to break the agreed embargo was the UK, and for political reasons. In June 1996 by order of education ministers in the British Government, the comparatively low ranking of England in mathematics was leaked to *The Times*, and was used in a front-page headline. The reason for doing this and thus incurring the wrath of the international community was because ministers wanted to announce the inclusion of mental arithmetic tests and a no-calculator paper in national tests at eleven and fourteen, and unfavourable international comparisons appeared to provide a legitimate reason for doing so.

The Times leak was immediately preceded by considerable media exposure given to the report *Worlds Apart?* (Reynolds and Farrell, 1996), an OFSTED-commissioned review of results of international surveys of educational achievement in which England had participated. An interesting feature of this review was that unlike most of the other research reports in this series it was not put out for tender.

The press exposure was accompanied by a well-advertised *Panorama* programme showing how the high position of Taiwan was achieved by whole class teaching methods, which were continually being recommended by Her Majesty's Chief Inspector at OFSTED. The *Panorama* programme was guilty of bias, drawing attention for example to 'the long tail of achievement' in England while failing to advertise the fact, previously brought to the attention of the programme producers, that the results of the lowest 10 per cent of pupils in Taiwan were no better than those in England.

Neither the *Worlds Apart?* report nor the *Panorama* programme chose to feature a major finding of the surveys reviewed, that up to that point no significant effect on attainment in mathematics due to different teaching methods had ever been detected. Indeed, in addition to running regression analyses of the cross-sectional data from 20 countries, the Second International Mathematics Survey (SIMS) (Burstein, 1992) had devoted considerable effort to a longitudinal study of value-added in eight countries with extensive analysis of different teaching methods. They concluded:

> All we can safely say (we hope) is that students do experience different types of instructional arrangements cross-nationally and that the influence of these arrangements generically appears to be weak relative to such matters as prior learning and the contents of learning opportunities during the course of study. (Burstein, 1992, p. 278)

The media attention given to *Worlds Apart?* was particularly odd since it contained no new data. The survey included data which was more than 15 years old, and even the most recent large-scale survey quoted had been reported more than four years earlier (Lapointe, Mead and Askew, 1992). In fact not only had these results been prominently featured in the media when they had first appeared, but *The Sunday Times* had from time to time recycled various aspects of them in order to maintain the impact of the message that standards were low and falling, and therefore an immediate return to traditional teaching methods was necessary.

Unsurprisingly there was one aspect of an international survey which, while reported in the literature (Lapointe, Mead and Philips, 1989), failed to hit any national headlines. In the IAEP (International Assessment of Educational Progress) 1988 survey among six countries, Korea came top in every aspect of mathematics except one. In logic and problem-solving, England and Wales were ahead not only of Korea but of all the other countries surveyed. Given that problem-solving is an area of mathematics much favoured by the CBI and British industry, and a focus of the recommendations in the Cockcroft Report (DES, 1982), this result might have been seen as something of a triumph for mathematics teaching in England. But since the agendas of the media and politicians at the time were to press for more traditional teaching, this positive result was never drawn to the national consciousness.

In contrast to the media-hype devoted to *Worlds Apart?*, the announcement of the age 13 results from the TIMSS survey was strangely muted. Instead of recycling old data, here at last was a major new post-National Curriculum source of apparently reliable data on the largest ever number of countries, and yet it was given little emphasis in most of the press. In contrast to the front-page leak in June, *The Times* merely ran a page 6 article 'English teenagers slump in world maths league'. In other papers the latest school league tables, or the seemingly improved overall results of the summer national tests, eclipsed the TIMSS results. Clearly the Department for Education and Employment had decided to release both league tables and national test data simultaneously with the international TIMSS press conferences in order to divert attention from disadvantageous international comparisons, which might reflect badly in the pre-election season on the extended period of Tory rule.

There was slightly more media excitement though over the announcement of the TIMSS age 9 results on June 11th, 1997. For example *The Independent* had a page 5 headline 'English come bottom of the class in maths', which itself demonstrated a certain journalistic innumeracy: later in the article and in the results table for countries with accepted samples which accompanied the headline, England was in fact shown to be 10th out of 17 countries. Under the adjacent headline 'Back to basics with daily dose of three Rs', Estelle Morris, a Labour minister, was quoted as using the TIMSS result as an excuse to push the proto-Tory policies of the newly elected Labour Government. These concentrated on numeracy and literacy, and included ensuring 'an hour a day' for 'the 3Rs' and that 'trainee teachers would be schooled in "traditional" teaching methods'. Only a few weeks earlier David Blunkett, the new Secretary of State, had been supporting a ban on calculators in the 5–7 age group in order to improve numeracy standards.

Ironically the futility of these proposed solutions was demonstrated by other findings reported in the TIMSS age 9 survey (Mullis et al., 1997). English primary schools on average in 1994 already spent between 55 and 60 minutes a day on mathematics, a time allocation which was only exceeded by three other countries (including one with worse results). Furthermore, English pupils who used calculators in some lessons in Year 5 performed better than those who never used them at all. Unfortunately results were not available for either England or Scotland on the effect of different teaching strategies, but in both the countries which are otherwise culturally closest, Australia and New Zealand, attainment was negatively associated with frequency of computational skills practice and positively associated with frequency of setting tasks involving mathematical reasoning.

While correlation should not be confused with causation, nevertheless these results hardly offer support to the new Government's policies. Thus as at school level, poor results can trigger inappropriate imposed solutions. At least the Government can console itself that its decision to reduce class size in primary schools may have a positive effect; the TIMSS data showed that in relation to primary class size, England has the 6th largest out of 25 countries, and the largest classes outside Asia.

Of course the media could have chosen to lead on the TIMSS age 9 results with a more accurate headline like 'England top of the class in geometry', reflecting the fact that English Year 5 pupils, tying with those in Hong Kong and Australia, had the highest mean score on the geometry sub-test, and were ahead of the remaining 23 countries. This is not an unimportant result, given that with the advent of multimedia software, spatial and graphical skills will assume ever greater importance, while the sort of laborious written calculations in which English pupils perform comparatively poorly, will assume even less.

Similarly the excellent science results at both age 9 and age 13 in TIMSS were largely ignored by both press and politicians. The rather complex message, that science (and geometry) scores had improved relative to other countries as overall mathematics scores fell, would have prevented attributions of blame to either teachers or teaching methods. It seems most likely that the unintended side-effects of the National Curriculum in changing the balance of time and focus were the real cause of the slight comparative mathematical decline. Hence Labour ministers would appear to be partly right in wanting to re-focus on numeracy (and literacy) and to de-emphasize other subjects at primary school if their aim is to do well in the international mathematics league tables in which traditional number skills feature strongly; no-one however seems to have thought it appropriate to stop to consider the likely effects on our science scores, nor more importantly what knowledge and skills will actually be most important for people to have in the next century.

Interestingly, the introduction of the National Curriculum itself provides one of the most significant examples of the use of international comparisons to justify policy. Sir Keith Joseph referred to the results of the SIMS survey in 1980–81 in proposing greater curricular control, in the form of attainment targets and assessment at primary level (DES/WO, 1995, p. 9).

When Kenneth Baker took over as Secretary of State he lost little time in announcing in his speech to the North of England Conference in 1987 not just a set of primary targets, but a fully specified National Curriculum. Again the major justification was the fact that we were falling behind in mathematics; in contemporary interviews he quoted the work of an economist from the National Institute for Economic and Social Research, Professor Sig Prais (Prais and Wagner, 1985).

Prais has been a significant influence on the government policy over a long period, using international comparisons of mathematical standards to argue, both directly with ministers and through *The Sunday Times* and Channel 4, for more traditional teaching methods like those used in his native Germany. He was appointed by Baker to the National Curriculum Mathematics Working Group, although he resigned when he was unable to engage the support of other members. He has attracted substantial funds from the Gatsby Foundation and elsewhere for a series of comparative studies (e.g. Burghes and Blum, 1995; Bierhoff, 1996). These have generally been very successful in attracting media attention, but fall short of academic rigour in such details as sampling, test design and control methods. Prais and his collaborators have, however, failed in competitive or peer-reviewed arenas, such as research council funding and publication within refereed academic journals.

Swiss methods of teaching number, currently being implemented at Prais' instigation in Barking and Dagenham schools, were also featured on the *Panorama* programme related to the *Worlds Apart?* publication. (Switzerland quietly replaced Germany as the model country for Prais since, partly for reasons explored later, the Swiss appear to do well in international comparisons, whereas more recently Germany has performed on a similar level to England; nevertheless the teaching methods and materials in the two countries are similar.) Although there is no rigorous independent evaluation of the Barking and Dagenham numeracy programme, the DfEE agreed to finance the work at a high level after the Gatsby Foundation withdrew their support. Both the then Secretary of State and the current Secretary of State, when Shadow Minister, have visited the project, and these visits and continual pressure by Prais were influential in leading first to the launch of the highly influential DfEE National Numeracy Project, under the Conservative Government, and more recently to the Task Force in Numeracy, under the Labour administration.

Pressure has been exerted on these two government-funded developments to use similar methods to those in Barking and Dagenham, a single national text decreeing the teachers' script and activities to be followed in each lesson, regardless of pupils' attainments and school context. Equally the Labour-inspired Task Force is clearly expected to address perceived low overall standards of numeracy by imitating more 'successful' countries. It is chaired by the principal author of *Worlds Apart?*, and has as a key member one of Prais' collaborators in carrying out international comparisons, and representation from Barking and Dagenham. Prais himself, meanwhile, continues to have influence under the Labour Government as an appointed member of a DfEE working group on educational research.

The reason for referring to this work is not that it is entirely without value, but to demonstrate how influential one person with conviction and determination, although with little experience in education or knowledge of rigorous educational research methods, can be on politicians and on the media by making constant reference to the low mathematics results of Britain in comparison to other countries.

In the next four sections some of the technical problems of drawing implications from international comparative studies will be discussed, leading to a concluding section.

Problems with International Comparisons — Sampling

One of the more helpful contributions of *Worlds Apart?* was to list some of the problems of making international comparisons. (However one should note that having listed these, Reynolds and Farrell proceed to largely ignore them in drawing conclusions which are sometimes inconsistent.)

One major problem is that of ensuring comparability between samples. It is particularly the case with small-scale studies that it is difficult to ensure that samples are genuinely representative. For example, selecting a small number of Barking and Dagenham primary schools to compare with those in Switzerland is unlikely to give a very favourable result for the UK (Bierhoff, 1996).

However even large-scale studies are not immune from the difficulty. Drawing on a devastating critique by Freudenthal (1975), I have noted elsewhere (Brown, 1996) the sampling inconsistencies of the First International Mathematics Study (FIMS) (Husen, 1967). (For example, the English sample was 'bizarre' due to the wrong instructions having been given to schools, leading to a mean age of 14.4 in a survey which was supposed to be comparing the performance of 13-year-olds.)

In the first three mathematics studies, FIMS, SIMS and TIMSS, of the IEA (International Association for the Evaluation of Educational Achievement), and in those of the IAEP (International Assessment of Educational Progress), there is a recurring problem about the definition of the sample. There is clearly continuing international disagreement as to whether what is being sampled is a particular age cohort, or a particular grade cohort. In the UK or the Pacific Rim it hardly matters, since pupils are allocated to grade level (year group) strictly by age, but in other European countries more than 25 per cent of pupils are outside the expected grade level as a result of being held back for examination failure. For example Figure 4.1 demonstrates the difficulty of comparing results in equivalent grades in Germany and Britain. (This data on difference in ages incidentally was not mentioned when *The Sunday Times* in May 1994 discussed selective item results in this report, comparing English results disadvantageously with those of the parallel German secondary school grades. More recently, the age 13 data in TIMSS, Beaton et al., 1996, suggest that grade-level standards in England are in fact roughly equivalent to those in Germany in spite of the fact that the average age of the German pupils is 8 months older.)

The problem of age or grade was solved in the First IEA mathematics study (FIMS) by reporting separate league tables for grade and age, with some countries occurring in one list only. This separation was rejected in the second study (SIMS) but the result was a fudging of the exact definition of the sample; three different definitions of which grade level was to be selected are given in three different official reports (Travers and Westbury, 1989; Robitaille and Garden, 1989; Cresswell

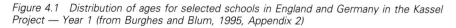

Figure 4.1 *Distribution of ages for selected schools in England and Germany in the Kassel Project — Year 1 (from Burghes and Blum, 1995, Appendix 2)*

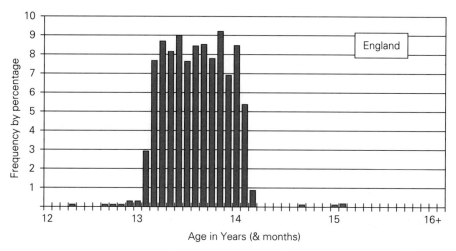

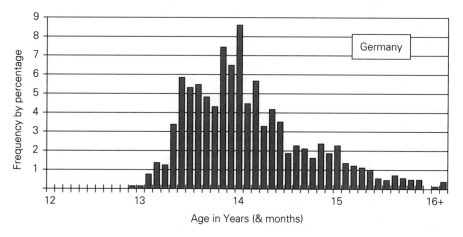

and Gubb, 1987). The IAEP, which has always put more emphasis on international league tables and less on school processes, thought they had solved the problem by asking for a sample of pupils born in a specific calendar year, but for ease of administration both the English and the Swiss insisted on the pupils being sampled only from specific grade levels (Lapointe et al., 1992). In the case of England, by changing the testing date it was possible to achieve the same mean and distribution for age as for other countries; however this was not possible for Switzerland because of the same 'repeating years' tradition as in Germany. Hence, in the reporting of the results it appears that the lowest 10 per cent of the attainment range scored very similarly in all countries except Switzerland, where there appeared to be no really low attainers (and hence also a high mean by European standards). It is also probably true that removing the lowest attainers, and replacing them by similar pupils with one, two or even three years' more experience, enables a more ambitious common curriculum (Bierhoff, 1996). Prais was able to use the deceptive absence of low attainers to argue for funds from the DfEE and Gatsby to translate outdated Swiss textbooks and to implement them in Barking and Dagenham.

In the latest TIMSS survey there are again severe difficulties of making fair comparisons due to the sampling methods (Beaton et al., 1996). All countries were asked to test the two adjacent grade levels which between them contained the greatest proportion of 13-year-olds. Although, as in FIMS, only Germany appeared to openly break the rules to its own advantage, the definition led to situations where again the lowest attaining 13-year-olds were omitted from the sample by virtue of having been held down a year or more. (Nine out of 39 countries excluded 20 per cent or more for this reason, including France, Germany, Portugal, Romania, while 10–20 per cent were excluded in 10 countries, including Ireland, the Netherlands, Austria, Hungary, Belgium and Spain. The comparable figure excluded for England was 1 per cent.) Similar problems only on a rather smaller scale were experienced in the comparison of 9-year-olds (Mullis et al., 1997). Given the close clustering of European results in TIMSS, this factor must have a substantial effect on the European rank orderings.

Similarly, the distribution of 13-year-olds between the two grade levels tested in TIMSS significantly affected the results, with the mean age of the sample in some countries, where most 13-year-olds were in the lower grade (e.g. Japan, with 91 per cent), being more than a year older than in others where most 13-year-olds were in the higher grade (e.g. Greece, with 85 per cent). Because of these inequities, the TIMSS reports (Beaton et al., 1996; Mullis et al., 1997) do in one table try to estimate median scores for 13-year-olds and 9-year-olds only. However this rather more valid version of the league table does not feature in the press summaries, and indeed the assumptions made to enable the estimate to be calculated introduce new problems.

Furthermore, there are significant numbers of pupils in some countries in schools which do not even form part of the population from which samples are drawn. For example in the SIMS surveys, the Netherlands excluded more than 17 per cent of pupils, mainly in special and vocational schools for low-attaining pupils, while France excluded 12 per cent of pupils in these schools. Correcting for this would have brought the results for both countries down to those for England. Similarly in the TIMSS report the reader has to work very hard to find the note which explains that only 32 per cent of Thai 13-year-old pupils attend school, which might go some way to explaining the fact that Thai results appear similar to those for England. It is clear that in general the mean scores for different countries must be strongly affected by the varying degrees of presence or absence in the sample of the lowest attaining pupils. It is surprising therefore that more effort has not been expended in dealing with this aspect of sampling. In other countries, whole sub-populations may even be missing (for example 4 out of 26 Swiss cantons and 1 German Land refused to form part of the sampled population for TIMSS).

Finally, many schools selected as part of the samples for international comparisons have refused to take part and not all have been replaced by equivalent alternatives. England has traditionally been one of the worst offenders, but in TIMSS several countries had higher refusal rates (e.g. in the Netherlands more than 75 per cent of schools approached refused to take part).

In all, 23 out of the 42 countries for which details are given in the age 13 TIMSS report did not properly fulfil the sampling requirements. In the case of 16 of the 23, including the Netherlands, Germany and Denmark, the discrepancies were thought serious enough to merit their results being separately listed. Thus it is necessary to carefully examine differences in the samples from different countries, especially regarding the exclusion of low attaining pupils, before interpreting the results.

Problems with International Comparisons — Forms of Reporting

Problems in ensuring equivalent samples in international comparisons have been discussed at some length because small differences can have major effects on the league tables. This is particularly the case since many countries tend to cluster together with very similar mean scores. Bracey (1996) points out that only a few percentage points may separate high and low-ranked nations: for example in SIMS geometry results the United States were ranked 16 out of 20 with 38 per cent; whereas Scotland, ranked 4th, scored only 6 percentage points more at 44 per cent (Robitaille and Garden, 1989). Similarly in SIMS, 12 European and/or Anglophone countries all had scores between 45 and 52 per cent, while in the IAEP study 10 such countries scored in the range 55 and 64 per cent (Lapointe, et al., 1992). This draws attention to the misleading practice of the media highlighting of ranks rather than mean scores.

It is a welcome departure that in the English report of TIMSS (Keys, Harris and Fernandes, 1996) the rankings are accompanied by reporting in the form of three bands of countries, those significantly above, significantly below, and those with scores not significantly different from those of England. This at least draws attention to the presence of clusters of countries with non-significantly different scores, as well as excluding the countries with the most pronounced sampling deficiencies.

The tendency to cluster is further disguised in TIMSS by reporting scores converted to an overall distribution over both the sampled years taken together, with a mean of 500 and standard deviation of 100, which appears to give a spread of scores for individual students running from below 250 to about 800. However if these scores are divided by 10 so as to express them on a similar scale to percentage examination scores, with a mean of 50, and individual scores running from 20 to 80, then again the clustering becomes apparent, with 24 out of 35 countries having estimated medians for 13-year-olds of between 47 and 52. Of the European/Anglophone countries only Flemish-speaking Belgium with 56 is above this range (but still below Hong Kong, Japan, Korea and Singapore), while only Spain, Portugal, Cyprus and two Baltic States are below it.

It is also misleading to give either ranks, means or medians without indicating the range of scores within each country. When the ranges were first illustrated in the IAEP study (Lapointe et al., 1992) it became clear that the ranges of individual students' scores within countries were surprisingly similar, going from a score of about 20 per cent for the lowest attainers to about 95 per cent. TIMSS has also adopted this practice (see Figure 4.2), although for each separate grade level, where

Figure 4.2 Distributions of scores in the TIMSS comparison of mathematics attainment among eighth grade students (Year 9) (from Beaton et al., 1996, Table 1.2, p. 26)

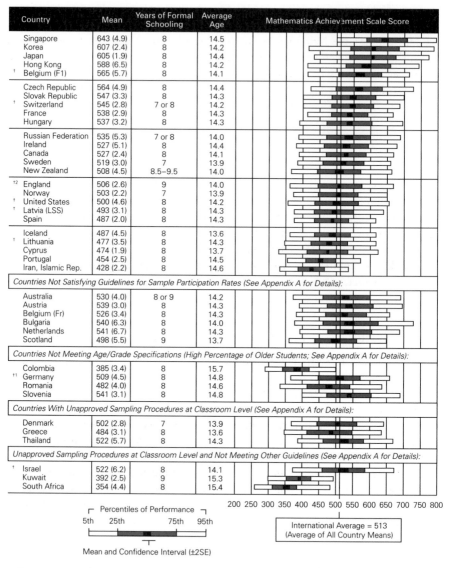

Country	Mean	Years of Formal Schooling	Average Age
Singapore	643 (4.9)	8	14.5
Korea	607 (2.4)	8	14.2
Japan	605 (1.9)	8	14.4
Hong Kong	588 (6.5)	8	14.2
† Belgium (F1)	565 (5.7)	8	14.1
Czech Republic	564 (4.9)	8	14.4
Slovak Republic	547 (3.3)	8	14.3
† Switzerland	545 (2.8)	7 or 8	14.2
France	538 (2.9)	8	14.3
Hungary	537 (3.2)	8	14.3
Russian Federation	535 (5.3)	7 or 8	14.0
Ireland	527 (5.1)	8	14.4
Canada	527 (2.4)	8	14.1
Sweden	519 (3.0)	7	13.9
New Zealand	508 (4.5)	8.5–9.5	14.0
†² England	506 (2.6)	9	14.0
Norway	503 (2.2)	7	13.9
† United States	500 (4.6)	8	14.2
† Latvia (LSS)	493 (3.1)	8	14.3
Spain	487 (2.0)	8	14.3
Iceland	487 (4.5)	8	13.6
† Lithuania	477 (3.5)	8	14.3
Cyprus	474 (1.9)	8	13.7
Portugal	454 (2.5)	8	14.5
Iran, Islamic Rep.	428 (2.2)	8	14.6

Countries Not Satisfying Guidelines for Sample Participation Rates (See Appendix A for Details):

Australia	530 (4.0)	8 or 9	14.2
Austria	539 (3.0)	8	14.3
Belgium (Fr)	526 (3.4)	8	14.3
Bulgaria	540 (6.3)	8	14.0
Netherlands	541 (6.7)	8	14.3
Scotland	498 (5.5)	9	13.7

Countries Not Meeting Age/Grade Specifications (High Percentage of Older Students; See Appendix A for Details):

Colombia	385 (3.4)	8	15.7
†¹ Germany	509 (4.5)	8	14.8
Romania	482 (4.0)	8	14.6
Slovenia	541 (3.1)	8	14.8

Countries With Unapproved Sampling Procedures at Classroom Level (See Appendix A for Details):

Denmark	502 (2.8)	7	13.9
Greece	484 (3.1)	8	13.6
Thailand	522 (5.7)	8	14.3

Unapproved Sampling Procedures at Classroom Level and Not Meeting Other Guidelines (See Appendix A for Details):

† Israel	522 (6.2)	8	14.1
Kuwait	392 (2.5)	9	15.3
South Africa	354 (4.4)	8	15.4

Percentiles of Performance
5th 25th 75th 95th
Mean and Confidence Interval (±2SE)

200 250 300 350 400 450 500 550 600 650 700 750 800

International Average = 513
(Average of All Country Means)

* Eighth grade in most countries.
† Met guidelines for sample participation rates only after replacement schools were included.
¹ National Desired Population does not cover all of International Desired Population. Because coverage falls below 65 per cent Latvia is annotated LSS for Latvian Speaking Schools only.
² National Defined Population covers less than 90 per cent of National Desired Population.
( ) Standard errors appear in parentheses. Because results are rounded to the nearest whole number, some totals may appear inconsistent.

Source: IEA Third International Mathematics and Science Study (TIMSS), 1994–95.

the sampling problems render the comparisons less valid, rather than for the 13-year-old cohort.

In TIMSS there is more variation between lowest and highest students in the different countries than in the IAEP study. Nevertheless it can be seen that again the ranges (illustrated from the 5th to the 95th percentile only) are wide compared to the differences in means between countries. It is also the case that the range of scores in England is not noticeably greater than that in many other countries. Indeed seven countries, including the four leading countries in the Pacific Rim, have greater standard deviations. Those countries with the smallest ranges and standard deviations tend to be those, like France, which practice a policy of maintaining homogeneous standards by holding low attaining pupils back a year.

Thus the view of many journalists, based on those of educationists such as Reynolds and Farrell (1996), that England has a wider range of achievement than other comparable countries is not strongly supported by the TIMSS results, nor by other recent data. Nor is the much quoted 'long tail of achievement' such a feature; indeed the range below the mean is less long than the range above it and is no longer than in many other countries, as is shown in Figure 4.2.

Thus in spite of misleading ways of presenting results, especially by league table rankings, the reality is that, correcting for sampling deficiencies, England tends to perform in mathematics in a similar way to most European/Anglophone countries, with neither a particularly wide range nor an especially long tail.

Problems with International Comparisons — Curriculum Match

One of the reasons why mathematics is the most tested subject in international comparisons is that it is thought to be culturally invariant and to depend less on ordinary language and more on internationally accepted symbol systems than other subjects. For this reason it is sometimes used, as in FIMS, as a surrogate measure to compare the effectiveness of different school systems. However as MacLean (1992) points out, the expectation that it would be a 'universal and culturally neutral subject turned out to be a chimera' (p. 10).

The degree of variation, in both the content of the mathematics curriculum and in the way this content is approached, is much greater than is normally suspected. Moreover differences in the degree of coverage of the curriculum tested, known as 'opportunity to learn', have been shown to be the strongest factor affecting differential performance among countries in international mathematics surveys (Burstein, 1992). For example England does not generally perform well in tests of number, but in many cases, for whatever reason, does not claim to cover the content of as many of the test items in this area as do other countries. Correspondingly, England generally does well in geometry, data handling and statistics, and in these areas teachers do cover most of the curriculum tested.

However, the relation between coverage and attainment is by no means perfect. For example the US claimed a perfect curriculum match in the age 13 TIMSS survey (presumably because they provided many of the items and as the major funders had a right of veto) but still scored below the international average. In contrast,

England, with a slightly higher score, considered that only 57 per cent of the items in the TIMSS tests were appropriate to the curriculum of most of the Year 8 students tested (Beaton et al., pp. B–4). Here and in the Year 4 comparisons England had one of the lower levels of match (although even poorer matches are reported by countries such as the Netherlands, Switzerland, Canada and Denmark).

Some idea of how this degree of mismatch arises is obtained from data collected by the IAEP study (Lapointe, Mead and Askew, 1992), which is presented in Table 4.1.

This table is compiled from responses from the teachers who taught the pupils tested, as to whether they had emphasized these topics 'a lot' over the previous year. While clearly they do not indicate the pupils' earlier experiences, the results at least indicate wide differences, for example in the amount of emphasis on fractions, percentages, measures, probability, statistics and algebra.

The two number areas in TIMSS are rather oddly called 'Fractions and Number Sense', and 'Proportionality'. It is perhaps not surprising, given the relative neglect of fractions by teachers in England shown in Table 4.1, that scores are relatively low in the first of these areas which contributes 34 per cent of the total mathematics items. But it would seem to be a matter of great national concern that England generally performs badly in number, and that curriculum coverage is lower than that in other countries. However, much depends on the nature of the items in the tests, in particular on the relevance of the aspects which English teachers do not claim to teach. For example adding complex fractions was specifically de-emphasized in the National Curriculum and postponed until older age groups, as it was considered to have little practical relevance for most pupils, although some importance for later mathematical and scientific work. It is very difficult, if the test items are not released, for anyone to interpret the results and their implications. It is not known exactly on which sorts of items English pupils perform worst, nor how much it matters.

In comparison to the TIMSS mathematics tests, which do not match our curriculum very well, in the science tests the match for England was much closer than for most comparable countries, especially for Year 8. This comparatively closer degree of match may at least partially explain our superior science performance.

Table 4.1   Percentages of teachers of 13-year-olds in 6 countries who said they emphasized topics 'a lot' (derived from information in Lapointe, Mead and Askew, 1992)

	England	Korea	Taiwan	Switzerland	France	USA
Whole nos.	49	47	33	75	43	49
Fractions	10	19	24	72	81	54
Decimals	44	30	15	81	57	52
Ratio	43	10	52	43	51	38
Per cent	50	3	7	41	23	42
Measures	63	15	9	70	48	38
Geometry	39	67	14	58	53	27
Stat'l disply	53	37	35	20	39	18
Probability	11	53	0	0	0	9
Stat'l calcn	29	11	15	0	17	13
Algebra	53	86	74	23	82	51

Other Factors Affecting Performance

In addition to the factors mentioned above, there are some other major reasons why England may be perceived as performing badly in mathematics in comparison to the Pacific Rim, and indeed in comparison to some other European countries.

The first is trivial but not necessarily insignificant, in that it relates to the atmosphere in which the tests are taken. Al Beaton, one of the organizers of TIMSS, reported that whereas the school he had observed in Korea made a great fuss of the occasion, with the pupils taking part marching in to the tune of the school band and urged to do their best for their country, the school in the US had kept back the pupils from a games lesson, advised them to go onto the next item if they found one difficult, and reassured them that the test results did not count towards their school grades. Thus the tests may not be a fair comparison of what pupils can do given enough motivation.

The second factor is more fundamental. Nowhere in these studies is there an attempt to measure the total time devoted to mathematics in different countries. However there are indications from SIMS and TIMSS data that mathematics is of relatively low status in England and occupies a correspondingly small proportion of time. For example, compared with most other countries homework time is minimal, and there is a low percentage of curriculum time in current and earlier years. Compared to Pacific-rim countries there is also low participation in private tuition, and a low number of obligatory days of school attendance per year. It has been calculated that altogether a Japanese pupil will on average devote at least twice as much time to mathematics each year as will an English pupil (Brown, 1996).

The third factor is setting and streaming practices. SIMS results suggest that highly differentiated curricula tend to produce the weakest results, probably because curriculum coverage has a strong influence on performance and pupils in lower sets often receive an impoverished curriculum.

Conclusion

Teacher trainers, officers in government agencies, primary teachers and heads, and secondary mathematics teachers are subject to stress from government to improve national ranking in mathematics, just as pressure is on teachers from school management to perform well in local league tables and OFSTED inspections. This can have a positive influence, but only provided time is taken to analyze carefully weaknesses and their causes, after which all parts of the education system can decide on a joint action plan to improve our standards.

Instead, international comparisons have been seized on as providing a perfect justification for whatever moves government, the media or others have decided need immediate implementation. For example, teaching methods have been under fire, although there is little evidence of their impact on overall performance. Meanwhile the major influences may lie elsewhere, in our setting practices, in the time devoted to mathematics, in the curriculum, or in the lack of professional development for teachers. Experimentation with different teaching methods is important, but only if there is rigorous external validation.

So far, however, there has been little sign of coordinated national debate about what mathematics it is most important for pupils to know, nor of how best to teach it. If international comparison tests do not correspond to National Curriculum priorities, then we should not be driven into what might be seen as anti-educational practices simply in order to improve our international league table position. One art we could profitably learn from other countries is how to make curriculum decisions that are rational and consultative, rather than dictatorial, hasty and ideologically driven.

References

BEATON, A.E., MULLIS, I.V.S., MARTIN, M.O., GONZALEZ, E.J., KELLY, D.L. and SMITH, T.A. (1996) *Mathematics Achievement in the Middle School Years: IEA's Third Mathematics and Science Study*, Chestnut Hill, Massachusetts: Boston College.

BIERHOFF, H. (1996) *Laying the Foundations of Numeracy: A Comparison of Primary Textbooks in Britain, Germany and Switzerland*, London: National Institute for Economic and Social Research.

BRACEY, G.W. (1996) 'International comparisons and the condition of American education', *Educational Researcher*, **25**, 1, pp. 5–11.

BROWN, M. (1996) 'FIMS and SIMS: The first two IEA International Mathematics Surveys', *Assessment in Education*, **3**, 2, pp. 181–200.

BURGHES, D. and BLUM, W. (1995) 'The Exeter Kassel Comparative Project: A Review of Year 1 and Year 2 results', in *Proceedings of a Seminar on Mathematics Education*, London: The Gatsby Foundation.

BURSTEIN, L. (1992) *The IEA Study of Mathematics III: Student Growth and Classroom Processes*, Oxford: Pergamon Press.

CRESSWELL, M. and GUBB, J. (1987) *The Second International Mathematics Study in England and Wales*, Windsor: NFER-Nelson.

DEPARTMENT OF EDUCATION AND SCIENCE/WELSH OFFICE; COMMITTEE OF INQUIRY INTO THE TEACHING OF MATHEMATICS IN SCHOOLS (1982) *Mathematics Counts (The Cockcroft Report)*, London: HMSO.

DEPARTMENT OF EDUCATION AND SCIENCE/WELSH OFFICE (1985) *Better Schools (Cmnd 9649)*, London: HMSO.

FREUDENTHAL, H. (1975) 'Pupils' achievements internationally compared — the IEA', *Educational Studies in Mathematics*, **6**, pp. 127–86.

HUSEN, T. (1967) *International Study of Achievement in Mathematics, Vols I and II*, Stockholm/New York: Almquist & Wiksell/Wiley.

KEYS, W., HARRIS, S. and FERNANDES, C. (1996) *Third International Mathematics & Science Study: First National Report, Part I*, Slough: NFER.

LAPOINTE, A., MEAD, N. and ASKEW, J. (1992) *Learning Mathematics (Report of the IAEP 1990/1 survey)*, Princeton, NJ: Educational Testing Service.

LAPOINTE, A.E., MEAD, N.A. and PHILLIPS, G.W. (1989) *A World of Differences: An International Assessment of Mathematics and Science*, Princeton, NJ: Educational Testing Service.

McLEAN, M. (1992) *The Promise and Perils of Educational Comparison*, London: Tufnell Press.

MULLIS, I.V.S., MARTIN, M.O., BEATON, A.E., GONZALEZ, E.J., KELLY, D.L. and SMITH, T.A. (1997) *Mathematics Achievement in the Primary School Years: IEA's Third Mathematics and Science Study*, Chestnut Hill, Massachusetts: Boston College.

NATIONAL COMMISSION FOR EXCELLENCE IN EDUCATION (1983) *A Nation at Risk: The Imperative for Educational Reform*, Washington, DC: US Government Printing Office.

PRAIS, S. and WAGNER, K. (1985) *Schooling Standards in Great Britain and West Germany*, London: National Institute for Economic and Social Research.

REYNOLDS, D. and FARRELL, S. (1996) *Worlds Apart? A Review of International Surveys of Educational Achievement Involving England (Ofsted Reviews of Research Series)*, London: HMSO.

ROBITAILLE, D.F. and GARDEN, R.A. (1989) *The IEA Study of Mathematics II: Contexts and Outcomes of School Mathematics*, Oxford: Pergamon Press.

TAVERNER, S. and WRIGHT, M. (1997) 'Why go modular?' *Educational Research*, **39**, 1, pp. 104–12.

TRAVERS, K.J. and WESTBURY, I. (1989) *The IEA Study of Mathematics I: Analysis of Mathematics Curricula*, Oxford: Pergamon Press.

Part Two

Theorizing the Debates

Chapter 5

Models of Effective Schools: Limits and Capabilities

Hugh Lauder, Ian Jamieson and Felicity Wikeley

Introduction

Research into school effectiveness is now at a crossroads. While there have been some important methodological developments which enhance our understanding of the contribution schools can make to educational outcomes, the research programme has been dogged by conceptual confusion and shaped by the political and ideological context in which it has operated (Thrupp, 1995). If we are to progress in our understanding of schools a new realism is required as to schools' limits and capabilities and we need to re-examine how research can inform this understanding.

A major difficulty with the debate over school effectiveness has been that only the dominant model, what may be called the received model (RM), has been the subject of discussion. An exclusive focus on this model by both its defenders and critics has meant that a version of the fallacy of too few options has been committed. A thoroughgoing re-appraisal of school effectiveness suggests that a truer picture would be that there is a range of models of school effectiveness. In this chapter we appraise two models of how schools work and their implications for effectiveness and practice, the *received* (RM) and the *heretical* (HM). We then seek to incorporate the insights of these two models in a third, the *contextual* model (CM).

The HM stands at the polar opposite of the RM in its fundamental assumptions and therefore serves to throw into sharp relief the advantages and disadvantages of the RM. But it too has its strengths and weaknesses hence the CM is an attempt at synthesis. These models are complex and not entirely mutually exclusive. The benefit of comparison is not merely, therefore, for the purposes of critique but to explore the extent to which elements of each can be brought together to create a model of school development in a defensible synthesis. We should emphasize that the models we present here are rational reconstructions[1] and hence are to be understood as ideal types. We begin by examining the (RM) according to Lakatos' account of the structure of research programmes.

Lakatos (1970) provides a helpful way of analyzing the structure of research programmes because his account of them is able to show the relationships between the different levels of theoretical proposition and the dynamics of theoretical evolution. In the case of the RM this is particularly helpful since it is often claimed that it lacks theoretical content and that this is one of its fundamental problems. Lakatos distinguishes between the hard core of a research programme, which provides the bedrock assumptions and 'vision' underlying the programme, and a protective belt of theories which can be adjusted in the light of anomalies or empirical challenges to the hard core vision and propositions of the programme. The hard core propositions are either untestable or remain immune from challenge by the protective belt of auxiliary hypotheses. However, in defining the vision or perspective of the research programme it also provides the framework for which concepts can be admitted and which cannot: in a sense it provides the rules which define the *universe of concepts* that are considered legitimate. The integrity of the research programme is dependent on the protective belt of theories adjusting to empirical challenge while remaining consistent with the propositions of the hard core.

Lakatos' analysis was intended for research programmes in the natural sciences. However, its utility for analyzing research programmes in the social sciences and in education has been established (e.g. Harris, 1979). Not all research programmes will conform exactly to Lakatos' template, however the RM can best be analyzed as a two tier structure of propositions which are more open to testing as we ascend from the hard core to the second tier or protective belt.

The Received Model

The RM refers to the mainstream tradition of school effectiveness research which was established in England by Rutter, Ouston, Mortimore and Maughan's *15000 Hours* (1979). We are aware that some theoretical assumptions of the model have been or are currently being modified in ways we shall subsequently acknowledge. However, for purposes of theoretical clarity and appraisal we present initally the ideal type model in what Lakatos called a 'rational reconstruction'. The hard core of this model is as follows:

1 Schools as organizations do have an effect on student outcomes in terms of exam success, in contrast say to the view that it is teachers rather than schools which have effects on students outcomes as Hanushek (1986) has argued; or to the view that when contextual variables are fully taken into account there is no significant difference between schools.
2 These school effects are not caused by chance *and* that effects that improve school performance, in relation to exam success, can be engineered on the basis of RM research.
3 Schools are like any other organization in that staff and children will respond to the systems, sanctions and rewards of a school so that successful re-engineering is possible. (This latter assumption is problematic at a number of levels which we will discuss subsequently in relation to the kind of value system that schools should embody. However, it is especially problematic in relation to children who are assumed to be (i) either malleable enough *to respond* to a school's organizational structures and practices

or (ii) rational egoists; that is, that they sufficiently understand their own self-interest to follow the sanctions and incentives created by the school and the external credential system. For example, Willis (1977) argued that the educational exchange of compliance for credentials lay at the heart of the school but that this was a form of 'rational' exchange recognized by working-class resisters and rejected because the 'terms of trade' were too unfavourable for them.)

4   That schools as organizations are structured as nested organizations. Following the theoretical work of Barr and Dreeben (1983), it is assumed that schools are part of a nested set of organizational relationships with central and/or local government as the broadest organizational structure and within that, the school, the department or other forms of sub-organization and the classroom. It is further assumed that effectiveness can be identified by analyzing the performance of each level and by inference the effectiveness of the relationships between each level.

5   Despite the fact that schools are nested in a wider organization it is assumed that there is a degree of relative autonomy between levels and between the educational system and society. Hence schools can generate effects independent of many of the factors external to the school which may impinge on exam outcomes.

It is worth noting that while the criticism is often made that the RM is an a-theoretical structure these hard core propositions when taken together generate a potential set of problems of the kind which have dogged sociology and the sociology of education, in particular, for some time. For example, debate over how to understand concepts of relative autonomy between levels or structures abound, particularly in Marxist sociology in relation to the state. Similarly, the idea that staff and especially children will merely respond to organizational structures invites comparison with the claims made by Bowles and Gintis (1976) that individuals are essentially passive in the face of the structures and demands of capitalist schooling. Far from being a-theoretical there is plenty in these assumptions to generate debate over the RM.

In addition to the hard core propositions the RM has also developed a set of internally created theoretical constructs about the nature of effective schools for its protective belt. Many have a remarkable similarity to some of the leading constructs and assumptions of contemporary management theory, although what the precise relationship of influence is between the RM and some of the tenets of management theory is unclear. Just as in management theory where the emphasis on high performing organizations has been understood in terms of leadership, clear goals, mission statements, the ethos of an organization and staff consensus, so it has been in the RM.

However, at this point there is a parting of the ways between the RM and elements of management theory, for the RM has generated these concepts from what indeed appears to be empiricist methods. At this level of the research programme the claim that the RM lacks theory appears far more convincing and indeed can be seen as a major problem, once the rhetoric surrounding these concepts is stripped away and their meaning probed. The technique used by RM for generating concepts like 'leadership' or 'ethos' is simply to operationalize these concepts with a battery of items which when combined 'add up' to 'leadership' or 'ethos'. If they then turn out to be significant they are regarded as important to school effectiveness. The theoretical rationale for operationalizing these concepts tends to rely on no more than 'common sense'. In this sense they have, at the least, an intuitive appeal to RM's audience but in fact these concepts can give the impression of far greater theoretical coherence. This is especially so of RM's key theoretical innovation that of 'ethos' or 'climate' — the view that what is key to a school's performance is the ethos of a school. It is a construct we shall examine in some detail when we consider the fundamental problems of the RM.

There are four ways in which a research programme like the RM can be criticized. The *first* is in terms of internal coherence and plausibility. Here the question is one of whether the key elements of RM do indeed cohere into a consistent vision which gives systematic direction to research to enable it to identify successful schools, what makes them successful and to generate the kind of prescriptions necessary to engineer success in less successful schools. The *second*, is to ask whether the progression of research has indeed been fruitful and consistent with the RM's hard core. The *third* is to ask whether the RM can guide practice so as to successfully re-engineer school organizations to improve performance. And, the *fourth* is to ask what has been omitted from RM's universe of theoretical constucts which may be important to an understanding of the ways schools work.

The Internal Coherence and Theoretical Strength of RM

The RM appears to be a coherent model both within its hard core assumptions and between the hard core and its protective belt of 'quasi managerialist' 'theories'. For example, it assumes that schools can be understood as organizations: that there is nothing generically different about schools from other organizations and this hard core assumption is reflected in its leading protective belt concepts. The notions of leadership, goal definition etc. are generic to any organization.

However, while RM's hard core may appear coherent it clearly has deep tensions within it since, as we have already indicated, it replicates some of the most profound problems in sociology and cognate disciplines. Moreover, its most fundamental assumptions about the nature of schools as organizations are open to interrogation. It is by a discussion of the Heretical Model that the problems associated with these hard core assumptions are most sharply revealed. For the moment, though, we wish to concentrate our attention on the protective belt of auxiliary hypotheses and especially on the notion of ethos or climate for it raises issues about the adequacy of RM to identify why some schools are successful and not others, and whether it can also provide sufficient guidance in the re-engineering of schools identified as less successful.

The introduction of the notion of school climate served at least two purposes: there was a political purpose in that school climate was used as an alternative construct to Coleman's notions of social class and racial mix in order to draw attention to the claim that schools could make a difference irrespective of social class composition (Thrupp, 1995). The concept also had a key role to play within the internal structure of the RM. Once a variety of factors were identified as 'producing' school effectiveness there had to be some organizing concept that could pull the constituent parts of the recipe together; ethos or climate appeared to do the trick. Now, there is no doubt that ethos can vary between schools and within schools, (something RM didn't take into account in its early work) and common sense would suggest that it might have an effect on teacher and student performance but in the Received Model, no theory of how ethos is created has ever emerged. Instead, it is merely defined according to an abritrary set of questionnaire items which has differed from one study to another (Miller and Fredricks, 1990). Ethos may be a fruitful idea but in research terms it remains suspended in the ether. Once we see that it does not work in pulling the variables identified as significant into a coherent account of how they should be combined to produce an effective school, it is a case of the Emperor losing some if not all of his clothes. Or, to put it another way, what appears to be a promise that the RM can explain school success in terms of 'ethos' and also provide lessons in good practice is a chimera.

The RM as a 'Progressive' Research Programme

One of the tests of a research programme is that it can generate fruitful research on the basis of theoretical and methodological innovation. Here there are clear examples of such 'progress'. Perhaps the most interesting in this respect is that of research into the levels beneath that of the school, such as the department (Harris, Jamieson and Russ, 1995; Sammons, Thomas and Mortimore, 1995). Such research, which gains its direction from the hard core assumption of 'nestedness', has been made possible by the development of hierarchical linear modelling techniques. This technique has also expanded the range of within and between school analyses that can be conducted, for example, in terms of the treatment by schools of different student groups. There has also been an extension of the RM into comparative analyses of school effectiveness (Reynolds and Farrell, 1996) and some focus on the obverse of the effective school — the failing school (Tomlinson, 1997). Within its own terms the extension of the research programme in this way can be seen as 'progressive'. However, some of the research within this tradition has also served to qualify the original rhetoric if not the premises of the research programme. There are four developments which are particularly noteworthy.

The first is that it has now been clearly established that the difference schools can make to life chances is limited. Somewhere between 85 and 90 per cent of the variance between schools is explained by what Willms and Raudenbusch (1989) have called type A characteristics, those intake variables over which the school has no control. The second is that the degree to which type B characteristics, those over which the school has some control, like policy etc., can in fact make a difference is open to question for all but outlier schools because of measurement uncertainty (Goldstein, 1996).

Two points should be made about these developments. The first is that they are modifications, they do not alter the basic theoretical structure. The second is that they are welcome and should be placed alongside the advances in insight that the RM has been able to generate (Gray, Goldstein and Jesson, 1996). While these developments make the achievements of the RM more substantial, if less controversial, they are a far cry from the early rhetoric of the initial founders of the RM. In particular, they raise questions about the authority of RM methods in identifying and guiding good practice.

Over and above these qualified advances there are still many questions unresolved with respect to the RM hard core proposition that schools can make a difference once intake characteristics and contextual variables have been taken into account. It is still an open question and one of considerable policy import as to whether type B characteristics can make a difference or whether contextual factors like the ethnic and social class mix of the student body explains much, if not all, of the remaining variance between schools. The reason why this remains a live debate is that different studies have measured different aspects of school processes and usually on a very restricted measure of school level and performance variables. For example, where a measure of a contextual variable has been taken into account it is often of a limited kind. In the UK it is often the number of students eligible for free school meals which stands as a proxy for the number children in poverty. Yet this is hardly a measure of the impact of different social class sub-cultures on school outcomes.

Similarly, although there have been calls to extend the range of school performance variables, studies that do so occur all too rarely. This leaves the RM open to the charge, frequently made, that it embraces a reductionist view of the aims of schooling and through default, if not design, buys into the prevailing government orthodoxy that the quality of schooling can be measured, almost exclusively, by test and exam performance. This is not a charge which is strictly accurate[2] but the limited measures to assess school effectiveness remains a weakness within the RM's own terms. By the same token, at least two crucial variables — those of student turnover and changes in school roll — have been systematically omitted yet they will, almost certainly, have a profound effect on school performance. We know that students living in poverty are likely to be highly geographically mobile, this has been documented for the United States (GOA, 1995) and New Zealand (Lauder et al., 1995) and there is evidence that something similar happens in the UK (Mortimore, 1988). We also know from the work of Coleman (1988) that students who do move schools frequently are heavily penalized in terms of educational performance, yet this is a variable that is rarely, if ever, incorporated in the RM's equations. Instability of school rolls also becomes a crucial issue in a market context due to schools entering a spiral of decline. Research by Hughes et al. (1997) has shown that a decline in school rolls due to market forces has a significant effect on school outcomes.

In its own terms the RM still has a long way to go to accumulate the kind of research evidence which would enable confident policy advice at the macro level to be given. However, at the micro level it encounters greater difficulties.

The RM's Capacity to Guide Practice

If the initial question of the RM was that of whether schools could make a difference, it followed that once differences in processes and outcomes, relative to intake, had been established, lessons as to how schools could be improved followed. These 'lessons' took the form of lists of the ingredients of what made an effective school. These ingredients were identified in the empiricist way described above. However, the leap from establishing that schools *could* make a difference to a recipe as to how schools could improve was too ambitious and begged a series of questions that remain unanswered to this day, despite a welcome sophistication in the development of quantitative techniques.

If, for a moment we assume that 'successful' schools are engineered by design not serendipity two related problems remain. We have seen that their theoretical basis is precarious due to the way they have been constructed but it is also the case that, for reasons we will discuss subsequently, they have omitted key variables in their analysis. These include those of the politics and culture of the school. By culture we mean the professional cultures of teachers and student sub-cultures, all of which we might expect to be riven by class, racist and patriarchal norms. Culture in this sense is a distant cousin of the anondyne notion of ethos yet we can expect both the culture and politics of a school to have a determinant effect on outcomes. Certainly, the work of Ramsay, Sneddon, Grenfell and Ford (1983) and Thrupp (1996) from New Zealand suggests that the class, ethnic composition and related student sub-cultures set the limits and possibilities to what schools can achieve.

These observations bring us, therefore to the issue of *translation*. To define a school, or a unit of it as effective is one thing. To get colleagues to accept this finding is another thing altogether as Reay (1996) and Wikeley (forthcoming) have so clearly shown. What is missing from RM is any recognition that the culture and politics of a school have a role to play in understanding not only why a school is or is not effective but in communicating the 'knowledge' gained from such research to significant 'others'. In turn this point raises the even more profound question of whether lessons from one school can ever be applied, more or less straightforwardly, to another. There is an analagous debate in the literature on organizational management and the conclusion there is that corporate organizations are so radically different in their culture, politics and strategic position that recipes for success cannot simply be transferred from one organization to another (Kay, 1997).

If the introduction of notions like politics and culture draw attention to the possible uniqueness of school contexts the further question is raised of what the RM has ommitted from its universe of concepts that is germane to understanding how schools work.

Hugh Lauder, Ian Jamieson and Felicity Wikeley

What the RM Has Omitted From Its Universe of Concepts

Perhaps what is most revealing about the RM is what it has ommitted by way of theoretical constructs. These include: little reference to school culture or politics as we have seen; little reference to the external policy environment — we call this the problem of the atomistic view of school effectiveness; little reference to those concepts which might be helpful in explaining school success and failure which *link* the external policy environment to the internal structuring of the school — what we will call border concepts. These problems culminate in what may be called the counterfactual issue. Namely, the RM's inability to identify, for example, the impact of major changes in the organization of teachers' work, and consider alternative, possibly more effective, ways of organizing schools. We deal with these issues in turn.

The atomistic view of school effectiveness

Part of the problem of seeking to transfer recipes for success is that schools are not islands, they form part of a system and their success and failure will be predicated on how other parts of the system act and change. In this respect focus on the school as the sole unit of analysis, may be convenient in political terms but it will not produce effective schools. To some extent the RM has acknowledged this by looking at the performance of LEAs as well as individual schools. The problem now is that the policy environment has changed to a quasi-market which has an impact on schools' performance (Hughes et al., 1996 and 1997) and in particular on those labelled as 'failing' (Thrupp, 1997; Tomlinson, 1997). There can be no sound analysis of what makes schools effective without taking into account the market context in which they operate.

Border concepts

Many of the concepts which are likely to inform our understanding of the nature of schools and their performance do not sit easily with the notion that schools as organizations can have effects on student outcomes independent of the wider social and policy context. The concepts of culture and politics, in particular, suggest that the assumption of relative school autonomy needs to be severely modified. For example, the idea that school outcomes are influenced by student sub-cultures which link to wider external sub-cultures suggests that we need to examine the way schools can respond to, change or modify these sub-cultures. In the ethnographic literature there is already a rich vein to be mined in this respect (Hargreaves, 1967; Lacey, 1970; Willis, 1977; Ball, 1981; Brown, 1987; and Jones, 1989) yet since notions of social class, racist and patriarchal cultures have played so little part in the development of the RM it is has not begun the task of theorizing these forms of interaction. This point raises the wider question of the relationship between quantitative and qualitative research (Thrupp, 1995) and it is one to which we shall return.

A second example of a border concept concerns that of the nature of teachers' work. The change to a market system of education has wrought a change in school values and practices as Ball (1990), Ball and Bowe (1992), Gewirtz, Ball and Bowe (1996), Grace (1996) and Menter et al. (1996) have shown. The role and professional ethic of teachers has changed, with a shift from colleagial to hierarchical modes of decision-making and an emphasis on 'leadership'. In addition there is now a major attempt to prescribe not only curriculum but teaching methods largely on the basis of comparative studies with school systems deemed to be more successful than England's on the Pacific Rim (Reynolds and Farrell, 1996). The question here is how have these externally imposed changes impacted on the performance of teachers? Just as schools may be able to mediate external sub-cultural influence within the school, the same issue arises with these external policy changes. How have schools responded to these changes, have they responded uniformly or have some done so with better processes and outcomes than others? Any adequate account of school practices and outcomes ought to be able to address these questions but the RM cannot. This point leads us to the third issue.

The counterfactual problem

The counterfactual problem for the RM is not that it cannot throw light on whether educational performance has been raised (see e.g. Gray and Jesson, 1996) but that it has no way of making a judgment as to whether the current system with its prevailing values and practices is the best way of raising educational performance. One way of doing this is to engage in comparative studies of school effectiveness, which is precisely what Reynolds and Farrell (1996) are doing. From the papers we have seen so far, however, the tradition of abstracted empiricism appears to dominate: in other words, the policy, cultural, political and historical questions have been ignored. The failure of these early papers within the Reynolds' project should not deter us from the important task of attempting to make sound counterfactual judgments. To continue with the example of Reynolds' work: OFSTED has justified attempts to raise test scores by emphasizing the need for whole class teaching on the basis of a review conducted by Reynolds of educational practices in some Pacific-rim countries. OFSTED may well be merely attempting to correct an undue emphasis on one teaching method to the exclusion of another however, the crucial issue must surely be in part a question not only of test results but how they are arrived at. For example, in the Pacific Rim there is a major concern with the lack of critical thinking and creativity amongst students (OECD, 1996) despite strong showings in international studies of educational performance. This is because policy-makers there take the view that the key to future economic competitiveness lies in the development of a creative workforce. In England the problem of how to raise basic educational standards while preserving or developing creativity is not even part of the public debate.

These criticisms suggest that the universe of concepts framed by the RM's hard core, is unable to meet these criticisms, although clearly in its own terms it is a 'progressive' research programme. If we are to move forward we now need to turn the Heretical Model because it issues a fundamental conceptual challenge to the RM's hard core.

The Heretical Model

The HM is so called because it denies what policy-makers and many researchers assume: that we can know why some schools are effective and others not and that we can engineer stable school structures and practices which will make less effective schools more effective. In the present policy climate such a view is clearly heretical.

The HM can be derived from the work of Stephen Ball and his colleagues at Kings College, London, but the key underlying idea is one that has been raised in the context of the effectiveness of teaching by several commentators (e.g. Monk, 1992; Whitehead, 1996). Ball's (1996) view is based on a rejection of:

> . . . the neat and totalising, essentialist, one-off forms of analysis that are normally applied to schools as organisations, both in characterisations in research and in public evaluations i.e. failing/successful, effective/ineffective etc. (p. 1)

Ball adopts this position on the basis of the assertion that:

> Schools are complex, contradictory sometimes incoherent organisations like many others. They are assembled over time to form a bricolage of memories commitments, routines, bright ideas and policy effects. They are changed, influenced and interfered with regularly and increasingly. They drift, decay and re-generate. (p. 1)

That this is just an assertion should not unduly trouble us, it has the same status as the hard core propositions within the RM. However, it touches on one of the fundamental problems of organization and management theory which is how organizations as rational structures can be engineered while also being creative and hence indeterminate in their strategies and responses to a changing environment. The problem is captured in the notion of 'loose coupling' which is designed to provide a theory which overcomes this problem:

> Loose coupling . . . allows organizational analysts to explain the simultaneous existence of rationality and indeterminacy . . . [it] suggests that any location in an organization (top, middle, bottom) contains interdependent elements that vary in the number and strength of their interdependencies. The fact that these elements are linked and preserve some degree of determinancy is captured by the word 'coupled' in the phrase 'loosely coupled'. The fact that these elements are also subject to spontaneous changes and preserve some degree of independence and indeterminance is captured by the modifying word loosely. The resulting image is of a system that is simultaneously open and closed, indeterminate and rational, spontaneous and deliberate. (Orton and Weick, 1990, pp. 204–5)

From an organizational perspective, the problem is that while this may be an accurate image it doesn't explain how the right combination of interdependency and indeterminacy can be arrived at. What this suggests is that schools can never be understood in a purely mechanical way, that a degree of indeterminacy is necessarily built in the very nature of organizations. In turn, this means that schools may always vary in their performance as they adapt to new environments and experiment. The claim, for example, that schools can be high reliability organizations cannot mean that they will not fail in some respects at some times.

However, Ball has two arguments which push the issue of indeterminacy in schools further, but, in contrast to the descriptive model depicted by Orton and Weick, he has two explanations for why indeterminacy is a necessary feature of schools as organizations. The most interesting but perhaps weaker explanation can be found in a much earlier work of Ball's (1987) in which he suggests that schools are loosely structured as a way of dealing with ideological diversity. In effect it is a political response to the fact that educational aims, methods and contents are open to debate. The response by heads or management teams to the difficulty the essentially contested nature of schooling poses is:

> . . . frequently contained by a deliberate policy of loose-coupling. Departments or other sub-units . . . are left to their own devices. Official school policy is open to interpretation or special arrangements are negotiated . . . once the loose-coupled or anarchic character of schools and their ideological diversity are recognised then the ever-present potential for conflict must also be accepted. (Ball, 1987, p. 15)

What Ball is pointing to here may be a unique feature of schools as organizations in that 'loose-coupling' is seen as a rational response to the contested nature of education. But this view is not merely a matter of politics but of values for it can be argued that schools should first and foremost be moral communities and that their organizational structure, including the politics of decision-making should reflect their essential nature. If schools are viewed in this light a further element of unpredictability is built into schools because there are no alogorithms or recipes by which moral decisions can be made. It is very much a matter of context.

However, in the current economic and political climate in which the state has lost many of the Keynesian levers of economic regulation and the importance of knowledge to the economy has risen, the state has turned its attention to what it can control. In this context, education is an obvious target for greater centralized control (Brown, Halsey, Lauder and Stuart Wells, 1997). Hence the essentially contested nature of educational aims is replaced by a set of government fiats as to the means and ends of education. In his (1996) paper Ball attempts to identify the methods used by the state to exercise control over values. He argues that a systematic change in the nature of teaching as a profession has been engineered by intellectual technologies such as Total Quality Management (TQM) which is: 'a relay device effectively linking government "mentalities" and policies with everyday organisational "realities"' (p. 13). In turn these relay technologies are part of the 'bigger picture, a larger transformation' produced by the 'larger ideological narrative and organisational structure of the "enterprise" culture' (p. 21).

In other words, the social technologies of the enterprise culture have reconstructed the identities of teachers as professionals in such a way as to minimize ideological debate and political conflict. Ball's is an explanation of the manufacturing of consensus. In the process he and his colleagues (Gewirtz, 1996; Reay, 1996) develop an important border concept for he raises questions about the appropriateness and merits of these new forms of professional identity construction for teachers.

Whatever the merits of this intriguing view there is another sense in which school performance can be seen as serendipitous, once intake characteristics and contextual variables have been accounted for. Although, in Ball's work it brings us once more back to the issues of values and democracy. This is quite simply the view that organizational 'success' might be a matter of luck because schools are so complex there is no way they can be defined by a single adjective or descriptor. Whatever focus is taken on a school will be at best partial.

This latter view does not entirely rule out the possibility of school improvement but it does place improvement attempts firmly in the hands of teachers within any particular school and it is linked to a particular form of decision-making. Since schools are multi-faceted and unique in their ensemble of history, policy, politics and culture it is only teachers inside the culture that can understand how best to improve the school. Moreover, since the school is such a complex organization, improvement must be the product of considerable debate and democratic decision-making. In this sense the HM generates a different view of professional practice and decision-making from that of the RM.

In his empirical work on the implementation of the National Curriculum (Ball and Bowe, 1992), there is clearly justification for the view that 'top down' prescriptions will be changed in unintended and unanticipated ways once applied in schools. This then leaves the teacher as professional with a high degree of *de facto* autonomy both within the school and in relation to government policy. Perhaps most importantly in this respect, teachers are seen not merely as the purveyors of others' values as government policy would have them but as authentic beings capable of exercising their own moral judgments.

As a critique of both state policy and the RM, this model provides a necessary corrective to many of the current orthodoxies. However, in the process it is in danger of ignoring past good practice in Britain and of some of the important insights that can be gained both from the RM and research into other successful programmes, for example, Reading Recovery. The key here is to create a model of school effectiveness which acknowledges the importance of teacher professional autonomy and the uniqueness of each school as an organization, while seeking to systematically improve all schools within the national system. As Green (1997) has argued, it is likely that decentralized systems do not have the capacity to deliver the highest potential standards of education for all, yet the argument of the HM if taken to its logical conclusion leads to a highly decentralized system of education. There has to be some structured way of being able to deliver good practice while acknowledging the importance of teachers as professionals.

With these points in mind we turn to the *Contextual Model*.

The Contextual Model

In attempting to sketch the contours of the contextual model (CM), certain parameters have been developed as a result of the consideration of both the RM and HM. Before bringing these to bear on the development of the contextual model we would reinforce one point which has been made by other contributors to this volume. Not all justifiable processes and aims of education can or should be measured quantitatively. For example, the processes and aims relating to schooling for a democratic education are extremely hard, if not impossible to quantify, yet few would deny the importance of such an aim. Part of the problem here is that quantitative methods and indicators are reified in the current political climate. Researchers operating within the precepts of the contextual model would be at pains to stress the importance and limitations of both quantitative and qualitative research in ways we shall subsequently discuss. What we take from this point in the development of the CM is the necessity to acknowledge the limitations of all research methods in fostering school improvement.

Research Questions

Schools in different contexts will have different capacities, potentials and limits. This then has a direct bearing on accountability, for schools cannot all be held accountable in the same way. Yet regulatory agencies like OFSTED in England and Education Review Office (ERO) in New Zealand clearly assume that schools in working-class areas should be considered to have the same capacities as other schools. They must make this assumption since it is typically working-class schools which are identified as 'failing'.

Research within the CM will fundamentally be concerned with the link between capacities, potentials and limits within specific social contexts and within specific positions within an educational market. The purpose is to ask under what conditions schools can best perform and how they should be held accountable. This approach would reject the notion that schools can be judged according to league tables or even judged fairly on the basis of value-added league tables if they do not also take account of the contexts we have referred to and which we know, in rather general terms, have an impact on school performance. League tables, however sophisticated, assume a continuum of performance but once these varying and interlocking notions of context are acknowledged as significant there can be no place for accountability based on such assumptions.

In this respect, it is also worth emphasizing that capacities and potentials must be viewed in terms of sustainability. Much of the present rhetoric about the effectiveness of schools is based on the identification of single cases of schools that appear to be successful in areas of great poverty. From this it is inferred that if one school can achieve in this way, all like schools can. This may be a fallacy. Working-class schools may well raise their achievement levels for a time but given the intense pressures on them it is unlikely that the level of achievement can be sustained. We know of no research which has shown that they can.

This then suggests that research within the CM should be longitudinal and should ask four kinds of related question: what impact does a school's community and intake have on its performance; what impact does the educational market have on a school's performance; under what conditions could schools perform better;

and how are we to develop contextual criteria for holding schools accountable? In asking these questions it should be emphasized that we are referring not only to the internal organization and performance of schools but of the way the relationship of schools to a community can be better organized. The perspective here cannot however be confined to a group of schools within a community but will necessarily have to link macro social and economic policy to the impact on education. For example, we know from Wilkinson's (1966) seminal work that it is not merely the fact of poverty, but the relative levels of inequality, that will have a bearing on family well-being and hence children's school performance. Such research needs to be taken into account.

Theoretical Resources

The CM would have no initial substantive theoretical commitments. As Lakatos points out, the hard core of a research programme does not emerge fully formed from the head of Zeus! It does, however, have a set of orientations and a set of theoretical resources. The key orientation would be that of openness where the RM is closed. Rather than assume that all schools can be made effective the CM would seek to interrogate this assumption. In a sense what the RM has done is to miss out certain basic steps in making the hard core assumptions that it does.

Central to this question is that of the relative autonomy of schools and the ways in which they may or may not be able to mediate those external influences represented by what we have called border concepts. While relative autonomy will always remain a problematic notion it is not a difficulty encountered by the RM alone. Indeed it is one which is explored by many of the ethnographic studies cited above. In the work of Hargreaves and Lacey, the schools' organization into streams exacerbates the problems of the class inequalities that students bring to schools. In contrast, Willis' lads merely 'bounce' off the school organization and moral system. The important point here is that in each of these studies a position is taken about the relationship of the school to the wider society and more specifically how the school may or may not be able to act to mediate external factors. The general point here is not that a position should be taken on the question of relative autonomy but rather to document the various circumstances in which schools may or may not successfully mediate external forces. In this sense the basic postulate should not be the closed assumption that schools are relatively autonomous but rather the question of the conditions under which they might be relatively autonomous. To say this does mean breaking with the proselitizing inference that because some schools can be relatively autonomous and hence 'effective', that all schools can.

An irony in considering the way that the the qualitative tradition may be used to develop a more sophisticated protective belt is that the two contributions that may be most fruitful — those of Brown (1987) and Thrupp (1996) — are notable for their absence or denial of any theory of relative autonomy of the school. Brown's work is of interest because he takes up the Durkheim-Bernstein theme of the *moral order* created by working-class students within the schools in his study. In his work this moral order is a resource of working-class culture rather than one fostered by the school, yet clearly there is a potential in this notion as a building block in the development of a theory of the school. Similarly, Thrupp's work is significant because he suggests that it is the social class mix of the students within a school which determines the 'moral order' and pedagogy of a school rather than the other way around. It then raises a further important question about the nature of causation in the way schools are structured.

Drawing on qualitative studies of this kind merely provides an illustration of the kinds of resources that can be drawn upon. Nevertheless what is already at hand provides a rich starting point in theorizing school processes and outcomes.

Methodology

The methodology of the CM would in the first and ideal instance involve both quantitative and qualitative study of schools within an educational market. Quantitative study would seek to establish over time the impact of markets on school performance. The quantitative element of such a study would also analyze school effects over time in the light of this analysis. Where schools in similar circumstances perform differently according to several indicators these would be investigated qualitiatively.

It should be emphasized that the quantitative part of this analysis should not be seen as unequivocally setting the parameters for school performance. We know that quantitative studies are themselves subject to error, even at the 'polar ends' of a continuum of performance.[3] Rather quantitative and qualitative work should be seen as operating within the context of a 'conversation' about a school's performance.

Accountability and Good Practice

The purpose of such studies should be threefold. The first is to test a central proposition of the HM by seeing, once a fully specified model of intake and contextual variables has been developed, whether schools remain stable over time in the limited sense of value-added with respect to effectiveness indicators. If they do not then we clearly need to ask why. If the answer is one of caprice and serendipity, as one version of the Heretical Model might suggest, then the remaining two purposes are thrown into jeopardy. Assume, however, that schools either are unstable for good reasons to do with experimentation or simply remain stable, then the next step would be to provide case studies of good practice. Whether they are acted upon will depend on how they are interpreted within the context of the culture, politics and values of a school, although clearly there would be an onus on schools to seek to improve by modelling appropriate good practice. Case studies do not constitute lists or recipes but are sources of critical reflection to be adapted and used by teachers in others schools in ways appropriate to their cultural contexts. This is to take seriously the issues concerning school cultures and values raised by the HM. From these studies and schools' responses to them should emerge contextual criteria of accountability not only for schools but for policy-makers.

Although we have been at pains to emphasize the contextual nature of good school performances we acknowledge that there is a place for governments to mandate what are considered good educational practices from around the world, so long as policy importation is done judiciously. The evidence so far suggests it has not. However, the key here is the way good practice is mandated. If it is done bureaucratically so that teachers are told to teach by a particular method for so many hours a day, it will fail because it will simply lead to a de-skilling of teachers. The success of being a good teacher lies in making the crucial contextual judgments as to when and how to apply particular pedagogies. Bureaucratic fiat will not address the crucial issue of how to teach children to be creative and independent, rather it is likely to lead to some aspects of the rote learning that the East Asian tiger economies are trying to escape.

Conclusion

What we are trying to do in offering a third model is to build on the the strengths of the other two models which will challenge current political orthodoxies. The 'Contextual' model of school effectiveness builds a middle ground between the Received and the Heretical models. Epistemologically it sits between the abstracted empiricism of the Received Model with its practitioner lists of characteristics, and the particularism of the Heretical Model. Taken to its logical conclusion the Heretical Model would run against the grain of teacher and school development in the UK. Before the advent of the National Curriculum, the UK with its devolved structure of schooling was highly innovative. In such a system the culture of sharing 'good practice' became ingrained. If it is assumed, as we do, that there are some identifiable characteristics of schooling that are systematically implicated in school effectiveness but that these are by no means recipes for success, the question of how knowledge of these good practices can once again be shared becomes paramount. The Contextual Model attempts to provide a sound research framework for achieving this aim.

Notes

1 A rational reconstruction does not necessarily relate to what researchers believe are their theoretical commitments but is a reconstruction of what they logically and historically have been committed to, independent of their own thinking. In this sense theories are not the property of individuals but are a resource that individuals work within and develop. Put another way, our concern is not so much with criticism of individual research projects but with a critique of the framework they operate within. The term was coined by Lakatos (1970). See the following discussion.

2 For example, with the development of Hierarchical Linear Modelling (HLM), league tables have been criticized because they assume that schools are the appropriate unit of appraisal and that they are stable in their performance over time. It should be added that there is a tradition which has developed alongside that of the RM that has used many of

its techniques to test policy prescriptions. Much of the work in this area has been undertaken in Scotland (see e.g. Gray, Mcpherson and Raffe, 1982; Willms and Mcpherson, 1997), New Zealand (Lauder et al., 1995; Harker and Nash, 1996; Hughes et al., 1996 and 1997) and the United States albeit often from a neo-liberal perspective (see e.g. Chubb and Moe, 1990). Research within this tradition is better understood as examples of a revamped political arithmetic (Brown et al., 1997) designed to bring to account official claims about government policy.

3   To give an example, in a study conducted by Lauder and Hughes (1990) one of the least performing schools in their sample — once intake and contextual variables had been taken into account — was a single-sex girls school with an apparently high socio-economic intake. However, this result is almost certainly misleading since the majority of high SES (socio-economic status) fathers who had been ranked in the category 'manager' had in fact been upwardly mobile but without high educational qualifications. It could be assumed that they had no cultural capital to pass on, hence the mean SES score of the school should have been lower than estimated. Even the most basic variables in school effectiveness research are theory impregnated!

References

BALL, S.J. (1981) *Beachside Comprehensive*, Cambridge: Cambridge University Press.

BALL, S.J. (1987) *The Micro Politics of the School*: London, Methuen.

BALL, S.J. (1990) *Educative, Inequality & School Reform: Values in Crisis! Inaugural Lecture*, Centre for Education Studies, Key's College, London.

BALL, S.J. (1996) 'Good school/Bad school', Paper presented to the BERA conference, Lancaster, September.

BALL, S. and BOWE, R. (1992) 'Subject departments and the "implementation" of National Curriculum policy: An overview of the issues', *Journal of Curriculum Studies*, **24**, 2, pp. 97–115.

BARR, R. and DREEBEN, R. (1983) *How Schools Work*, Chicago: University of Chicago Press.

BOWLES, S. and GINTIS, H. (1976) *Schooling in Capitalist America*, London: Routledge.

BROWN, P. (1987) *Schooling Ordinay Kids*, London: Tavistock.

BROWN, P., HALSEY, A., LAUDER, H. and STUART WELLS, A. (1997) 'The transformation of education and society', in HALSEY, A., LAUDER, H., BROWN, P. and STUART WELLS, A., (eds) *Education, Culture, Economy and Society*, Oxford: Oxford University Press, Chapter 1.

CHUBB, J. and MOE, T. (1990) *Politics, Markets and America's Schools*, Washington: The Brookings Institute.

COLEMAN, J., CAMPBELL, E., HOBSON, C., MCPARTLAND, J., MOOD, A., WEINFELD, F. and YORK, R. (1966) *Equality of Educational Opportunity*, Washington: US Government Printing Office.

COLEMAN, J. (1988) 'Social capital in the creation of human capital', in HALSEY, A., LAUDER, H., BROWN, P. and STUART WELLS, A. (eds) *Education, Culture, Economy and Society*, Oxford: Oxford University Press, Chapter 4.

GENERAL ACCOUNTING OFFICE (USA) 'Elementary school children: Many change schools frequently harming their education', Report to the Hon. Marcy Kaptur, House of Representatives, Washington D.C. Author.

GEWIRTZ, S. (1996) 'Post-welfarism and the reconstruction of teachers' work', Paper presented to the BERA Conference, Lancaster, September.

GEWIRTZ, S., BALL, S. and BOWE, R. (1995) *Markets, Choice and Equity in Education*, Milton Keynes, Open University Press.

GOLDSTEIN, H. (1996) 'Relegate the league tables', *New Economy*, winter, 3, pp. 199–203.

GRACE, G. (1995) *School Leadership: Beyond Education Management: An Essay in Policy Scholarship*, London: Falmer Press.

GRAY, J., GOLDSTEIN, H. and JESSON, D. (1996) 'Changes and improvements in schools' effectiveness', *Research Papers in Education*, **11**, 1, pp. 35–51.

GRAY, J. and JESSON, D. (1996) 'A nation on the move? The nature and extent of school improvement in the 1990s', Paper from the Improving Schools Research Project, Homerton College: Cambridge.

GRAY, J., MCPHERSON, A. and RAFFE, D. (1983) *Reconstructions of Secondary Education: Theory, Myth and Practice in Scotland Since the War*, London: Routledge and Kegan Paul.

GREEN, A. (1997) 'Educational achievement in centralised & decentralised systems', in HALSEY, A., LAUDER, H., BROWN, P. and STUART WELLS, A. (eds) *Education, Culture, Economy & Society*, Oxford: Oxford University Press.

HANUSHEK, E. (1986) 'The economics of schooling: Production and efficiency in public schools', *Journal of Economic Literature*, **24**, pp. 1141–77.

HARGREAVES, D. (1967) *Social Relations in a Secondary School*, London: Routledge and Keegan Paul.

HARKER, R. and NASH, R. (1996) 'Academic outcomes and school effectiveness: Type A and type B effects', *New Zealand Journal of Educational Studies*, **32**, 2, pp. 143–70.

HARRIS, K. (1979) *Education and Knowledge*, London: Routledge.

HARRIS, K.A., JAMIESON, I. and RUSS, J. (1995) 'A study of "effective" departments in secondary schools', *School Organisation*, **15**, 3, pp. 283–99.

HUGHES, D., LAUDER, H., WATSON, S., HAMLIN, J. and SIMIYU, I. (1996) *Markets in Education: Testing the Polarisation Thesis*, Wellington: Ministry of Education.

HUGHES, D., LAUDER, H., WATSON, S., STRATHDEE, R. and SIMIYU, I. (1997) *School Effectiveness: An Analysis of Differences Between Nineteen Schools on Four Outcome Measures Using Hierarchical Linear Modelling*, Wellington: Ministry of Education.

JONES, A. (1989) 'The cultural production of classroom practice', *British Journal of Sociology of Education*, **10**, pp. 19–31.

KAY, J. (1997) *The Business of Economics: Competition, the Stakeholder Economy, Business Strategy*, Oxford: Oxford University Press.

LACEY, C. (1970) *Hightown Grammar*, Manchester: Manchester University Press.

LAKATOS, I. (1970) 'Falsification and the methodology of scientific research programmes', in LAKATOS, I. and MUSGRAVE, A. (eds) *Criticism and the Growth of Knowledge*, Cambridge: Cambridge University Press, pp. 91–195.

LAUDER, H. and HUGHES, D. (1990) 'Social inequalities and differences in school outcomes', *New Zealand Journal of Educational Studies*, **25**, pp. 37–60.

LAUDER, H., HUGHES, D., WASLANDER, S., THRUPP, M., MCGLINN, J., NEWTON, S. and DUPUIS, A. (1995) *The Creation of Market Competition for Education in New Zealand*, Wellington: Ministry of Education.

MENTER, I., MUSCHAMP, Y., NICHOLLS, P., OZGA, J. and POLLARD, A. (1997) *Work and Identity in the Primary School*, Milton Keynes, Open University Press.

MILLER, S. and FREDERICKS, J. (1990) 'The false ontology of school climate effects', *Educational Theory*, **40**, 3, pp. 333–42.

MONK, D. (1992) 'Education productivity research: An update and assessment of its role in education finance reform', *Education, Evaluation and Policy Analaysis*, **14**, 4, pp. 307–32.

MORTIMORE, P., SAMMONS, P., STOLL, L., LEWIS, D. and ECOB, R. (1988) *School Matters: The Junior Years*, Wells: Open Books.

OECD (1996) *The Korean Education System*, Seoul: Ministry of Education.

ORTON, J. and WEICK, K. (1990) 'Loosely coupled systems: A reconceptualisation', *Academy of Management Review*, **15**, 2, pp. 203–23.

RAMSAY, P., SNEDDON, D., GRENFELL, J. and FORD, I. (1983) 'Successful and unsuccessful Schools', *Australian and New Zealand Journal of Sociology*, **19**, pp. 272–304.

REAY, D. (1996) 'The micro-politics of the 1990s: Staff relationships in secondary schooling', Paper presented to the BERA Conference, Lancaster, September.

REYNOLDS, D. and FARRELL, S. (1996) *Worlds Apart*, London: OFSTED.

ROBINSON, V. (1993) *Problem-based Methodology: Research for the Improvement of Practice*, Oxford: Pergamon Press.

RUTTER, M., OUSTON, J., MORTIMORE, P. and MAUGHAN, B. (1979) *Fifteen Thousand Hours*, Somerset: Open Books.

SAMMONS, P., THOMAS, S. and MORTIMORE, P. (1995) '*Accounting for variations in academic effectiveness between schools and departments*', Paper presented at ECER Conference, September.

THRUPP, M. (1995) 'The school mix effect: The history of an enduring problem in educational research, policy and practice', *British Journal of Sociology of Education*, **16**, pp. 183–203.

THRUPP, M. (1996) 'The school mix effect', Unpublished PhD Thesis, Education Department, Victoria University of Wellington.

THRUPP, M. (forthcoming) 'Exploring the politics of blame: School inspection and its contestation in New Zealand and England', *Comparative Education*.

TOMLINSON, S. (1997) 'Sociolological perspectives on failing schools', Paper given to the Sociology of Education Conference, University of Sheffield, January.

WHITEHEAD, J. (1996) 'Living educational theories and living contradictions: A response to Mike Newby', *Journal of Philosophy of Education*, **30**, 3, pp. 457–62.

WIKELEY, F. (forthcoming) Dissemination of Effectiveness Research as a Tool for School Improvement, *School Leadership and Management*, **18**, 1.

WILKINSON, R. (1996) *Unhealthy Societies: The Afflictions of Inequality*, London: Routledge.

WILLIS, P. (1977) *Learning to Labour*, Farnborough, Saxon House.

WILLMS, D. and McPHERSON, A. (1997) 'Equalization and improvement: Some effects of comprehensive reorganization in Scotland', in Halsey, A., LAUDER, H., BROWN, P. and STUART WELLS, A. (eds) *Education, Culture, Economy and Society*, Oxford: Oxford University Press, Chapter 45.

WILLMS, D. and RAUDENBUSCH, S. (1989) 'A longitudinal hierarchical linear model for estimating school, effects and their stability', *Journal of Educational Measurement*, **26**, 3, pp. 209–32.

Chapter 6

Educational Studies, Policy Entrepreneurship and Social Theory[1]

Stephen J. Ball

In this chapter I intend to reflect upon my practice as an educational researcher and theorist and, in more general terms, consider the current state of educational studies. In doing so I shall allow myself to be playful and perhaps at times outrageous. I am not attempting to be definitive. What I offer here is coming close to an approximation of something I might hope to say more clearly in the future. The spirit of what I am attempting, and some of the substance I wish to argue, are conveyed rather effectively in the following quotation from Michel Foucault:

> I wouldn't want what I may have said or written to be seen as laying any claims to totality. I don't try to universalize what I say; conversely what I don't say isn't meant to be thereby disqualified as being of no importance. My work takes place between unfinished abutments and anticipatory strings of dots. I like to open out a space of research, try it out, then if it doesn't work try again somewhere else. On many points . . . I am still working and don't yet know whether I am going to get anywhere. What I say ought to be taken as 'propositions', 'game openings' where those who may be interested are invited to join in; they are not meant as dogmatic assertions that have to be taken or left en bloc . . . (1991, pp. 90–1)

My proposition, then, my 'game opening' here, is that educational studies is in a sorry state and in danger of becoming sorrier. That is to say, the weak grammars of educational studies, those concepts, relations and procedures upon which it rests, are becoming weaker (Bernstein, 1996). In Bernsteinian terms, the serial segmented structures, those differentiating rituals which distinguish us from each other and from other fields of knowledge, are becoming more detached and insulated from one another. As Basil Bernstein might put it, the invisible light that shines wanly within the knowledge structures of educational studies is in danger of being snuffed out entirely.

It is hardly novel to suggest that the discourses and knowledge structures of educational studies are shifting in response to the political and ideological repositioning of the academy and of scholarship. It is important to make it clear that the state of affairs I am addressing here is, at least in part, symptomatic of a more wholesale reworking of the relationship between higher education and research and the state. However, the resultant changes in the practices of scholarship seem particularly marked and particularly paradoxical in the field of educational studies. More specifically, what I have called the sorry state of educational studies seems to me to stem in part from both the wholesale appropriation of other 'unreflexive' and utilitarian languages *and* the internal lack of dynamism, exacerbated by intellectual isolationism as educational studies pointedly ignores significant theoretical developments in cognate fields. The problem with educational studies, I am arguing, is that we are both too open to other discourses and not open enough.

This state of affairs is my topic. I want to spend some time exploring the problems with educational studies as I see them; I shall then consider the role of theory in reconstituting a new present for educational studies and conclude with some brief thoughts about the nature of theorizing and the problem with theory. While bearing in mind the initial disclaimer quoted above, I will have, necessarily, to indulge in some generalizations. I must also acknowledge from the start that I will leave my argument only partially developed and I will leave it with embedded contradictions. At times I will be likely to appear self-destructive and perhaps intellectually schizophrenic. I shall leave the reader to judge. I must also acknowledge that what I say may have somewhat less relevance to some disciplines within educational studies than it does to others.

To begin, I want to take as my particular case in point my own discipline — the sociology of education — but, as I say, I intend my thesis to be more generalized. I shall rehearse a kind of vulgar history of the discipline in order to establish what I call the **reincorporation** of educational studies.

British sociology of education had its beginnings in, that is it was initiated and primarily disseminated from, the London School of Economics (LSE). The methods and politics of the subject were, from the late 1930s to the late 1960s, driven by the methods and politics of the LSE. This placed education as part of the post-war social reconstruction of Britain and as part of the establishment of a modern welfare state. The concerns of researchers were focussed *initially* upon the problems of mass participation in the education system and the debilitating effects, for some children, of economic and material deprivation. The sometimes unarticulated assumption of the handful of education researchers at work at this time appeared to be that if these extrinsic sources of inequality could be removed or ameliorated then the repeatedly evident and apparently tight bond between educational attainment and social class could be broken; leaving residual differences which could be explained in others ways — like in terms of intelligence or selection bias. Crucially, the particular focus upon social class differences served to establish social class as the major, almost the only, dependent variable in sociological research for the next 40 years. During this period, through the work of particular 'universal intellectuals', the sociology of education aspired to, and occasionally achieved, a positive and influential relationship with policy-making. Particular policy solutions, based upon the outcomes of empirical research, were pursued, particularly in relation to Labour Party policy-making. Both the discipline and its politics and its relationships to policy were set within the grooves of an unproblemmatic, progressive, utopian modernism. This was the enlightenment project writ small. Research linked to ameliorative state policies focused upon the achievement of equality *and* prosperity — the better educated we are the better off we are, individually and collectively. The discourse of this policy optimism was founded upon notions like the 'wasted pool of talent' and 'compensatory education'.

As we know, this dual optimism (that attached to the welfare state and that embedded in the practices and discourses of the discipline itself) did not last. In the 1970s the academic discourse of programmatic optimism was to be dramatically and decisively replaced by one of radical pessimism. The interpretations of the causes and solutions of inequality scattered to the winds. Policy became an irrelevance as the reproduction of unequal social relations were discovered to be lurking stubbornly in every classroom nook and cranny and every staffroom conversation; while at the same time they were rooted in the abstract needs of the state and the inevitable and inescapable requirements and workings of the economy. The teacher as cultural dope was now the subject of derision from all sides for failing to deliver either fairness or prosperity. A relationship between research and policy (at least at national level) was now not just pointless but also politically incorrect. Educational researchers found themselves grounded between negativity and complicity. With the collapse of the relationship between educational research and policy and the beginnings of a growing suspicion of liberal expertise within educational politics, the vacuum in the arena of educational policy-making was skilfully filled by the organic intellectuals of the New Right.

In the 1980s, things became more complicated as class analysis was displaced as the primary variable and race, gender and, later, disability and sexual orientation, came to the fore both in analytical perspectives and in a new but tentative liaison between theory and practice. But race and gender studies were only two parts of a more thorough-going fragmentation of the sociology of education as some researchers began to turn their attention to and then attach themselves to the industry of educational reform. While some one-time and would-be sociologists and other educational researchers now reinvented themselves as feminists or anti-racists, and indeed brought to educational studies a much needed infusion of invigorating new theory, others began to take on new identities as 'school effectiveness researchers' and 'management theorists'. Around this latter kind of work, a new relationship *to* policy or rather *inside* policy was forged. Issues related to system design, analysis of provision and social justice were replaced by implementation studies focused on issues like 'quality', 'evaluation', 'leadership' and 'accountability'.

In the 1990s, whole areas of the sociology of education, specifically, and educational studies generally have been thoroughly reincorporated into the political project and discourse of policy and of educational reform. In some respects the discipline has come full circle. This reincorporation can be interrogated by rehearsing Brian Fay's distinction, also used by Gerald Grace, between policy science and policy scholarship (Fay, 1975). Fay defines policy science as 'that set of procedures which enables one to determine the technically best course of action to adopt in order to implement a decision or achieve a goal. Here the policy scientist doesn't merely clarify the possible outcomes of certain courses of action, he actually chooses the most efficient course of action in terms of the available scientific information' (1975, p. 14). This, Fay suggests, is a type of 'policy engineering': the 'policy engineer . . . is one who seeks the most technically correct answer to political problems in terms of available social scientific knowledge' (p. 14). Here policy is both de-politicized and thoroughly technicized; the perview of the policy scientist is limited to and by the agenda of social and political problems defined elsewhere and by solutions already embedded in scientific practice, this is what Fay calls 'the sublimation of politics' (p. 27). It also produces, I suggest, another effect, that is — by a combination of financial restructuring and Faustian deal-making — 'the taming of the academy'. As a result, research perspectives and research funding are increasingly tightly tied to the policy agendas of government: the already weak autonomy of higher education having been redefined as part of the cause of the nation's economic problems.

This problem-solving technicism further rests upon an uncritical acceptance of moral and political consensus and operates within the hegemony of instrumental rationalism or as Fay puts it 'man (sic) must plan, and the function of the social sciences is to provide the theoretical foundation that makes this planning possible' (p. 27). In this scientific and technical project for research, the debates and conflicts which link policies to values and morals is displaced by bland rationalist empiricism, and the best we can aspire to is to be 'integrated critics' (Eco, 1994). But again other effects are produced here. Firstly, this instrumental, rational empiricism is implicated and interested in the social construction of those subjects about whom it speaks, in relation to whom it construes problems and constructs solutions. It has produced what Donzelot calls the 'landscape of the social' within which it then acts (I return to this later). Furthermore, in this 'will to knowledge' and the complex interplay between knowledge and the objects of its concern, the very nature of 'the social' is captured and constrained by social science's classifications and nosologies and by the drive to achieve parsimonious and totalizing conceptions of social structures and processes. The epistemic assumptions of order, structure, function, cause and effect are variously mobilized to represent 'the social' and in doing so work to exclude many of the mobile, complex, ad hoc, messy and fleeting qualities of lived experience. We become locked into the simple but powerful and very productive assumption that 'the social' is susceptible to parsimonious and orderly totalizing conceptions. Or to use a slightly different lexicon, drawing again from Foucault (1977), we can say that:

> In appearance, or rather, according to the mask it bears, historical consciousness is neutral, devoid of passions and committed solely to truth. But if it examines itself and if, more generally, it interrogates the various forms of scientific consciousness in its history it finds that all these forms and transformations are aspects of the will to knowledge: instinct, passion, the inquisitor's devotion, cruel subtlety and malice . . . (p. 162)

Perhaps it would be helpful at this point if I were to develop an example of policy science at work in a way which begins to illustrate some of the variety of points I have adumbrated above. 'Management theory' offers one example on which I have written previously (Ball, 1990 and 1994) so let me move away from that slightly by considering the relationships between management theory and school effectiveness research. Again my style of analysis draws on Foucault, in particular I shall employ his 'master trope' — reversal. I will thus be seeking the negative activity of discourse.

Management theories as modes of objectification place human beings as subjects — to be managed. This is a 'discourse of right' which legitimates the exercise of authority. Its primary instrument is a hierarchy of continuous and functional surveillance. Effectiveness research can be seen to have played a crucial role in laying the groundwork for the reconceptualization of the school within which management discourse operates and has played its part in providing a technology of organizational measurement and surveillance. By technology here I refer to 'coherent or contradictory forms of managing and activating a population' which, like Bentham's panopticon, lend themselves to polyvalent tactical applications.

First, effectiveness studies and school-difference studies re-centred the school as the focus of causation in explanations of student performance and variations in levels of achievement; displacing or rendering silent other explanations related to the embeddedness of education in social and economic contexts. And in so far as the gaze of 'effectiveness' provided a scientific basis for the possibility of 'blaming' the school, it fitted perfectly (in terms of theoretical unity) into the discourses of derision which targetted schools as 'causes' of general social and economic problems within society at large. In addition, the focus on measurable outcomes also articulated directly with the political process of the commodification of education involved in the creation of an education market.

Second, this research provided a scientific concomitant to the political re-emphasis on excellence, diversity and selection and the attempt to develop methods of appraisal which can be used to identify (and punish) 'weak' and 'inadequate' teachers and this feeds into systems of incentive- and performance-related pay.

Third, the effectiveness studies developed a technology of control which enables the monitoring and 'steering' of schools by applying 'neutral' indicators; and in its ambition effectiveness research continually attempts to 'tap' and measure more of that which is schooling, including 'the "deep structure" of pupil attitudes and perceptions' (Reynolds, 1990, p. 21). Thus, significant discursive and disciplinary work is done by effectiveness research, which is even further reaching in its implications when linked to notions of accountability, school review and school development planning. Here we may see the play and effects of power and domination at work in the direct relationships and immediate structures of school organization. These are 'the panopticisms of every day' which are constructed and enacted 'below the level of emergence of the great apparatuses and the great political struggles' (Foucault, 1979a, p. 223).

In effect, through such schemes, teachers are entrapped into taking responsibility for their own 'disciplining'. Indeed teachers are urged to believe that their commitment to such processes will make them more 'professional'. Moreover, effectiveness is a technology of normalization. Such research both constructs a normative model of the effective school and abnormalizes the ineffective or 'sick' school. In relation to the concepts of 'review', 'development' and 'self-evaluation' it then draws upon the 'confessional technique' (an admission of transgressions and a ritual of atonement) as a means of submission and transformation. The secular confession is founded on the notion of normal as against abnormal transposed from the religious opposition of sin and piety. Such a transposition is most clearly evident in the methods of 'appraisal'.

The normalizing effects of 'effectiveness' are noted by Laurie Angus. In a recent review of school effectiveness literature, he comments that 'predictability and efficiency are valued to the extent that schools would surely become dramatically more boring places than they are already' (Angus, 1993, p. 343). He goes on to suggest that

> not only is there a lack of engagement with sociological (or other) theory, but also effectiveness work is largely trapped in a logic of common sense which allows it, by and large, to be appropriated into the Right's hegemonic project . . . it advocates an isolationist, apolitical approach to education in which it is assumed that educational problems can be fixed by technical means and inequality can be managed within the walls of schools and classrooms provided that teachers and pupils follow 'correct' effective school procedures. (p. 343)

By such means 'normalizing judgements' are turned upon the whole school and each school is set in a field of comparison — which again articulates with other current aspects of educational policy. An 'artificial' order is laid down, 'an order defined by natural and observable processes' (Foucault, 1979a, p. 179). The definitions of behaviour and performance embedded in the order and the norm are arrived at 'on the basis of two opposed values of good and evil' (p. 180). The good school and the bad school, effective and ineffective practice. Through 'value-giving' measures the constraint of a conformity that must be achieved is introduced.

If self-examination fails, the expert, the consultant, the moral disciplinarian is at hand to intervene with their models of 'effective practice'. In this role the scientific and the moral are tightly intertwined. In effect, given the logic of management, ineffectiveness is seen as a disorder of reason and as such susceptible to cure by the use of appropriate techniques of organization.

I could go on but my point here is to begin to explore an aspect of educational study and educational research by employing a different theoretical language and theoretical perspective, to focus upon unintended and overlooked consequences, so as to render our practice critically problemmatic. I am also seeking to demonstrate some of the ways in which our research and 'scientific' conceptualizations can be tied back into broader political projects and social processes and to the functions of managing and neutralizing social problems. A facade of objectivity obscures this process and further empowers the research enterprise with the capacity to categorize, professionalize and contain a specified social problem.

By employing this kind of critical reflexivity we can re-envision educational studies as a whole as a disciplinary technology, part of the exercise of disciplinary power. Management, effectiveness and appraisal, for example, as I have suggested, work together to locate individuals in space, in a hierarchical and efficiently visible organization. In and through our research the school and the teacher are captured within a perfect diagram of power; and the classroom is increasingly one of those 'small theatres', in which 'each actor is alone, perfectly individualized and constantly visible' (Foucault, 1979a, p. 200). It is thus that *governmentality* is achieved through the minute mechanisms of everyday life and the application of 'progressive' and efficient technical solutions to designated problems. Governmentality is 'the ensemble formed by the institutions, procedures, analyses and reflections, the calculations and tactics, that allow the exercise of this very specific albeit complex form of power, which has as its target population' (Foucault, 1979b, p. 20).

It is in this way that epistemological development within the human sciences, like education, functions politically and is intimately imbricated in the practical management of social and political problems. The scientific vocabulary may distance the researcher (and the manager) from the subjects of their action but, at the same time, it also constructs a gaze, a focus of analytical, critical and/or therapeutic attention that renders the 'landscape of the social' ever more visible. Through methodical observation the 'objects of concern' identified in this landscape are inserted into a network of ameliorative or therapeutic practices. The point is that the idea that human sciences like educational studies stand outside or above the political agenda of the management of the population or somehow have a neutral status embodied in a free-floating progressive rationalism are dangerous and debilitating conceits.

But now I have run ahead of myself and I want to return to Fay's work to consider the alternatives to policy science more closely. Fay (1975) offers two alternatives to policy science; one is interpretive social science, and the other is critical social science. Both are familiar enough I think not to require extensive discussion here, except to say this: Fay argues that 'an interpretative social science promises to reveal to the social actors what they and others are doing, thereby restoring communication by correcting the ideas that they have about each other and themselves' (p. 90).[2] Now that may be an over-simplification, but I shall let that go at present and note Fay's comment that interpretative social science is deeply conservative in that 'it leads to reconciling people to their social order' (p. 91). That may be equally contestable but again I shall leave that argument for another time. Fay's second alternative, critical social science, rests on the proposition that 'social theory does not simply offer a picture of the way that a social order works; instead, a social theory is itself a catalytic agent of change within the complex of social life which it analyses' (p. 110). Now this is an attractive and popular intellectual position for policy scholars. It is a position I find, at least some of the time, personally comfortable and conducive. But is it a real *alternative* to the failings that Fay finds in policy science? Only partially I think.

We need to think carefully here about the use and meaning of terms, especially those in Fay's final phrase 'a catalytic agent of change within the complex of social life which it analyses'. I have three nagging and related problems with this formulation. First, social science, here, is set over and against the social, social life, which it acts upon and analyzes but is not part of. The critical social scientist is not seen as part of the struggle for 'truth' but is placed above and outside it with clean hands and clean conscience, representing the 'conscience of society as a whole'. Social scientists are not seen to have interests, careers or identities at stake here, they are free moral agents, unencumbered by everyday ideological limitations and personal ambitions. The second worry is that 'the critical' in critical social science is too limited and does not extend to a reflexive consideration of the ways in which social science constitutes 'the social' and its own ethical subjects; in this case the 'falsely conscious' and those of 'raised consciousness'. This spartan and familiar duality, upon which the critical social scientist then works, does significant injustice to the 'complex of social life' to which Fay himself refers and trades on a rather simplistic notion of unified and stable social subjects. Third, in the educative, revelationary role which Fay attributes to the critical social scientist, an uncritical rationalism and progressive humanism are smuggled back into the social scientist's practice, in the form of 'consciousness raising'; which is achieved by offering to social actors 'an alternative conception . . . of what they are' — a simple essentialism. I am not arguing that Fay's model of critical social science is irredeemably flawed but its epistemological emphases are in danger of collapsing it back into that which it seeks to distinguish itself from. Cohen (1993) makes the point more dramatically:

> I propose to withdraw the automatic 'cognitive advantage' of university critical writing, on the grounds that no such advantage is warranted: our writings are out-fitted for the grooves of 'reason', 'society', 'need' — each of which is a cosmos of mythology unto itself. In making this withdrawal, I am more or less expressing 'no confidence' in the essential activities of the modern university. (p. x)

So can I discern still another position in all this? Is there another, a fourth way? In the way things like this are supposed to work it is probably incumbent upon me to attempt to do so. But I will make my attempt in a rather elliptical fashion I am afraid. Before doing so I shall return once more to Fay's distinctions.

I want to extend Fay's nosology: alongside policy scholarship, policy engineering and policy science we also now need to recognize the role in educational studies of **policy entrepreneurship**. I intend the term to carry a variety of meanings but it rests primarily on the proselytizing, and in some cases the sale, of 'technically correct answers'. The policy entrepreneur is committed to the application of certain technical solutions to organizations and contexts which are taken *a priori* to be in need of structural and/or cultural change. The entrepreneur's interests, in terms of identity and career, are bound up directly and immediately, rather than once removed, as in the case of policy science and critical social science, with the success of their dissemination. We might pick out 'the self-managing school' as an example of one such focus of dissemination, 'enterprise in higher education' is another, 'teacher appraisal' another, 'mentoring' and 'partnership' in initial teacher education are others. However, currently, particularly under New Labour, school effectiveness provides the clearest example of the power and effect of policy entrepreneurship.

As almost a mirror image of the school, family, social class nexus of the educational studies of the 1950s and 1960s, school effectiveness provides a new *zeitgeist* for educational reform in the 1990s. Social contexts and social demographies are stripped away to 'expose' and position schools in isolation; to be inspected, evaluated and compared by 'the difference' they make. The social patterns and economic trends which link together large numbers of failing schools, especially in the secondary sector, are systematically neglected in the attention given to leadership, vision, management, and ethos. The gaze of research has shifted once more, away from the pathologies of the home, the workings of capital, and political biases and distortions, to land upon the skills and competences of teachers and headteachers.

Indeed teachers and headteachers generally are rendered as ensembles of skills and competences — depersonalized. School effectiveness is the most asociological of the new educational studies and perhaps for that reason the most attractive to politicians, of virtually all persuasions. By removing context and complexity school effectiveness renders education eminently manageable and maleable. It translates directly into judgment and 'improvement'. It feeds into what Thrupp (1998) calls the 'politics of blame'. 'Savage inequalities' (Kozol, 1991) are magically tamed, decoupling education from homelessness, unemployment, poverty and racism. Institutional turbulence, social segregation and social mix, and resource allocation are set aside in favour of an arid, technical reductionism. Concomitantly education is depoliticized in at least two senses. Firstly, 'Knowledge and curriculum are generally regarded as unproblematic and it is assumed that students must simply learn them' (Angus, 1993, p. 343). Secondly, home–school relationships are homogenized and reduced to the anodyne rhetoric of partnership. 'Neglect of pupil cultures and family cultures, which are also class cultures means a neglect of agency' (Hatcher, 1996, p. 40).

Once again there is an intellectual trade between government and educational studies, a new economy of ideas and a new generation of single-idea policy advisers. It might be said that in all this the referent that we call 'school' has disappeared and become a floating 'target' of signification by policy solutions. The promotion of humanity is subordinated to the promotion of efficiency. School effectiveness is in some sense the zenith of modernist intellectualism, a final accommodation between popular meaning and social research. An accommodation which, perhaps not surprisingly, gives rise to *Sun-style* headlines — 'Failing Schools Named'; 'Incompetent Teachers to be Sacked' — strident in their simplifying terror. Of course all of this fits neatly with various other punitive populist measures on the New Labour agenda — curfews for young people, zero tolerance (on the streets and in schools), the harassing of beggars, workfare. The use-value of such research is clear. It cuts through the cultural overcoding which typifies much academic writing to achieve statist forms and language. A form of writing that 'exceeds what is expected of it', that offers 'semantic fixes' of a variety of sorts.

Furthermore, school effectiveness is now among the UK's invisible exports — its entrepreneurs tour the world with their overhead transparencies to deliver effectiveness 'gigs' to various audiences keen for a policy 'high' to 'fix' their school or school system. In Africa, school effectiveness software is now available for sale. In the UK, school effectiveness seminars do good business in out of town hotels.

It is possible again to situate such developments in a broader social and political context. In the era of late modernity the urge to represent is verging on the obsessional and forms of certainty have become valuable commodities as we seek to know the world a little better than those with whom we compete and assert greater and more detailed control over our environment. Unmediated knowledgability has its attractions and its price in many fields of the human sciences (cf. Beck, 1992).

This then is my backcloth. In epigrammatic form I want to suggest now that we have too much knowledge and not enough understanding. I want to put some epistemological distance between myself and the developments I have been reviewing. I want to celebrate theory. I wish to argue that the absence of theory leaves the researcher prey to unexamined, unreflexive preconceptions and dangerously naive ontological and epistemological *a prioris*. I shall wail and curse at the absence of theory and argue for theory as a way of saving educational studies from itself.

As a further aside, it is important to note that the collapse, or abandonment, of theory within educational studies has its parallels elsewhere in the field of education, for example in the removal of theory work from teacher education courses and the concomitant reduction of teacher development to a matter of skills and competencies and on-the-job learning. Teaching, like educational studies, is thus reconstituted and depoliticized. It is changed from being an intellectual endeavour to being a technical process. Indeed this coincidence of change is in no way surprising, these technologies are all part of the same contemporary *dispositif* — the unity of a discourse through a period of time, 'a limited space of communication'.

But how can theory help? What is the point of theory? The point is that theory can separate us from 'the contingency that has made us what we are, the possibilities of no longer seeing, doing or thinking what we are, do or think' (Mahon, 1992, p. 122). Theory is a vehicle for 'thinking otherwise'; it is a platform for 'outrageous hypotheses' and for 'unleashing criticism'. Theory is destructive, disruptive and violent. It offers a language for challenge, and modes of thought, other than those articulated for us by dominant others. It provides a language of rigour and irony rather than contingency. The purpose of such theory is to de-familiarize present practices and categories, to make them seem less self-evident and necessary, and to open up spaces for the invention of new forms of experience.

Now such a register, I realize, grates upon the anglo-saxon, positivist, utilitarian ear. We prefer our intellectualism expressed in the more sober tones and nuances of semantic deliberation and rational planning. Within the British tradition, intellectualism, science or scholarship often only seem to be regarded as valid and useful when weighed and measured by concrete outcomes. Chris Shilling (1993) made just this point in a review of a collection of papers drawn from recent work in the sociology of education. He took it as a sign of the times that the editors 'should have to justify the sociology of education, and by implication their own collection, by a highly reflexive positioning of it within an essentially utilitarian tradition of research based upon measuring the social outcomes of educational policies' (p. 103). He goes on to describe the sociology of education as 'a discipline which has been in decline in Britain for far too long' (p. 103). In effect the sociology of education and educational studies are in a state of 'intellectual stagnation', most particularly we are experiencing what Randall Collins refers to as the 'loss of cultural capital', that is the neglect of significant ideas, concepts and theories. Or as Shilling puts it in his review: 'Quite simply, the contributors to this volume have paid insufficient attention not only to previous traditions in the sociology of education, but to the most important current developments in sociology. Contemporary sociological theories in such areas as modernity, postmodernity, structuration, self-identity, the civilising process, consumption, and the body have much to offer the study of education' (p. 111). All of this relates back to my initial point about the dangers of isolation, but it also illustrates again the basic transition, both cultural and structural, which is under way in educational studies, a transition from intellectual intelligence to technical rationalism.

But the point about theory is not that it is simply critical. In order to go beyond the accidents and contingencies which enfold us, it is necessary to start from another position and begin from what is normally excluded. Theory provides this possibility, the possibility of disidentification — the effect of working 'on and against' prevailing practices of ideological subjection. The point of theory and of intellectual endeavour in the social sciences should be, in Foucault's words, 'to sap power', to engage in struggle to reveal and undermine what is most invisible and insidious in prevailing practices (see Siraj-Blatchford, 1994). Theories offer another language, a language of distance, of irony, of imagination. And part of this, as Sheridan puts it is 'a love of hypothesis, of invention' which is also unashamedly 'a love of the beautiful' (1980, p. 223) — as against the bland, technical and desolate languages of policy science and policy entrepreneurship. However, in taking such a stance intellectuals cannot simply seek to reinhabit the old redemptive assumptions based upon an unproblemmatic role for themselves in a perpetual process of progressive, orderly growth or development achieved through scientific and technological 'mastery' or control over events or by the assertive re-cycling of old dogmas and tired utopias. 'The regime of "truth" gave the intellectual, whose business truth was, a certain "universal" status' (Sheridan, 1980, p. 222). This is no longer available or desirable. The process of disidentification also involves a transformation of intellectuals and their relationship to the 'business of truth'. The post-epistemological theorist will eshew the scientific claim to originality, discovery and the improvement of the human condition. What I am groping towards here is a model of the educational theorist as a cultural critic offering perspective rather than truth; engaged in what Eco (1994) calls 'semiotic guerrilla warfare'. Or to put it another way:

> Criticism is a matter of flushing out that thought (which animates everyday behaviour) and trying to change it: to show that things are not as self-evident as one believed, to see that what is accepted as self-evident will no longer be accepted as such . . . As soon as one can no longer think things as one formerly thought them, transformation becomes both very urgent, very difficult and quite possible. (Foucault, 1988, p. 154)

For Foucault, freedom lies in our ability to transform our relationship to the past, to tradition and much less in being able to control the form and direction that the future will take. In the mad scramble of late modernist life we seem to need to latch on to elusive images of who we are and what our existence means. But in the place of such rigid and anterior norms and discourses, we must, as Richard Rorty suggests, locate a playing field on which ideas are toyed with and radical ironies explored. In Rorty's post-epistemological view, edifying conversations, rather than truth-generating epistemological efforts must be the staple of a post-structural social science (Rorty, 1979). To quote Foucault again 'I think that there are more secrets, more possible freedoms, and more inventions in our future than we can imagine in humanism as it is dogmatically represented on every side of the political rainbow' (1988, p. 15).

But will any theory do? I think not! We must consider *how* as well as *why* we employ theory. Theory can, and often does, function to provide comforting and apparently stable identities for beleaguered academics in an increasingly slippery world. Theory can serve to conjure up anterior norms and lay its dead hand upon the creativity of the mind. Too often in educational studies theory becomes no more than a mantric reaffirmation of belief rather than a tool for exploration and for thinking otherwise. Such mantric uses of theory typically involve little more than a naming of spaces. This is what Dale (1992) calls 'theory by numbers'. The map simply needs to be coloured in rather than researched. We all too easily become stuck in what Althusser (1975) calls a 'descriptive theory', a transitional phase in theory development, based upon a 'special kind of obviousness' (p. 133). 'Every descriptive theory' he argues 'thus runs the risk of "blocking" the development of the theory. . . .' The paradox of critical social science is that our rational, humane utopias are always formed within the discourses, dispositifs and epistemes from which we seek to escape. It is the past that is the problem here not the future.

There is another sense in which we need to think about how we theorize and that relates to the ambition of our enterprise and the style and scope of our endeavours. On the one hand, there is a kind of theorizing that is parsimonious, certain and closed. This is also typically a hard-edged, in some ways peculiarly male, form of knowledge. More often than not critical social science takes this form and is as a result both too sure of itself and too bold in its ambitions. On the other, there is a kind of theorizing that rests upon complexity, uncertainty and doubt and upon a reflexivity about its own production and its claims to knowledge about the social. What I am trying to convey here is beautifully expressed by Teresa de Lauretis who describes feminist theory as requiring

> leaving or giving up a place that is safe, that is 'home' — physically, emotionally, linguistically, epistemologically — for another place that is unknown and risky, that is not only emotionally but conceptually other; a place of discourse from which speaking and thinking are at best tentative, uncertain, unguaranteed. (1990, p. 138)

Disindentification as a practice for educational studies will almost certainly involve a loss of identity, of universal status, it will threaten our certainty and our sense of usefulness. But maybe those things have been swept away anyway. The question is do we reiterate our tired, anterior, mantric theories, do we do whatever we have to to make ourselves useful as technicians of social management, or do we re-invent ourselves as intellectuals and cultural critics?[3]

I realize in all this that I am teetering between fatalism and scepticism (Sawicki, 1991, and others note the same problem), an uncomfortable but nonetheless sometimes productive position to find oneself in. Perhaps I am occupying what de Lauretis calls the 'eccentric' perspective. Nonetheless, I take some heart from a comment by Andre Gorz, who wrote, 'The beginning of wisdom is the discovery that there exist contradictions of permanent tension with which it is necessary to live and that it is above all not necessary to seek to resolve'.[4]

Stephen J. Ball

Notes

1 This is a twice reworked paper: a first version was given as the Annual Address to the Standing Conference for Studies of Education, at the Royal Society of Arts, London, 4th November 1994; a second appeared as an article in the *British Journal of Educational Studies*, 1995, **43**, 3, under the title 'Intellectuals or technicians: The urgent role of theory in educational studies'. I am grateful to the editors for their permission to re-use the paper.
2 Rorty (1989, p. xvi) for example, places ethnography rather differently.
3 One of the most common responses to the original version of this text was to ask whether I am leaving myself and educational studies open to the criticism that the point of philosophy is not simply to describe the world, but to help to change it. My text may be read as deficient in those terms but I intend to convey very much the opposite message. I would see a specific and situated politics, a politics of the immediate, of the every day, of the personal as the logical concomitant of my arguments. Furthermore, I am counselling both boldness and modesty. Boldness in relation to the specifics of power; both in our own backyards and in our research sites. Modesty in our normative claims and in our general political ambitions. But this is a dangerous politics very different from the safe, fictive revolutionism that remains a la mode in some parts of the academy.
4 I am grateful to Jo Boaler, Alan Cribb, David Halpin, Iram Siraj-Blatchford, Maria Tamboukou and Jack Whitehead for their comments on earlier versions of the text. Some of which I have acted upon, others of which remain as food for thought, for further writing and further conversations.

References

ALTHUSSER, L. (1975) *Lenin and Philosophy and Others Essays*, London: Verso.
ANGUS, L. (1993) 'The sociology of school effectiveness', *British Journal of Sociology of Education*, **14**, 3, pp. 333–45.
BALL, S.J. (1990) 'Management as moral technology: A luddite analysis', *Foucault and Education: Disciplines and Knowledge*, London: Routledge.
BALL, S.J. (1994) *Education Reform: A Critical and Post-structural Approach*, Buckingham: Open University Press.
BECK, U. (1992) *Risk Society: Towards a New Modernity*, Newbury Park, CA: Sage.
BERNSTEIN, B. (1996) *Pedagogy, Symbolic Control & Identity: theory, research, antique* London: Taylor Francis.
COHEN, S. (1993) *Academia and the Luster of Capita*, Minnesota: Minnesota University Press.
DALE, R. (1992) 'Recovering from a pyrrhic victory? Quality, relevance and impact in the sociology of education', in AMIOT, M. and BARTON, L. (eds) *Voicing Concerns*, Wallingford: Triangle.
DE LAURETIS, T. (1990) 'Eccentric subjects: Feminist theory and historical consciousness', *Feminist Studies*, **16**, 1, pp. 133–46.
ECO, U. (1994) *Apocolypse Postponed* (edited by R. Lumley), London: BFI Publishing.
FAY, B. (1975) *Social Theory and Political Practice*, London: Allen and Unwin.
FOUCAULT, M. (1977) *Language, Counter-Memory, Practice: Selected Essays and Interviews*, Ithaca, NY: Cornell University Press.
FOUCAULT, M. (1979a) *Discipline and Punish*, Harmondsworth: Peregrine.

FOUCAULT, M. (1979b) 'On governmentality', *Ideology and Consciousness*, **6**, 1, pp. 5–22.

FOUCAULT, M. (1988) *Michel Foucault: Politics, Philosophy and Culture — Interviews and Other Writings 1977–1984*, New York: Routledge.

FOUCAULT, M. (1988) 'Truth, power, self: An interview with Michel Foucault', *Technologies of the Self*, Amherst: The University of Massachusetts Press.

FOUCAULT, M. (1991) 'Questions of method', *The Foucault Effect: Studies in Governmentality*, Brighton: Harvester/Wheatsheaf.

HATCHER, R. (1996) 'The limitations of the new social democratic agendas: Class, equality and agency', in HATCHER, R. and JONES, K. (eds) *Education Under the Conservatives: The Response to the New Agenda of Reform*, Stoke-on-Trent: Trentham.

KOZOL, J. (1991) *Savage Inequalities*, New York: Crown Publishing.

MAHON, M. (1992) *Foucault's Nietzschean Genealogy*, Albany: State University of New York Press.

REYNOLDS, D. (1990) 'Research on school/organizational effectiveness: The end of the beginning', in SARAN, R. and TRAFFORD, V. (eds) *Management and Policy: Retrospect and Prospect*, London: Falmer Press.

RORTY, R. (1979) *Philosophy and the Mirror of Nature*, Princeton, NJ: Princeton University Press.

SAWICKI, J. (1991) *Disciplining Foucault: Feminism, Power and the Body*, New York: Routledge.

SHERIDAN, A. (1980) *Michel Foucault: The Will to Truth*, London: Tavistock.

SHILLING, C. (1993) 'The demise of the sociology of education in Britain', *British Journal of Sociology of Education*, **14**, 1, pp. 105–21.

SIRAJ-BLATCHFORD, I. (1994) *Praxis makes Perfect: Critical Educational Research for Social Justice*, Ticknall: Education Now Books.

WRIGHT-MILLS, C. *The Sociological Imagination*, Harmondsworth: Penguin.

Chapter 7

School Effects in Postmodern Conditions

Bob Lingard, Jim Ladwig and Allan Luke

> Economism is a form of ethnocentrism. Economism recognises no other form of
> interest than that which capitalism has produced, through a kind of real operation
> of abstraction, by setting up a universe of relations between man and man [sic]
> based, as Marx says, on 'callous cash payment' and more generally by favouring
> the creation of relatively autonomous fields, capable of establishing their own
> axiomatics (through the fundamental tautology 'business is business', on which
> 'the economy' is based). (Bourdieu, 1990, pp. 112–13)

Introduction

'Economism' in education is more than a plethora of governmental and bureaucratic
imperatives. Rather, it marks out a host of normative assumptions and prescriptions
about: the kind of 'culture' the school is and should be; its 'intercultural' relations
with affiliated governmental systems and communities; and which of its many and
varied cultural representations and productions can be used to evaluate it. In current
debates over the drift of schooling and education towards economic rationalism,
Bourdieu's comments remind us again what we should have recalled from our intro-
ductory educational evaluation textbooks, but tend to forget in everyday practice:
that there are no trans-cultural, neutral or universal indicators of 'value', whether
that value is conceived of in terms of 'performance', 'efficiency', 'effectiveness' or
'outcomes'. But they also suggest that 'economic rationalism', the 'new economism',
and 'managerialism' are not simply 'wrong' in any absolute political or moral sense.
They are in and of themselves articulations of a particular cultural standpoint, a
now dominant set of assumptions, discourses and beliefs. In this light, perhaps our
argument with economic rationalism in education is a matter of, among other things,
cultural politics, a matter of disputed epistemic standpoints about what might count
as an educational culture, who should participate in and benefit from that culture,
and what the signs, indicators, and markings of such a culture might be.

In this chapter, we argue that any substantive rethinking of school effectiveness needs to take into consideration emergent conditions of New Times (Morley
and Chen, 1996), and will require a reframing of how we conceptualize the 'effects',
'outcomes', 'products' and 'functions' of schooling — the terms themselves artefacts
of an industrial era. In order to understand the socio-political significance and utility

of school effectiveness research, that research needs to be reconnected with the school effects research which emphasizes schooling's contribution (or otherwise) to the production of social inequality and equality in new educational conditions and contexts; that is, the school effectiveness literature needs to be dragged beyond a preoccupation with the comparative performance of schools and students on a narrow range of achievement indicators — both through the tracking of how schools constitute and reconstitute 'difference' in the population, and indeed through the ongoing problematization of the 'value' of such indicators in a shifting socio-demographic environment. Only then, we argue, can school effectiveness research inform a politics of education and intervention in educational policy debates in a way that does not simply tautologically reinforce the assumptions of industrial era schooling. How schools 'make a difference' has to address the focal questions raised by New Times and postmodernity: the various hybrid forms of difference in identity, knowledge, competence, textuality, and institutions emerging across post-industrial nation states, however differentially in terms of the actual variable spread and permutation of such changes in the very distinctive, yet interconnected, local environments of traditionally urban and rural areas, rust-belt and silicon valley communities, edge cities and new suburban spaces (Harvey, 1993).

We are, of course, sceptical of any claim that such a reconstituted school effectiveness research agenda can tell us all we need to know for such purposes. We are reminded here, when thinking about the striving for a full research-based, quantitative account of school effects, of Lyotard's (1984, p. 55) utilization of an observation by Borges: 'An emperor wishes to have a perfectly accurate map of the empire made. The project leads the country to ruin — the entire population devotes all its energy to cartography.' There are many other questions to ask with respect to schooling, and other important theoretical and research tasks, than narrow con-ceptualizations and measures of school effectiveness. Thus, more specifically, we are sceptical that the 'black holes of ignorance' (Reynolds, 1994b, p. 1) within extant school effectiveness research can be perfectly filled. Additionally, we are wary of the political purposes for which school effectiveness research can be used in the political context briefly outlined above and pursued again in the following sections of this chapter.

We begin with a fuller account of the political context of the school effectiveness movement, initially tracing its genealogy and then synergy with the managerialism of the postmodern state. We then go on to distinguish between the school effective-ness literature and the school effects research. In rejecting and critiquing the former, we warn of the danger of throwing out totally any acceptance that we can develop some technical, empirical, and indeed, quantitatively informed knowledge about whether or not schools can make a difference. However, we will argue that to be of use in contemporary educational politics, school effects literature needs to be augmented by some form of postmodernist politics which acknowledges the different, diverse and hybrid identities students bring to schools. The pivotal move we want to make here is to replace the term 'effectiveness' with the term 'effects', radically redefined in terms of a host of knowledge/discourse and power effects of institutional life. In so doing, we want to move school effectiveness from a conception of the unified subject (student), and schools as pieces of adaptable industrial machinery, to an understanding that the school is one institution among many contributing to the hybrid formation of knowledge, identity and practice in the changing life-worlds of work and unemployment, leisure and consumption, and civic and community life. Hence the need in this context to refashion the reinscribed school effectiveness research with a postmodernist understanding of the possibilities and idiosyncrasies of local sociologies, for it seems that the current construction of school effectiveness research is better suited to systemic accountability purposes than to developmental and political attempts to improve schooling in equity terms.

Genealogical Traces of School Effectiveness

The school effectiveness literature marks the convergence of two historical developments: available discourses on what might count as institutional, administrative and pedagogical 'performance' and 'effectiveness' in schools, and corporate managerialism as the dominant approach to the reconstruction of secular schooling in the postmodern state. Performativity and managerialism: like so many other of the phenomena and conditions of New Times these are neither new phenomena nor without precedents in residual institutional traditions and practices. The first historical development, then, relates to research and theorizing about the capacity of schools to make a difference. The school effectiveness research from the US and the UK is primarily concerned with seeing student academic outcomes as the 'difference' that can be made. The second key enabling factor for the school effectiveness literature relates to the changing political and economic conditions and emergent state structures that frame contemporary politics of education and education politics.

The crude and obvious conclusion is that the 'school effectiveness' literature is an artefact of the new managerialism. The discourses on school effectiveness are historical extensions of the industrial and technical approaches to the quantification and control of curriculum and instruction, including both the 1930s Taylorist attempts to treat schools as factories and farms with maximal product 'yield', and postwar human capital attempts to maximize the outcome of educational investment in developed and newly industrializing countries (Sweetland, 1996). What is perhaps unprecedented is the new epistemology of local self-management and self-surveillance, that schools (whether we conceive of them as franchises, branch plants, or agents of local chaos and independent corporate 'free radicals') should in effect develop technologies of the (institutional) self that enable 'steering from a distance'. While the technocratic model of education was premised on direct centralized control (as in Fordism and monopoly capitalism), the emergent managerial models involve self-monitoring, local self-regulation, and local reportage and discursive self-reconstruction (as in 'Toyotoism' and new age corporate capitalism) by central jurisdictions that, indeed, may have no visible 'heart' or nexus of power (cf. Eco, 1985).

In education, we have seen the reframing of relationships between central offices (and their systemic strategic plans) and schools, which have been 'granted' more autonomy to achieve the goals established by such plans and to prove their achievement through various performance indicators. 'Steering at a distance' is one apt descriptor of this hollowed-out, yet more narrowly outcomes focused, state structure and *modus operandi* (Kickert, 1991). Better outcomes (effectiveness) and better proof of outcomes are expected of a less well-funded schooling system. Outcomes here refer to individual and school performance on a range of academic measures, some are summative evaluation instruments designed for centralized reporting purposes, others are incidental data whose validity for the task of centralized 'steering' may be suspect: standardized achievement tests, matriculation examinations, truancy and suspension rates, diagnostic formative evaluation, teacher credential levels and professional development participation, etc. There is also a visible reframing of questions about 'equity' and 'opportunity' among marginalized and 'at risk' student bodies and communities: where such groups become liabilities against school-wide performance 'league tables' and ratings systems, and/or levers for funding based on percentages of eligible equity clientele. In either case, we would argue that there has been a return of the individual deficit subject and a move away from socio-cultural explanations of student performance within this contemporary policy regime (Lingard, 1997). Such constructions of 'outcomes' are, of course, not the only way in which contemporary policy could operate; indeed, it is the contention of this chapter to stake the claim to an alternative.

More generally, this preoccupation with outcomes can be seen as part of the performativity (Lyotard, 1984) redolent of the postmodern culture which accompanies the other political developments alluded to. In turn, this is related to a widespread agnosticism towards meta-narratives — an emphasis instead upon performance in 'the age of delegitimation and its hurried empiricism' (Lyotard, 1984, p. 52). It is in this policy context of an emphasis on academic outcomes from schooling delivered at the lowest cost against a backdrop of collapsed meta-narratives and increased social and values differentiation that school effectiveness research becomes attractive to policy-makers. Indeed, Yeatman (1994, p. 117) notes that the 'performativity' of the postmodern state works as 'a principle of selective closure in respect of the information overload and social complexity' and the 'open politics of voice and representation' of the social movements which it confronts. School effectiveness research is attractive in this way precisely because of its refusal of grand narratives, its suspension of normative cultural assumptions, and because it refuses to profess an epistemological standpoint or moral position. Such research resonates with the new techniques of governmentality. But, as Lyotard would be the first to insist, this government incredulity towards pedagogical morality and educational philosophy in effect constitutes a culture and a narrative in and of itself (Luke, 1997). The school effectiveness literature is founded on a narrative about the success of technocratic quantification.

The metaphor of steering at a distance, however, implies that someone is indeed steering, or at the least that the system is on autopilot; Eco (1985) has critiqued the assumption that the state within capitalism has a 'heart' or central form of agency. Nonetheless, policy is putatively about steering. The policy literature is, however, replete with evidence of resistance to this circuit of power within the policy cycle

(Ball, 1994) and there is also an element in this policy regime which puts in place a type of self-surveillance in the process of impression management of performance at local sites. In many ways, though, this is still a modernist approach to the state, to techniques of governmentality, and to conceptualizations of power. There are other circuits of power (Clegg, 1989; Hindess, 1996) in which schools operate; these are best understood in terms of Foucault's conception of power as dispersed not centrally controlled, relational, productive, and expressed not possessed. Elizabeth Grosz (quoted in Caine and Pringle, 1995, p. xi) expresses this nicely as, 'power can be thought of as running around and through us, like honey, in various states of fluidity and congealment'. Foucault's distinctions between power as domination, or as expressed through the techniques and rationalities of government, or as relational 'structures of action' which are 'unstable and reversible' (Hindess, 1996, p. 97) are important here. And while local sites are being reconstituted by global flows (Appadurai, 1996), there is the space of play and fluidity at the local sites within educational systems. Here we also need to consider the new hybrid identities, discourses and texts in the local sites of communities and schools.

The State and the Political and Policy Context of School Effectiveness Research

In postwar social sciences, theorizing of the state occurred in two distinctive 'waves'. Until the 1970s it was neglected in liberal, functionalist, US-developed political science and sociology which tended to focus on institutions and groups, casting individuals in identifiable roles. During the 1970s neo-Marxist sociology refocused on the significance of the state, as did feminist theory subsequently. More recently, with the global resurgence of market liberalism and the enhanced significance of the market over the state as the major societal steering mechanism within nations, and in a context of poststructuralist theory and postmodernist feminism, the state has been deemed of secondary theoretical or political use: secondary specifically to the significance of multinational corporations and economies; globalized social, cultural and economic fields; and indeed, emergent transnational social formations and movements and supranational political organizations, as well as the reconstitution of the local by these flows of globalization. While recognizing these political and economic changes, we argue that the postmodern state remains important in theoretical and political terms (cf. Hinkson, 1996). However, we acknowledge that it has been reconstituted, both structurally and procedurally, in its emergent relationship with the (not so) 'free market' (Hinkson, 1996).

Within the globalization literature there are dichotomous 'besieged' or defiant' accounts of the nation state in relation to the flows of globalization (Reus-Smit, 1996). Again we argue that the state remains important, but now works in different ways and sits in a 'mutually constitutive relationship' with 'emerging global structures and processes' (Reus-Smit, 1996, p. 163). At the same time, the nation state continues to play a key role in mediating and regulating how globalization is reconstituting both the national and the local, influencing through regulation, legislation, direct and indirect financial control local uptakes of and participation in globalized multinational economies.

It is the postmodern state which provides a fertile ground for school effectiveness research and its utilization within contemporary schooling policy. How so? Within nations the state has been restructured with such changes often described under the rubrics of 'new public management' (Hood, 1995) or 'corporate managerialism' (Considine, 1988). Here private sector management practices are utilized to restructure the bureaucracy to ensure a narrower focus on goals, more efficient delivery of services, and enhanced capacity to respond to change. In contrast to older style Keynesian bureaucracies, the postmodern state is about achieving clearly articulated, but narrowed, outcomes at lowered structural costs, rather than emphasizing broad outcomes and a fetishized procedural exactness (Lingard, 1996). The resultant hollowed-out structure — akin more to a coathanger rather than a pyramid (Evatt Research Centre, 1989) — is supposedly better able to respond to change than the sclerotic, 'red-tapeism' of the older style state bureaucracies (Yeatman, 1990). The alleged results, then, of these new state economies and systems are flexibility, local responsiveness, flattened hierarchies and decentralized decision-making, and, indeed, increased efficiency and innovation. Not coincidentally, these mirror the claims made about school-based management.

Various factors — including globalization, the fiscal crises supposedly inherent in the ongoing expansion of expectations associated with Keynesianism, the search for a post-Keynesian settlement, and fragmentary impulses in society contingent upon the flows of globalization (Taylor, Rizvi, Lingard and Henry, 1997, p. 80) — have contributed to this restructuring of the state. Cerny (1990) describes this state as 'competitive' in character. By this he means that within a globalized economy the chief goal of the state at the national level has become the need to ensure the international competitiveness of the putative national economy. This becomes in turn a meta-policy (Yeatman, 1990) which sets the parameters for the extent and nature of provision for the full range of public policies, including schooling. Fiscal rectitude by the state, encompassing cuts in expenditure and the move to greater user pays approaches, is the result. This new state 'steers at a distance' by articulating within its various departments strategic goals which have to be achieved by those down the line responsible for the delivery of the service. The accountability of the latter is measured through the development of a technicist range of performance indicators which are promiscuous in respect of goals and are the means by which the state now steers in an *ex post facto* fashion.

Culturally there are other significant developments. As already noted, with the proliferation of difference and new epistemologies associated with feminism, postcolonialism and poststructuralism, there is a scepticism or agnosticism about a large variety of grand narratives — 'incredulity toward metanarratives' is the central feature of the postmodern condition according to Lyotard (1984, p. xxiv). It is here that 'a generalised spirit of performativity' (Lyotard, 1984, p. 45) takes on relevance. The postmodern state adopts a technicist *modus operandi* against a backdrop of 'delegitimation' and proliferating difference in which the emphasis is upon 'maximizing output' and 'minimizing input' rather than narratives of emancipation.

As Lyotard (1984, p. 51) suggests, the question is no longer 'Is it true?' but 'What use is it?' combined with a concern for 'Is it efficient?' Such data, Lyotard (1984, p. 51) suggests, are '"nature" for postmodern man (sic)' related to the emphasis upon high performativity.

Performativity then is a simultaneous expression of high modernity with its centralized attempts to control and the postmodern with its play of difference and dispersed, localized relations of power in a context of 'manufactured uncertainty' (Giddens, 1994, p. 4) and doubt concerning meta-narratives. Anna Yeatman (1994) put it this way:

> The performative state is the response of vertically integrated control agendas to the conditions of postmodernity. If there cannot be a substantive community of ends shared by a legitimate elite of master subject citizens (the private proprietors of households), and the dissonance of irresolvably multiple perspectives of difference is introduced, the most sensible move is to abandon the substantive game of modern citizenship in favour of performativity. (pp. 112–13)

We can see here the coming together of the high modernity of techniques and passion for control (steering) with the postmodernist scepticism towards big picture narratives and epistemologies, and the collapse of consensus, as one expression of what can be seen as the postmodern.

It is in this state/political context that we would argue school effectiveness research (and the entire competency movement and new reductionist forms of state testing) resonates with the needs of state policy-makers and exudes a real synergy with the state's desire to 'steer at a distance' at the lowest cost. The achievement of the narrowed goals of schooling is measured against test results which most often work with a reductionist definition of what is being measured, perhaps best exemplified in literacy testing in the Australian context. This is the way the state steers at a distance. The state also needs to hold to a view which accepts that schools can be manipulated as technical systems and that they can make a difference, at least in a performance, if not so much in an opportunity sense, concerns for which are largely erased from this policy regime. Here, enter the school effectiveness research which fits with the technicist character of steering through performance measures, set against reduced political expectations of individuals, who are regarded as being responsible for their own performance and well-being. We see here the return of the individual deficit subject in postmodern times with both schools and school students dislocated from their social contexts and conceptualized as unified industrial machines (Luke, 1997) and at the same time political questions about the goals of schooling effaced by technical ones.

The school effectiveness research, then, fits within the modernist, industrial — Fordist if you will — aspects of the contemporary restructuring of school systems. However, there is also a range of postmodern changes going on simultaneously which cannot be accounted for by focusing simply on the modernist elements of contemporary developments, and anyway schools respond to other pressures than those of the state's attempt at steering. Ball (1994, p. 11) picks up on this when he observes that: 'Policy as practice is "created" in a trialectic of dominance, resistance and chaos/freedom.' Schools are located in other spaces than the simple dominance/resistance binary as suggested within much of the policy literature (Ball, 1994, p. 11). As Ball again notes: 'There is just more to school and classroom life than this, a third space — other concerns, demands, pressures, purposes and desires' (p. 11). In that context and before arguing the need for a postmodernist reconceptualization of the concept of effects, in the next section of this chapter we show why work on school effectiveness literature needs to be reconnected to the school effects literature.

Distinguishing the School Effectiveness and School Effects Literatures

How we conceptualize the 'difference' we refer to when we use the terminology of 'making a difference' is central to our argument. The task for the social scientist in New Times might be, to paraphrase Bateson (1972), to figure out which differences make a difference, why and where, but in sociocultural and economic environments that no longer present a normalized and normative background (of, say, monoculture, monolanguage, and degendered subjects) against which to measure 'exceptional' students and communities. Following Bateson, the question is not 'What are the effects of schooling?': rather the questions become, 'What counts as an effect?' and 'What effects make a difference, for whom, when and how?' In New Times, difference is the norm and rapid change in institutional and social structures is proceeding apace.

Nevertheless, the discourse of 'school effectiveness' has carried cross-national appeal. From early inceptions in the US (see, for example, Purkey and Smith, 1983 for a review), to the distinctively British origins best known amongst UK readers (Mortimore et al., 1988), to multiple other national contexts (see Reynolds et al., 1994b), the basic logic of attempting to identify just what characteristics of schools seem to contribute to desired outcomes clearly has been part of the larger transnational transformation of state governance discussed in the previous section. Recent publications from some of these self-proclaimed 'leading British researchers in school effectiveness and school improvement', indicate that the authors of such research are concerned to develop close ties with school policy and practice (Gray et al., 1996, p. viii), by linking with the more school-focused, qualitatively researched, 'school improvement' tradition in the UK while focusing strongly on the outcomes of schooling.

For all its ubiquity and attempt to connect across national boundaries and paradigmatic divides, the UK-based and aligned 'school effectiveness' literature lives out a massive irony. That is, even while the authors of such research claim to build from early studies of school effects (typically citing the 1966 James Coleman equal opportunity studies), and while they attempt to link into other traditions, the school effectiveness tradition per se, seems to have either ignored or at least failed to come to terms with the more long-standing and more empirically sophisticated US sociological tradition of examining the effects of schooling within a broader status-attainment sociology. Also, such cross-national work fails to understand how the flows of globalization (Appadurai, 1996) are challenging the salience of the national and reconstituting local/global relations.

The importance of recognizing the intellectual and historical affiliation between school effectiveness research and sociological school effects research lies in understanding the broader social and political implications of such an academic endeavour. Recognizing such a connection will not be news to most sociologically minded educational researchers, of course; but, we believe much of the theorizing and critique of school effectiveness tends to apply too narrow a view of its tradition. We argue that while the tradition on which such research has been built has been most often taken as part and parcel of a 'functionalist' or 'systems' paradigm, the political and social consequences of such research can in fact be quite ambiguous. Further, we suggest that by placing the logic and analytical framework of school effectiveness research into its broader intellectual/historical context, it can be seen that such research endeavours could contribute significantly to struggles for socio-educational equity.

To place the school effectiveness literature within such a historical context is a relatively straightforward matter. Aside from any critique that might be generated in response to the ways in which school effectiveness researchers respond to (or rather fail to respond to) questions of educational equity, the question of what schools might contribute to educational outcomes has been directly grounded in the 1960's examination of educational opportunity. Citing the Coleman study themselves, school effectiveness researchers build from the finding that although social background differences did, in the Coleman studies, account for the lion's share of differential educational outcomes, schools themselves were found to play a part in contributing to outcomes. For authors such as Peter Mortimore and his colleagues, recognizing the influence of social background contributed to what these authors see as the 'view that the influence of school can only be trivial' and diverted attention from the observation that 'schools vary a great deal' (Mortimore et al., 1988, p. 1). Such a positioning is interesting in itself because it reveals, first a mistaken interpretation of the early studies of educational inequities, and, secondly, the basis on which school effectiveness literature has been able to develop without reference to the developments within the sociological tradition it claims as its oppositional grounding point. This self-positioning of the school effectiveness research is most interesting because it leads the way to reconnecting the basic question of school effectiveness to more politically productive examinations of schooling.

That is, while it is the case that studies of educational inequality gave reason to dampen overly optimistic expectations about what schools could do to alleviate social inequalities outside of schools, the one finding that has been most central in the development of sociological studies of school effects came from the finding that it was not differences between schools that affects achievement most significantly, but differences within schools. This finding — one of the unexpected results of the Coleman study that has been corroborated time and again in many countries — is a central plank of the 'tracking' (streaming) studies in the US, the UK and many other countries. In the words of Gamoran and Berends:

Part of the impetus for survey research on tracking was not to understand the effects of track assignment *per se*, but to discover a within-school source of variation in student achievement . . . This effort came in response to the findings of the Coleman report . . . and others . . . that variation between schools had relatively little to do with individual achievement outcomes. Because achievement varies within schools more than between them, it made sense to consider aspects of students' experiences that differ within schools. (1987, p. 416)

Two things are apparent from Gamoran and Berends' observation. First, it is clear that the school effectiveness interpretation of these findings overlooked the main attributable source of school-based variations in educational achievement (within-school variation). Secondly, it is clear that the whole tradition of studying within-school variations is sidelined once researchers take 'the school' as a unit of analysis in itself.

Studies in this long tradition of examining school effects are numerous and address a wide range of questions: from understanding the organizational demands that lead to curriculum differentiation; to understanding the social models implied by various forms of tracking (whether they operate meritocratically or not); to understanding the various effects of tracking; to understanding what the key features are that contribute to various effects attributable to internal school curriculum organizations (the rigidity of track placements, differentiation amongst teachers, etc); to examining effects according to different curricular areas or subjects. (For a current curriculum-focused review at the time, see Oakes, Gamoran and Page, 1992; we should at least note that this tradition has been very productive even since that review.)

Those familiar with the current and long-lasting tracking debates in the US will recognize that the tradition of measuring within-school effects has played a major role in questioning the social role of schools in terms of justice. After all, once it is recognized that the notion of schools offering equal opportunities is demonstrably false, even when research employs the most ostensibly conservative scientific methodologies, the basic assumptions of liberal justice get called into question. What may not be recognized, however, is how these studies have helped develop research into school restructuring that squarely tackles not only the question of equal educational opportunities, but of equitable educational outcomes. Here, researchers drawing from the US sociological school effects research have been able to frame research questions and produce research results that should be of significant interest to anyone concerned with social justice and education. That is, in its studies of school restructuring, the federally funded Centre on the Organization and Restructuring of Schools, based at the University of Wisconsin-Madison, from 1991–95 demonstrated that some schools in the school restructuring movement not only have been able to produce higher educational achievement outcomes overall, but also that school restructuring can produce more equitable student outcomes (Newmann and Associates, 1996). Such a finding is so rare as to be virtually non-existent in the educational research canon of (post)modern, (post)industrialized countries, and clearly of major import when assessing the value of examining school effects.

By making the connection between the school effectiveness tradition and what we have called the 'school effects' tradition, we hope to have demonstrated two fairly straightforward points. First, we think it is clear that the development of 'school effectiveness' studies has only partially drawn on the sociological tradition which has examined the outcomes of schooling. In so doing it has left undeveloped key avenues of research that can contribute to understanding the social and political effects of schooling. Secondly, it is also clear that the basic framework of examining school effects need not necessarily contribute to ill-advised and unjust educational policy developments. Indeed, the example offered by the work of Newmann and his colleagues demonstrates that studies in school effects may well offer more sound and solid evidence on which to develop educational policy. However, the concept of school effects needs to be a more nuanced one to take account of the condition of postmodernity.

A Postmodernist Reconceptualization of School Effects

As already noted, Lyotard (1984) provides grounds for a critique of the 'grand narratives of modernity'. One of the key educational narratives of modernity has concerned 'effectiveness', derived from the 'cult of efficiency' described by Callahan (1962). School effectiveness has been viewed as the production of differential patterns of educational achievement, and now indeed in terms of 'value-addedness'. The problem raised by this is the relative impoverishment of what is seen to count as achievement: measured in conventional terms of skills, behaviours, knowledges and competences, these narrow conceptions are in fact historical artefacts of industrial-era versions of schooling and constructions of the modernist human subject. In this way, the discourses of school effectiveness are premised on not so grand meta-narratives drawn from behaviourism, Fordism and the industrial state. The very assumption of school effectiveness frames up the question of effects in terms of those ostensible industrial effects of schooling in the production of mechanistically framed and conceived phenomena. In this regard, Lyotard's work raises a set of questions about the teleological presuppositions of school effects and other literatures.

What Lyotard also does is problematize the ethics of progress: a largely overlooked aspect of his work is the degree to which his is a counter-teleological argument. Specifically, the very onto/phylogenetic assumptions underlying models of human development, curriculum development and sequencing, and pedagogy are based on the production of the postwar-skilled, monocultural, male, 'rational' subject. A key effect shared by Lyotard and Foucault's work is to return us to a re-theorizing of effects — one that does not presuppose effects as the logical ends of linear actions, developments, dialectics and histories, but rather a postmodern concept of effects that allows for hybridity, idiosyncrasy, difference, and indeed, local and pragmatic accidents. Lyotard's work on games suggests a move towards a more ecosystemic model of simultaneous effects and anticipated chaos, as against models of singular causes or black boxes. As with Foucault's model, Lyotard's explanation of the systemic nature of change even suggests that the steering at a distance model is flawed, insofar as it assumes that there is a cognate heart to state power, that indeed there is a driver or, at the least, principled autopilot at work in the seat of power. By this account, the school begins to look more like the complex ecosystems described in the ethnographic and symbolic interactionist literatures and the poststructuralist studies of schools as arenas of micropolitics, instead of the industrial machine model endemic to industrial modernism, especially as manifest in much educational administration and psychology.

None of this precludes a political economy of, or focused empirical research on school effects, but both need to be repunctuated within different metaphors. Here the conceptual frameworks of Bourdieu and Foucault lead to such a rethinking of metaphors: schools are local sociologies, ecosystemic contexts that are nested and embedded within larger layers of state intervention, etc, etc. For example, one of the most provocative, but overlooked elements of Foucault's work, was his attempt to re-theorize the consequence of discourse in terms other than those of empirical science's attempt to establish cause–effect relationships. Insofar as the school effects literature is looking for causal relations within a relatively linear and restricted conceptual cosmos, it is at odds with a broader political understanding of schooling in postmodern conditions. Classical experimental searches for independent and dependent variables fail to theorize context, not in its humanist configuration, but rather context itself as a knowledge effect, for example, through failing to see through the theorizing effect of constructing 'the school' as an *a priori* of analysis.

To carry the argument further, in a manner consistent with Ladwig's (1994) conceptualization of educational policy as a social field *sui generis* (as distinct from the fields of schooling and the state), placed within a heterogenous and complex constellation of social fields such 'effects' research could be rendered useful. Both Bourdieu's and Foucault's work call our attention to how institutions act as variable fields of power, where discourse is put to work to constitute subjects and effects. Neither Bourdieu nor Foucault disbar material, extra-discursive conditions and consequences, but such a conceptualization suggests that the *petit* sociologies — the local sociologies at work in schools and regions (Luke, 1995) — may generate effects that are unanticipated from the centre where policy, curriculum, and so on are shaped. What the Foucauldian model of local effects suggests is that in effect steering is done locally in idiosyncratic, counter-discursive ways.

Where standard policy implementation studies speak of 'mutual adaptation' in attempts to understanding local variation, the socio-political frameworks constructed in our appropriations of Foucault, Lyotard, Bourdieu and others allow a more multi-layered, multi-focused analysis of school effects. Hence, the task of a study of effects would be to examine hosts of factors and how together they constitute fields of power, defining, repositioning, classifying and producing knowledge, and knowing and known subjects. If we shifted the focus, then it would be on to how schools participate in the production of the knowing, speaking, subject. Analyzing schooling as operating within fields of power, as social fields where varying kinds of capital and knowledge/power configurations are put to work locally (often in line with central foci but also against and/or within), is our way of turning the debate over school restructuring into a more productive set of questions to be readdressed and reframed.

Conclusion: Towards a Critical Cultural Empiricism

We are not opposed to empiricism *per se*, but rather to the 'hurried', 'abstracted' and decontextualized 'empiricism' of school effectiveness research. Indeed, we would argue that empirical research about school effects has played an important role politically. But while the school effectiveness literature risks, to borrow from Bourdieu, misrecognition of effects in terms of their ostensive agency, that is, focusing on schools, rather than recipient subjects, a refurbished school effects literature may offer us an alternative. In this sense, the type of reconceptualization for which we argue here is an example of what Ladwig (1996, p. 164) has referred to as 'constructing a science with an attitude'.

For example, think about the whole post-war sociology of education within the political arithmetic tradition which documented the class-based inequalities in education, and then subsequent work which documented inequalities in relation to gender, race and ethnicity and their intersections with each other and with class. Consider also how a misreading of empirical data has been one important element in the 'What about the boys?' backlash against feminist-inspired reform policies and practices for girls in education (Mills and Lingard, 1997). Empirical research on school effects is important in political terms, and as just one element in policy and practice interventions. Certainly, the goals of schooling cannot be determined through such research (after all, even in classical 'scientistic'/Kantian terms the 'ought' cannot be derived from the 'is'), any more than normative curriculum goals and social practices in New Times can be derived from descriptive assessment studies of Old Times. Effectiveness in definitional terms is a concern with the level of achievement of goals. With respect to schooling, these goals have to be decided in a normative way through democratic socio-political discussion and should take account of current and future social arrangements, including the emergent postmodernism.

The school effectiveness literature works with a modernist and industrial conception of the school and student within a narrow and reductionist definition of 'school effectiveness', all of which find some synergy with the modernist recidivism of emergent state structures, but at the same time fail to connect with the postmodern elements of the present. More accurately, then, the state itself now works in hybrid, modernist–postmodernist ways, clearly evidenced in the fetish for performativity with its (modernist) desire for control, yet (postmodernist) rejection of a framing meta-narrative and epistemology. Such state structures and their accompanying *modus operandi* do indeed seek to 'steer at a distance'.

However, there are other circuits of power in which schools are located, unmediated by the state and policy and affected as well by the reconstitution of the local by the flows of globalization. There are also today hybrid student identities and (many) schools function as new (post-Fordist) workplaces. We have suggested that the school effectiveness literature needs to be reinscribed with the school effects research and that the concept of effects itself needs to be given a postmodernist inflection. To the extent that such an exercise is an explicit attempt to 'poach from the mainstream' (Ladwig, 1996), it is a considered political strategy to engage directly in the field of the state.

To reiterate, we would not want to reject research-based attempts to find out in what ways schools might be able to make a difference, with difference conceptualized as the potential to interrupt the reproduction of inequality and the production of homogenized subjects. Here there is much work to be done in theorizing and researching relations between equality and difference (Young, 1990; Yeatman, 1994; Taylor et al., 1997, Chapter 7) and conjoining a politics of recognition with a politics of redistribution (Fraser, 1995).

We have argued that such research on school effects needs to take conceptual account of these societal and theoretical changes — what we might call a 'considered empiricism'. There is a need for a provisional postmodernist politics of pastiche which seeks to work together such research with the sort of political account suggested in the argument of this chapter. This might provide some purchase on effective political and policy interventions in education at the present hybrid modernist–postmodernist moment, what has been called the condition of postmodernity (Harvey, 1989).

We began this chapter by citing Pierre Bourdieu's comment that 'economism' is a form of ethnocentrism. An implication of Bourdieu's comments is that the assignment of the 'remorseless economic logic' of the market as the principal denominator of social worth, clearly demarcated as superior to 'other' domains of the 'sacred' and 'subjective', is a cultural assignment and cultural judgment. The school effectiveness literature here creates yet another such sociological binarism, namely between questions of institutional performativity, effectiveness and efficacy on the one hand, and those 'soft' pedagogical issues of identity, subjectivity, and pedagogical 'experience' on the other.

Our argument here is not against economic rationalism per se, as has been the tendency of most sociological critiques of the effects of the management literature on schooling. Rather, it is to suggest that the discourses of 'effects' have framed up our understandings of the kinds of symbolic and material capital and the kinds of subjectivities produced, reproduced and transformed by schooling in culturally limiting ways; ways that, while well suited to the practices of industrial cultures and economies, may need whole scale re-envisioning and reworking for the present.

As we rethink the profoundly and fundamentally modernist assumption of the institution of schooling — that it exists to produce quantifiable symbolic and institutional capital of 'value' in the social fields of material and symbolic production (cf. Carrington and Luke, 1997) — perhaps a new vocabulary is necessary, one which begins to reframe and rethink the mentalism and mechanism of 'outputs' and 'effects'. Perhaps the difference that schools can make is in something other than the production of credentials, of rational minds, skills and competence levels. Perhaps the difference can be conceptualized, analyzed and, even, measured in terms of the new kinds of citizen sensibilities, bodily and cultural practices, and indeed kinds of discourses and cultural productions that are generative and redistributive for new conditions, rather than simply reproductive of existing divisions of wealth, discourse, gender and labour. That re-envisioning will require pedagogical imagination, sociological imagination and, indeed, a new empirical rigour that the old testimonials to the real (test scores, output indicators and the like) are incapable of generating. We see the argument of this chapter as just one contribution towards the generation of such an experimental vocabulary for talking about the consequences of schooling in the unsettled and uncertain arena of new social, cultural and economic configurations in globalizing, postindustrial nation states. That new work, as Bourdieu suggests, will focus on the new domains of school and work as cultures, and not simply as economies.

References

APPADURAI, A. (1996) *Modernity at Large: Cultural Dimensions of Globalization*, Minneapolis: University of Minnesota Press.

BALL, S. (1994) *Education Reform: A Critical and Post-structural Approach*, Buckingham: Open University Press.

BATESON, G. (1972) *Steps To an Ecology of Mind*, New York: Ballantine Books.

BOURDIEU, P. (1990) *The Logic of Practice*, Cambridge: Polity Press.

CAINE, B. and PRINGLE, R. (eds) (1995) *Transitions: New Australian Feminisms*, Sydney: Allen and Unwin.

CALLAHAN, R.B. (1962) *Education and the Cult of Efficiency*, Chicago: University of Chicago Press.

CARRINGTON, V. and LUKE, A. (1997) 'Literacy and Bourdieu's sociological theory', *Language and Education*, **11**, 2, pp. 96–113.

CERNY, P. (1990) *The Changing Architecture of Politics: Structure, Agency and the Future of the State*, London: Sage.

CLEGG, S. (1989) *Frameworks of Power*, London: Sage.

COLEMAN, J., CAMPBELL, E.Q., HOBSON, C.J., McPARTLAND, J., MOOD, A.M., WEINFELD, F.D. and YORK, R.L. (1966) *Equality of Educational Opportunity*, Washington: D.C.: National Centre for Educational Statistics.

CONSIDINE, M. (1988) 'The corporate management framework as administrative science: A critique', *Australian Journal of Public Administration*, **47**, 1, pp. 4–19.

ECO, U. (1985) *Travels in Hyperreality*, London: Picador.

EVATT RESEARCH CENTRE (1989) *State of Siege: Renewal or Privatisation for Australian State Public Services?* Leichhardt: Pluto Press.

FRASER, N. (1995) 'From redistribution to recognition: Dilemmas of justice in a "Post-Socialist" society', *New Left Review*, July–August, pp. 68–93.

GAMORAN, A. and BERENDS, M. (1987) 'The effects of stratification in secondary schools: Synthesis of survey and ethnographic research', *Review of Educational Research*, **57**, 4, pp. 415–35.

GIDDENS, A. (1994) *Beyond Left and Right: The Future of Radical Politics*, Stanford California, Stanford University Press.

GRAY, J., REYNOLDS, D., FITZ-GIBBON, C. and JESSON, D. (eds) (1996) *Merging Traditions: The Future of Research on School Effectiveness and School Improvement*, London: Cassell.

HARVEY, D. (1989) *The Condition of Postmodernity*, Oxford: Blackwell.

HARVEY, D. (1993) 'Class relations, social justice and the politics of difference', in KEITH, M. and PILE, S. (eds) *Place and the Politics of Identity*, London: Routledge, pp. 41–66.

HINDESS, B. (1996) *Discourses of Power: From Hobbes to Foucault*, Oxford: Blackwell.

HINKSON, J. (1996) 'The state of postmodernity: Beyond cultural nostalgia or pessimism', in JAMES, P. (ed.) *The State in Question: Transformations of the Australian State*, Sydney: Allen and Unwin, pp. 196–223.

HOOD, C. (1995) 'Contemporary public management: A new global paradigm', *Public Policy and Administration*, **10**, 2, pp. 104–17.

KICKERT, W. (1991) 'Steering at a distance: A new paradigm of public governance in Dutch higher education', Paper presented to European Consortium for Political Research, University of Essex.

LADWIG, J.G. (1994) 'For whom this reform? Outlining educational policy as a social field', *British Journal of Sociology of Education*, **15**, 3, pp. 341–63.

LADWIG, J.G. (1996) *Academic Distinctions: Theory and Methodology in the Sociology of School Knowledge*, London: Routledge.

LINGARD, B. (1996) 'Educational policy making in a postmodern state', *The Australian Educational Researcher*, **23**, 1, pp. 65–91.

LINGARD, B. (1997) 'The disadvantaged schools program in Australia: Caught between literacy and the local management of schools', *International Journal of Inclusive Education*, **2**, 1.

LUKE, A. (1995) 'Getting our hands dirty: Provisional politics in postmodern conditions', in SMITH, R. and WEXLER, P. (eds) *After Postmodernism: Education, Politics, Identity*, London: Falmer Press, pp. 83–97.

LUKE, A. (1997) 'New narratives of human capital: Recent redirections in Australian educational policy', *The Australian Educational Researcher*, **24**, 2, pp. 1–21.

LYOTARD, F. (1984) *The Postmodern Condition: A Report on Knowledge*, Minneapolis: University of Minnesota Press.

MILLS, M. and LINGARD, B. (1997) 'Masculinity politics, myths and boys' schooling: A review essay', *British Journal of Educational Studies*, **45**, 3, pp. 276–92.

MORLEY, D. and CHEN, K. (eds) (1996) *Stuart Hall: Critical Dialogues*, London: Routledge.

MORTIMORE, P., SAMMONS, P., STOLL, L., LEWIS, D. and ECOB, R. (1988) *School Matters: The Junior Years*, Somerset: Open Books.

NEWMANN, F. and ASSOCIATES (1996) *Authentic Achievement: Restructuring Schools for Intellectual Quality*, San Francisco: Jossey-Bass.

OAKES, J., GAMORAN, A. and PAGE, R. (1992) 'Curriculum differentiation: Opportunities, outcomes, and meanings', in JACKSON, P. (ed.) *Handbook of Research on Curriculum*, New York: Macmillan.

PURKEY, S.C. and SMITH, M.S. (1983) 'Effective schools: A review', *The Elementary School Journal*, **83**, 4, pp. 427–52.

PURKEY, S.C. and SMITH, M.S. (1985) 'School reform; The district policy implications of the effective schools literature', *The Elementary School Journal*, **85**, 3, pp. 353–89.

REUS-SMIT, C. (1996) 'Beyond foreign policy: State theory and the changing global order', in JAMES, P. (ed.) *The State in Question: Transformations of the Australian State*, Sydney: Allen and Unwin, pp. 161–95.

REYNOLDS, D., CREEMERS, B.P.M., NESSELRODT, P.S., SCHAFFER, E.C., STRINGFIELD, S. and TEDLIG, C. (eds) (1994a) *Advances in School Effectiveness Research and Practice*, Oxford: Pergamon.

REYNOLDS, D., TEDDLIG, C., CREEMERS, B.P.M., CHEONG CHENG, Y., DUNDAS, B., GREEN, B., EPP, J.R., TROND, E.H., SCHAFFER, E.C. and STRINGFIELD, S. (eds) (1994b) 'School effectiveness research: A review of the international literature', in REYNOLDS, D., CREEMERS, B.P.M., NESSELRODT, P.S., SCHAFFER, E.C., STRINGFIELD, S. and TEDLIG, C.

(eds) *Advances in School Effectiveness Research and Practice*, Oxford: Pergamon, pp. 25–51.

SWEETLAND, S.R. (1996) 'Human capital theory: Foundations of a field of inquiry', *Review of Educational Research*, **66**, pp. 341–60.

TAYLOR, S., RIZVI, F., LINGARD, B. and HENRY, M. (1997) *Educational Policy and the Politics of Change*, London: Routledge.

YEATMAN, A. (1990) *Bureaucrats, Technocrats, Femocrats: Essays on the Contemporary Australian State*, Sydney: Allen and Unwin.

YEATMAN, A. (1994) *Postmodern Revisionings of the Political*, New York: Routledge.

YOUNG, I.M. (1990) *Justice and the Politics of Difference*, Princeton, N.J.: Princeton University Press.

Chapter 8

High Reliability Organizations and Liability Students — The Politics of Recognition

Roger Slee

Introduction

Running against the political grain, the chapters in this book collectively call to account school effectiveness research and the school improvement movement. This chapter will not rehearse the substance of other chapters by once again presenting a general rebuttal to the effectiveness research and its application through the growing 'school improvement' industry. I will, however, take up the organizing question '*effective for whom?*' to challenge the growing appeal of school effectiveness research to some of those arguing for inclusive schooling for disabled students.

Disabled students introduce a level of diversity and educational instability which undermines current discourses of effectiveness. I shall argue that the 'high reliability organization' as the 'cutting edge' model for the effective school (Reynolds, 1995) advances a form of Taylorism (see Hamilton, Chapter 2) which is functionalist and ineluctably assimilationist, and that like educational management discourses, the rhetoric of school effectiveness and school improvement is deployed as a moral technology (Ball, 1990). The high reliability organization is used by Reynolds to imply comparability between schools and flight control operations, nuclear power plants and surgical theatres. For some the reductionism of this discursive metaphor may appeal (Barber, 1996), for others it deflects from the profoundly damaging effects of the National Curriculum, the marketization of schooling and the introduction of league tables as the new educational benchmarks (Ball, 1994; Ball, Chapter 6; Grace, Chapter 9; Hamilton, Chapter 2).

The central argument of this chapter is that having hitched its wagon to a managerialist political discourse which, when linked to the politics of league tables, back-to-basics movements and raising standards, school effectiveness research narrows to instrumental benchmarks and shuns the more democratic aspirations of the public education project (Rose, 1995). Inclusive education is not deployed in this paper as an ideological shorthand for assimilation. Rather, it embraces the politics of recognition and understands disablement as cultural politics and not as a technical problem of product delivery. Such an argument challenges the normalizing project of the 'effective school'.

For those readers who find it curious that an educator can apparently argue against school effectiveness, against 'raising standards' and 'back-to-basics' slogans, I would urge that they eschew the reductionism concealed within the populist noise of these slogans which distracts us from more fundamental questions about schooling and its beneficiaries (Ball, 1988). This chapter also warns against hasty generalizing across cultural contexts (Fukuyama, 1996). I am nervous about the mass appeal of comparative test scores as a guarantee of improved outcomes for all children, and mindful of what Tony Booth refers to as the 'positivists' fallacy' — 'that a generalization abstracted from individual cases has validity for each case' (Booth, 1995, p. 101).

In the following section of this chapter, special educational needs and the politics of the educational liability, I examine deeply embedded conceptual tensions within the various discourses and tactics of 'inclusive schooling'. This brief discussion will foreground a consideration of the claim that 'effective schooling research and the school improvement movement is likely to improve the performance of children with special educational needs' (Ramasut and Reynolds, 1993, p. 236). While the focus of this analysis is the relationship between disabled students and the effective schooling discourse, I also suggest that other groups of marginalized students will not be well served by this notion of effectiveness (Gewirtz, Ball and Bowe, 1995; Gillborn and Gipps, 1996). In so doing it is not my intention to cast schools and teachers as the new villains in the production of disablement. More specifically I seek to demonstrate the complex roles of education policies and discourses and unequal social relations in the production of disablement and educational failure. The narrowly defined terms of performativity within this discourse must exclude 'unstable students' in order to protect the demand for goal certainty advocated in political treatises such as *Worlds Apart?* (Reynolds and Farrell, 1996). The recognition and celebration of difference is not a glittering prize for the school effectiveness researcher.

Special Educational Needs and the Politics of the Educational Liability

Writing in 1987, Len Barton questioned the self-evidence of Warnock's popularized notion of 'special educational needs' to argue that it was a euphemism for the failure of schools. Where a child was unable to succeed, the failure became the student's. This pathologizing of failure moved the school — its organization, curriculum, preferred pedagogy and attitude toward difference — out of the diagnostic frame. Special educational needs became an all-embracing metaphor for the defective child. In turn, the functional label of 'special educational needs child' has metaphorically become a refugee camp for the casualties of schooling. Black students who are excluded at an ever-increasing rate (Sewell, 1997; Parsons, 1996) have long been described as having special educational needs (Tomlinson, 1981) because of their failure in racist educational contexts (Troyna, 1993). Under-achieving boys whose attention is unsustainable in the traditional and increasingly competitive constellation of the National Curriculum and narrowing teaching methods are being diagnosed as suffering from Attention Deficit Hyperactivity Disorder (ADHD) (Slee, 1995). Individual student pathology deflects from the harder questions about the exclusionary imperatives of educational markets expressed through league tables, test scores and 'failing schools' that are unable to simultaneously exhibit the preconditions for the 'effective' containment of difficult children and the raising of their GCSE scores.

It has to be said that Mary Warnock (1982), some four years after the publication of her landmark report into special educational provision in England and Wales, *Special Educational Needs — Report of the Committee of Enquiry into the Education of Handicapped Children and Young People* (DES, 1978), returned to the notion of special educational needs with critical intent:

> Perhaps the main reason for the newly apparent poverty of special needs is in its definition . . . or rather its lack of definition . . . the concept of 'special need' carries a fake objectivity. For one of the main, indeed almost overwhelming, difficulties is to decide whose needs are special, or what 'special' means. (Warnock, 1982, p. 372)

The conceptual 'flabbiness' identified by Warnock presented a discursive opportunity to an established special education industry of considerable power and influence to move more directly into the regular classroom to administer to an increasing number of 'defective' or special educational needs children. While a series of modifications have been made to the language of special education, continuity exists within the enduring episteme. The discourse of special education has donned the rhetorical costumes of integration and inclusion. However, the special educational emperors expose the flesh of the medical model of disability. It is worth considering this a little further to demonstrate the appeal of school effectiveness and school improvement for the special educational fraternity.

Integration in Victorian Education (Ministry of Education, Victoria, 1984) established the policy framework for 'increasing the participation of students with disabilities, impairments and problems in schooling in the regular classroom'. In some ways this document represented a radical departure from previous interventions, such as Mary Warnock's report, by arguing that the integration of students with disabilities, impairments and problems in schooling was a rights issue. Semmens (1993, p. 110) outlines the five organizing principles which were set down as guides for the progress of more integrative practice:

- every child has a right to be educated in a regular school;
- categorization is personally and educationally unhelpful;
- school-based resources and services are more conducive to education than segregated specialist arrangements;
- collaborative decision-making (rather than expert direction) enables all participants to share in decisions and own outcomes; and
- all children can learn and be taught.

Notwithstanding the liberal intent of these principles, hindsight reveals the re-articulation of the epistemology and practice of traditional special education through the discourse of integration (Slee, 1993a). Time also exposes weaknesses in the so-called 'Integration Report' which provided the spaces for the extension of special educational interventions and the disablement of more students in Victorian state schools. Let us consider two of these weaknesses.

Who Needs to be Integrated?

First was the malleability of the descriptors used to identify which students could be the subjects (objects) for integration. Students with *disabilities, impairments and problems in schooling* is an almost limitless term of reference. If we contemplate the last coupling of words, *students with problems in schooling*, the grounds for intervention invites considerable professional interpretation. Not surprisingly this became a bureaucratic device for crisis displacement. Disruptive students were pathologized as the 'socially-emotionally disturbed' and integration became a dis-cursive tactic for acquiring additional resources for the surveillance and regulation of difficult students. Perhaps the clearest and most ironic expression of this discip-lining intent (Focault, 1977) was the sanctioning of off-site behaviour units as a part of integration policy. In Australia, John Lewis (1993) enlists the Victorian (the Australian state of Victoria) Ministry of Education Compendium of Statistics to demonstrate a number of trends that were less than integrative. First, resources did not follow students moving from the segregated special schools to regular classrooms. Second, increasing numbers of students already within the regular classroom were being re-classified as 'integration students' and subject to expert interventions and treatments. Third, enrolments in special schools did not decline so that resources could be moved from the segregated sector to the mainstream. Fourth, the 'end of special education' panic in fact shielded a steady movement of its influence and traditional practices into the regular classroom. Overall, integration policy in Victoria, as elsewhere, established an additional funding line to protect schools from change. Rather than address the complex social and educational pathologies that disabled different students, schools could bid for the bank-rolling of the containment and social control of the different students.

The Educational Conditions for Disablement and Enablement

The second weakness of the 'Integration Report' was its failure to consider the articulation of exclusion within the deep culture of schooling mediated through curriculum, pedagogy and school and classroom organization. In this discussion, therefore, school organization is used as an abbreviation for a whole range of organ-izational structures and procedures. Instead, the focus of the report was limited to the bureaucratic structures for implementing the recommendations of the report and to the procedural requirements for the allocation of 'integration resources' to disabled students. It was this distributive conception (Rawls, 1972; Rizvi and Lingard, 1996;

Slee, 1996) of integration that locked the theatre of policy into the machinations of ascertainment and allocation. Paradoxically the medical model became deeply inscribed within integration in Victorian schooling. There had to be a diagnosis of the child's disability, impairment and/or problem in schooling and its extent in terms of the financial requirements for placement into the mainstream regular class with minimal disruption to that setting. Thenceforth integration was the work of diagnosticians, bureaucratic resource acturists and classroom integration teachers and aides. Little wonder that the concentration of disputes over integration fixed upon resource requirements. This distributive conception of the integration educational project has international convergence. Whether discussing the Code of Practice and its implementation in schools in the London Borough of Westminster, the enactment of Public Law 94, 142 in Alabama or the exclusion of a student from Birkdale Primary School in Brisbane, Australia (Meadmore and O'Connor, 1997), the terms of reference are limited to the pathology of the child and material requirements for the school to support the relocation of the defective child.

The exclusion of disabled students is not solely effected through the physical environment of the school. Disablement is fundamentally located in the complex configurations of cultural politics (Oliver, 1990). Cultural politics are played out in settlements over what counts as worthwhile knowledge and how this is to be taught (Whitty, 1992; Apple, 1996; Ball, 1994). The form and content of the settlement over school curriculum structures educational relationships. Some students will be sponsored for success, others will be marginalized, academically disabled and excluded (Polk, 1984).

The exclusion of a child therefore does not simply present a technical problem requiring a bureaucratic solution through changed levels of resourcing and expert professional interventions. The diagnostic probes must be broadened to reveal all of the shifting constituent elements of the disabling educational relationships — the school, the individual learning requirements of the student, the narrowly prescribed curriculum, the teaching and learning methods, the physical arrangement of the classroom and beyond, the attitudes of teachers and students to difference.

In other words, students may be disabled by the narrowing parametres of the curriculum and/or they may be disabled by the methods employed for teaching and learning. Resolution must therefore challenge the institutional infrastructure of schooling. Just as Oliver (1990) has encouraged us to change the focus of the interrogation from the disabled person to the social context that disables or enables people, so too for schooling. This corresponds with similar cultural and political struggles for other groups of students oppressed by schools. The challenge for gender equity was not how to make girls better able to cope with and fit into patriarchal schooling. The struggle was to eliminate the articulation of sexism through the curriculum, through teaching methods, through evaluation and assessment techniques, through gendered hierarchies in the educational workforce, through the unequal allocation of space and resources, through affirming role models and so on (Weiner, 1995; Kenway, 1990; Yates, 1994). Barry Troyna applied similar perspective to expose the lack of analytic rigour and the problematic politics of the 'saris, samosas and steel bands' posture of multiculturalism in the classroom.

> ...in contrast to multi-culturalism, anti-racism... rejects the view which sees racism as primarily an individual problem. Nor do anti-racists endorse the voyeuristic imperatives of multiculturalism in which 'they' rather than 'us' become the subject of scrutiny. (Troyna, 1993, p. 26)

Liberal thinking and educational practice are not enabling. They are not, to use the now ragged slogan, empowering. Liberal theories of disability are essentialist and universalizing. Disability is understood as part of the defective pathology or psyche of the damaged individual. The challenge for the liberal educator is to procure the requirements for supporting the placement of this 'abnormal' child in the regular classroom. The struggle is to amass the material resources, shape tolerant attitudes from classroom peers and to mobilize the specialist personnel to minimize the interruptions to the normal operation of the regular classroom. Frequently, integration and inclusion are the discursive cloak for the re-articulation of assimilation (Branson and Miller, 1989). It becomes a normalizing quest (Ball, 1990; Rose, 1989) where schools get on with business as usual.

Completing the grip of liberal essentialism is achieved through the growing imperative of ensuring that trainee teachers have compulsory units in special needs where they are taught about human defect. To be sure it is explained in terms of making schools more supportive, but it is rare for these courses to be staffed by other than 'special educators'. Seldom are students invited to explore social models of disability (Oliver, 1990) as a way of encouraging student teachers to imagine the possibility of different voices contributing to the reconstruction of an education system which disables greater numbers of students now that more students have to stay in schools for longer periods of time following the collapse of the unskilled labour market (Polk and Tait, 1990; Marginson, 1993; Slee, 1995).

The False Promise of School Effectiveness

For some time now many of those arguing for 'inclusive education' have turned to the effective schooling research to suggest that by improving school organization disabled students' educational outcomes are more likely to benefit (Ainscow, 1991; Slee, 1993; Reynolds and Ramasut, 1993). School effectiveness represented a healthy line of resistance to the deficit bound medical models of special education and the provision of schooling for students with 'special educational needs'. Indeed David Reynolds (1991 and 1995) and Louise Stoll (1991) have participated in the 'conversations' to this end and suggested the scope for improvement for disabled students if they are educated in 'effective schools' modeled on high reliability organizations (Reynolds, 1995).

This line of argument has had its critics (Fulcher, 1993; Booth, 1995). Fulcher has long argued that '...social life is inadequately theorized or understood by (moral) reference to good and bad practice' (1989, p. 43). The danger in signing up to the school improvement charter is that there is a separation of the school from education policy and from social context. What transpires is a process of naming and shaming whereby schools are blamed for being solely responsible for educational failure and drastic measures are introduced to improve failing schools. That these measures frequently involve systematic population cleansing such as was the case in the Ridings School and large injections of funding previously not delivered to the school is not dwelt upon by those chronicling the new histories of schools which are 'turned around'.

The appeal of school effectiveness is understandable when we consider the origins of the research paradigm and reform movement. Again I will resist the temptation to fill space by rehearsing its history. This is readily available in this book (see chapters 5 and 9) and elsewhere (Reynolds, 1982 and 1985; Creemers, 1994). The point to make is that studies by Coleman et al. (1966), Jencks et al. (1972) and Plowden (CACE, 1967) collectively argued that schools had minimal independent influence on the development and educational outcomes of their students. However, in the United States, Edmonds (1979) and Brookover et al. (1979), and in Britain, Power et al. (1967), Reynolds (1976) and Rutter et al. (1979) radically interrupted this established educational orthodoxy to suggest that schools *could* make a difference, that there was a school effect. Why was it, they asked, that some schools in similar catchment areas were able to produce greater levels of student achievement or lower rates of truancy and disruption than others? The answer they found was in like characteristics of the more effective schools. The logic is compelling in its simplicity. The lists of factors of the effective school grew and became the basis for the 'school improvers' to move out to teachers to show them how to replicate effectiveness through the emulation of the five, seven, nine, thirteen factors (Lezotte, 1989; Levine and Lezotte, 1990).

The swing in the pathological site of defect from the student to the teacher and the school is attractive for those arguing inclusion. Ainscow puts it most clearly:

> Since I regard these traditional approaches as limiting opportunities for some children, I believe that school systems must find better ways of conceptualising and responding to educational difficulties. . . . In attempting to conceptualise educational difficulty in a more positive way we can more usefully see pupils experiencing difficulty as indicators of the need for reform. They point to the need to improve schooling in ways that will enable them to achieve success. . . . It is worth adding at this stage that I believe that such reforms would be to the benefit of all pupils. Consequently the aim is *effective schools for all*. (Ainscow, 1991, p. 3, author's emphasis)

To his credit Ainscow was searching for, and this continues (1995), a more robust theory of disablement in education off the back of which school reform could be generated. Like others at that time, including myself (Slee, 1991), the pattern was to use school effectiveness research and school improvement schedules to host that reform. However, the epistemology of school effectiveness and the suggested educational stratagems of the 'school improvers' were unavoidably functionalist — school improvers never refer to the ways in which the National Curriculum is prohibitive to disabled students or cultural minorities — and contributed to enduring disablement. Moreover, the great danger was to narrow policy to school or classroom operation and remove the discursive preconditions for the normalizing educational project. Others (Whitty 1997; Ball, Chapter 6) identify profound problems in the conception, methodology and applications of school effectiveness research. If we return to our questions *effective for what?* and *effective for whom?*, the promise of school effectiveness is thrown into relief against the 'savage inequalities' (Kozol, 1994) of schooling for those who schools were never really intended to include.

Effectiveness is measured through a range of data, its principal claims derived from scores from paper and pencil tests of non-verbal reasoning, arithmetic, reading and oral comprehension, and classroom observation schedules. The first set of questions to address revolve around validity and reliability as we stretch such tests across regional, national and cultural boundaries. The second set of questions address concerns about who is excluded from these measurement instruments. Reducing complex contextual realities to 'intake variables' or background 'noise', as Angus observes (1993), strengthens ideologies of cultural deficit for which schools must compensate (Davies, 1996). Davies (1996, p. 98) calls on the Congress of Manes in Brazil to strengthen the point:

> Our public schools are geared toward an ideal child. One who does not need to struggle for survival; who is well fed; who speaks the school's language, who knows how to handle a pencil and is capable of interpreting symbols, and who is stimulated by parents through all sorts of means. As this is not the reality of the Brazilian families, the schools do not have the right to impose these criteria, which are valid for the middle class, upon its students' majority. Its task is to educate Brazilian children as they actually are . . . (Leonardo, 1993, p. 75)

Effective for what? What do these improved scores actually mean when set against changing contexts for students. Does less truancy or a higher or lower standardized test score mean a great deal if schools are unable to deliver in their basic promise of a transition to a meaningful adult life of work? Are we asking the right outcome questions? Do we forfeit knowledge of the substantial achievements of so-called failing or ineffective schools within and for their communities through the blinkered vision of the selective measures (Rose, 1995)?

Let us now consider recent educational policies in the United Kingdom and the relationship of school effectiveness research, promiscuous in its appeal to both the Conservative and New Labour education administrations, to the general thrust of policy.

The Effective Disablement of Students — Some Contemporary Policy Barbarisms

Heward and Lloyd-Smith (1990, p. 21) observe that the Education Reform Act in England and Wales 'is a development that threatens the new directions in special education policy and may reinstate the former assumptions [of rigid categorization and segregation] with greater force'. Pressing schools to operate within an educational marketplace has changed the terms of reference for the educational mission, as Gold and her colleagues point out:

> Arguments about good practice have now to be viewed in terms of opportunity costs. How will those schools which have decided to take on whole school special needs policies maintain that commitment and keep the department and policy central to the school? . . . Outside the school in the education marketplace, will the presence of children with special educational needs attract new pupils? Will schools decide not to have any students with special educational needs if their presence affects enrolment? It remains to be seen whether market forces make philosophies about whole school provision for children with special educational needs either too expensive or too problematic. (Gold, Bowe and Ball, 1993, pp. 54–5)

The claims that the Education Reform Act would deliver choice and diversity have proven false. 'Choice' and educational markets appear to revalorize existing social class divisions and inequalities:

> The point is not that choice and the market have moved us away from what was a smoothly functioning egalitarian system of schooling to one that is unfair. That is crude and unrealistic. There were processes of differentiation and choice prior to 1988 (within and between schools). Some skillful and resourceful parents were always able to 'work the system' or buy a private education or gain other forms of advantage for their children. But post-1988, the stratagems of competitive advantage are now ideologically endorsed and practically facilitated by open enrolment, the deregulation of recruitment and parental choice. Well resourced choosers now have free reign to guarantee and reproduce, as best they can, their existing cultural, social and economic advantages in the new complex and blurred hierarchy of schools. (Gewirtz, Ball and Bowe, 1995, p. 23)

Whitty (1997) recently reissued his challenge to school effectiveness research on the occasion of his lecture commemorating the 50th anniversary of Karl Mannheim's death. The silence of school effectiveness on the structure of inequality and its failure to acknowledge that '. . . one conclusion to be drawn from a reading of the pioneering Fifteen Thousand Hours research (Rutter et al., 1979) is that, if all schools performed as well as the best schools, the stratification of achievement by social class would be even more stark than it is now' (Whitty, 1997, p. 156). He goes further to identify the pathologizing of schools which converges in the neo-liberal rhetoric of both Conservative and New Labour educational discourses and the effective schools research and school improvers' discourses:

> . . . it sometimes seems that not only neo-liberal rhetoric, but also some forms of educational research, take the discursive repositioning of schools as autonomous self-improving agencies at its face value rather than recognising that, in practice, the atomisation of schooling too often merely allows advantaged schools to maximise their advantages. For those schools ill-placed to capitalise on their market position, the devolution of responsibility can lead to the devolution of blame. (Whitty, 1997, p. 156)

The creation of better schools, in part, relies on their success in recruiting 'desirable' as opposed to 'undesirable' students (Gewirtz, et al., 1995, pp. 141–3) to communicate the correct image to their prospective client group. Once again this is not new and, as Gewirtz and her colleagues observe, is deeply sedimented in teachers' discourse. My point is that recent education policy does not challenge old assumptions about deficiencies in students' class, cultural, familial and or physiological pathologies. Recent policy reasserts and extends pathological explanations for student failure. As competition intensifies the identification of these undesirable students — liability students — spreads and more find themselves as the recipients of special educational interventions. Paradoxically, however, some students such as girls who formerly were devalued by schools, inadvertently and surprisingly, may be advantaged by the machinations of the market.

The National Curriculum in the United Kingdom has, as Whitty (1992) and Apple (1996) observe, forged a coalition between the Conservative cultural restorationist (Ball, 1994) education agenda and the neo-liberal advocacy of the market as the operational engine house. The calls for modern efficient school operations, the raising of standards through common curriculum and national testing to produce a better unit of human capital to increase the competitive economic edge and the romanticized notion of traditional values and standards are fused together (Apple, 1996, p. 31). The comprehensive curriculum which engages with the worlds inhabited by the student is subjected to a discourse of derision (Ball, 1994, p. 39), demonized and replaced by a 'political but depoliticized, authoritative curriculum of tradition' (Ball, 1994, p. 39). This *curricular fundamentalism* denies the plurality of student identities, instead demanding, and checking through national testing, a return to the 'agreed' basic knowledge and skills. The effective school secures both students' and teachers' compliance to this regime and trains them in the basics. It is behaviourist, in that it demands particular pedagogical forms. It is dismissive of 'trendy teaching', that form of teaching which advocates differentiation, critical inquiry, cooperative learning, cross-age tutoring, peer assessment, action research and un-tracking (Slavin, 1989; Mehan et al., 1996). A teleological, theoretical, enterprise school effectiveness does not properly engage with the complexity of life in schools. As Ball correctly observes it is an organizational algorithm for upping outcome measures distinguished more by its political promiscuity than by its analytical rigour.

Nowhere does the effective schools research enter into considered debate about the educational value nor the politics of the National Curriculum. It is a given. Effective schools research augments the league tables of schools' achievements in GCSE results to demonstrate the aggregate value-addeds of selected student cohorts. It is silent on questions of curriculum. Its motivation is a belief that raising achievement levels in particular forms of knowledge will enhance the competitive economic edge of the nation state. Hence in this rearticulation of human capital theory, the superficial fascination with the tiger economies of the 'far east' (Reynolds and Farrell, 1996) and its behaviourist pedagogical inclinations. I say superficial as Reynolds' concern about cultural complexity has not so far been seriously examined throughout his work (Reynolds, 1995).

School effectiveness is largely silent on, or under-theorizes, matters of equity (Sammons, Hillman and Mortimore, 1995). Equity is submerged within the rhetorical exhortation of the achievement in test scores. The effective school will need to monitor its student cohort carefully to see who presents for the counting. In this way the special educational fraternity will be sanguine in the knowledge that their industry is preserved or more precisely reconfigured within the effective school. Effective schooling and the school improvement movement (Barber, 1996) is blind to a searching interrogation of outcome. Test scores become ends. Questions of student destinations have no truck in this genre of research and writing. Explicit discussions of values and the type of society to which schools articulate/adhere are ignored. Instead, effective schooling coheres with the assumed self-evidence of the discourse of the Education Reform Act and the raising standards chorus.

Such a discourse is bound to produce failure. Its failure is racialized (Gillborn and Gipps, 1996; Sewell, 1997), it is class specific (Ball, 1994), it is gendered (Weiner, 1995; Kenway, 1990) and it reproduces disabilism (Oliver, 1996). The language of inclusive education which advocates a politics of recognition is discordant with the preconditions of the highly reliable organization. Inclusive education is dismissive of the assimilationist imperative of school effectiveness and the National Curriculum. Students are the stuff of schools. They should not be liabilities or impediments to the organizational mission. Difference is to be valued and our discussion of what is to be prized as educational success should not be closed down by disarmingly straightforward recipes (Barber, 1996). This chapter concedes the difficulty of addressing educational failure and the policy context and social conditions which contribute to the disablement of some student identities and calls for more careful and theoretically robust responses.

Acknowledgment

Gaby Weiner and Stephen Ball read a previous draft of this chapter and I am grateful for their helpful comments to which I have attempted to respond.

References

AINSCOW, M. (1991) 'Effective schools for all: An alternative approach to special needs in education', in AINSCOW, M. (ed.) *Effective Schools For All*, London: David Fulton Publishers.

AINSCOW, M. (1995) 'Special needs through school improvement: School improvement through special needs', in CLARK, C., DYSON, A. and MILLWARD, A. (eds) *Towards Inclusive Schools?* London: David Fulton Publishers.

ANGUS, L. (1993) 'The sociology of school effectiveness', *British Journal of Sociology of Education*, **14**, 3, pp. 333–45.

APPLE, M. (1996) *Cultural Politics and Education*, Buckingham: Open University Press.

Roger Slee

BALL, S.J. (1988) 'Comprehensive schooling, effectiveness and control: An analysis of educational discourses', in SLEE, R. (ed.) *Discipline and Schools: A Curriculum Perspective*, Melbourne: Macmillan.

BALL, S.J. (1990) 'Management as moral technology: A luddite analysis', in BALL, S.J. (ed.) *Foucault and Education: Disciplines and Knowledge*, London: Routledge.

BALL, S.J. (1994) *Education Reform: A Critical & Poststructural Approach*, Buckingham: Open University Press.

BARBER, M. (1996) *The Learning Game*, London: Gollancz.

BARTON, L. (ed.) *The Politics of Special Educational Needs*, London: Falmer Press.

BOOTH, T. (1995) 'Mapping inclusion and exclusion: Concepts for all?', in CLARK, C., DYSON, A. and MILLWARD, A. (eds) *Towards Inclusive Schools?* London: David Fulton Publishers.

BRANSON, J. and MILLER, D. (1989) 'Beyond policy: The deconstruction of disability', in BARTON, L. (ed.) *Integration: Myth or Reality?* London: Falmer Press.

BROOKOVER, W.B., BEADY, C., FLOOD, P., SCWEITZER, J. and WISENBAKER, J. (1979) *Schools, Social Systems and Student Achievement: Schools Can Make a Difference*, New York: Praeger.

CENTRAL ADVISORY COUNCIL FOR EDUCATION (CACE) (1967) *Children and Their Primary Schools* (*The Plowden Report*), London: HMSO.

COLEMAN, J.S., CAMPBELL, E., HOBSON, C., McPARTLAND, J., MOOD, A., WEINFELD, F. and YORK, R. (1966) *Equality of Educational Opportunity*, Washington: US Government Printing Office.

CREEMERS, B. (1994) 'The history, value and purpose of school effectiveness studies', in REYNOLDS, D., CREEMERS, B.P.M. and NESSELRODT, P.S. (eds) *Advances in School Effectiveness Research and Practice*, Oxford: Pergamon.

DAVIES, L. (1996) 'The management and mismanagement of school effectiveness', in TURNER, J.D. (ed.) *The State and the School: An International Perspective*, London: Falmer Press.

DEPARTMENT FOR EDUCATION AND SCIENCE (DES) (1978) *Special Educational Needs — Report of the Committee of Enquiry into the Education of Handicapped Children and Young People* (*The Warnock Report*), London: HMSO.

EDMONDS, T. (1979) 'Effective schools for the urban poor', *Educational Leadership*, **37**, 1, pp. 15–27.

FOUCALT, M. (1977) *Discipline and Punish: the birth of the prison*, Hammondsworth: Penguin.

FUKUYAMA, F. (1996) *Trust: The Social Virtues and the Creation of Prosperity*, New York: Penguin Books.

FULCHER, G. (1989) *Disabling Policies*, London: Falmer Press.

FULCHER, G. (1993) 'Schools and contests: A reframing of the effective schools debate', in SLEE, R. (ed.) *Is There A Desk With My Name On It? The Politics of Integration*, London: Falmer Press.

GEWIRTZ, S., BALL, S.J. and BOWE, R. (1995) *Markets, Choice and Equity in Education*, Buckingham: Oxford University Press.

GILLBORN, D. and GIPPS, C. (1996) *Recent Research on the Achievements of Ethnic Minority Pupils*, London: HMSO.

GOLD, A., BOWE, R. and BALL, S.J. (1993) 'Special educational needs in a new context: Micropolitics, money and *Education for All*', in SLEE, R. (ed.) *Is There A Desk With My Name On It? The Politics of Integration*, London: Falmer Press.

HEWARD, C. and LLOYD-SMITH, M. (1990) 'Assessing the impact of legislation on special education policy', *Journal of Education Policy*, **5**, 1.

JENCKS, C.S., SMITH, M., ACLAND, H., BANE, M.J., COHEN, D., GINTER, H., HEYNS, B. and MICHELSON, S. (1972) *Inequality: A Reassessment of the Effect of the Family and Schooling in America*, New York: Basic Books.

KENWAY, J. (1990) *Gender and Education Policy: A Call for New Directions*, Geelong: Deakin University Press.

KOZOL, J. (1994) *Savage Inequalities: Children in America's Schools*, New York: Harpe Collins.

LEONARDO, A. (1993) 'CIEP: A democratic school model for educating disadvantaged children in Brazil', in LEVIN, H. and LOCKHEED, M. (eds) *Effective Schools in Developing Countries*, London: Falmer Press.

LEVINE, D.U. and LEZOTTE, L.W. (1990) *Unusually Effective Schools: A Review and Analysis of Research and Practice*, Madison, WI: The National Center for Effective Schools Research and Development.

LEWIS, J. (1993) 'Integration in Victorian schools: Radical social policy or old wine?', in SLEE, R. (ed.) *Is There A Desk With My Name On It? The Politics of Integration*, London: Falmer Press.

LEZOTTE, L.W. (1989) 'School improvement based on the effective schools research', *International Journal of Educational Research*, **13**, 7, pp. 815–25.

MARGINSON, S. (1993) *Education and Public Policy in Australia*, Cambridge: Cambridge University Press.

MEADMORE, D. and O'CONNOR, P. (1997) 'Benchmarking disability', *International Journal of Inclusive Education*, **1**, 2, pp. 163–74.

MEHAN, H., VILLANNEVA, I., HUBBARD, L. and LINTZ, A. (1996) *Constructing School Success: The Consequences of Untracking Low-achieving Students*, New York: Cambridge University Press.

MINISTRY OF EDUCATION — VICTORIA (1984) *Integration in Victorian Education — Report of the Ministerial Review of Educational Services for the Disabled*, Melbourne: Victorian Government Printer.

OLIVER, M. (1990) *The Politics of Disablement*, London: Macmillan.

OLIVER, M. (1996) *Understudy Disability: From Theory to Practice*, London: Macmillan.

PARSONS, C. (1996) 'Permanent exclusions the schools in the 1990s: Trends, causes and responses', *Children & Society*, **10**, 3, pp. 177–86.

POLK, K. (1984) 'The new marginal youth', *Crime and Delinquency*, **30**, pp. 462–80.

POLK, K. and TAIT, D. (1990) 'Changing youth labour markets and youth lifestyles', *Youth Studies*, **9**, 1, pp. 17–23.

POWER, M.J., ALDERSON, M.R., PHILLIPSON, C.M., SCOENBERG, E. and MORRIS, J.N. (1967) 'Delinquent schools?', *New Society*, 19 October, pp. 542–3.

RAMASUT, A. and REYNOLDS, D. (1993) 'Developing effective whole school approaches to special educational needs: From school effectiveness theory to school development practice', in SLEE, R. (ed.) *Is There A Desk With My Name On It? The Politics of Integration*, London: Falmer Press.

RAWLS, J. (1972) *A Theory of Justice*, Oxford: Oxford University Press.

REYNOLDS, D. (1976) 'The delinquent school', in WOODS, P. (ed.) *The Process of Schooling*, London: Routledge and Kegan Paul.

REYNOLDS, D. (1982) 'The search for effective schools', *School Organisation*, **2**, 3, pp. 215–37.

REYNOLDS, D. (ed.) (1985) *Studying School Effectiveness*, London: Falmer Press.

REYNOLDS, D. (1995) 'Using school effectiveness knowledge for children with special needs — The problems and possibilities', in CLARK, C., DYSON, A. and MILLWARD, A. (eds) *Towards Inclusive Schools*, London: David Fulton Publishers.

REYNOLDS, D. and FARRELL, S. (1996) *Worlds Apart? A Review of International Surveys of Educational Achievement Involving England*, London: HMSO.

RIZVI, F. and LINGARD, B. (1996) 'Disability, Education & the Discourses of Justice', in CHRISTENSEN, C. and RIZVI, F. (eds) *Disability & the Dilemmas of Education & Justice*, Buckingham: Open University Press.

ROSE, M. (1995) *Possible Lives: The Promise of Public Education in America*, New York: Penguin Books.

ROSE, N. (1989) *Governing the Soul: The Shaping of the Private Self*, London: Routledge.

RUTTER, M., MAUGHAN, B., MORTIMORE, P. and OUSTON, J., with SMITH, A. (1979) *Fifteen Thousand Hours: Secondary Schools and their Effects on Children*, Cambridge M.A.: Harvard University Press.

SAMMONS, P., HILLMAN, J. and MORTIMORE, P. (1995) *Key Characteristics of Effective Schools: A Review of School Effectiveness Research*, London: OFSTED.

SEMMENS, R. (1993) 'Implementing policy: Some struggles and triumphs', in SLEE, R. (ed.) *Is There A Desk With My Name On It? The Politics of Integration*, London: Falmer Press.

SEWELL, T. (1997) *Black Masculinities and Schooling: How Black Boys Survive Modern Schooling*, Stoke-on-Trent: Trentham Books.

SLAVIN, R. (ed.) (1989) *School and Classroom Organisation*, Hillsdale, N.J.: Erlbaum.

SLEE, R. (1991) 'Learning initiatives to include all students in regular schools', in AINSCOW, M. (ed.) *Effective Schools For All*, London: David Fulton Publishers.

SLEE, R. (1993a) 'The politics of integration — New sites for old practices?', *Disability, Handicap & Society*, **8**, 4, pp. 351–60.

SLEE, R. (1993b) 'Inclusive learning initiatives: Educational policy lessons from the field', in SLEE, R. (ed.) *Is There A Desk With My Name On It? The Politics of Integration*, London: Falmer Press.

SLEE, R. (1995) *Changing Theories and Practices of Discipline*, London: Falmer Press.

SLEE, R. (1996) 'Inclusive Education in Australia? Not Yet!' *Cambridge Journal of Education*, **26**, 1, pp. 19–32.

STOLL, L. (1991) 'School effectiveness in action: Supporting growth in schools and class-rooms', in AINSCOW, M. (ed.) *Effective Schools For All*, London: David Fulton Publishers.

TOMLINSON, S. (1981) *Educational Subnormality: A Study in Decision-making*, London: Routledge and Kegan Paul.

TROYNA, B. (1993) *Racism and Education: Research Perspectives*, Buckingham: Open University Press.

WARNOCK, M. (1982) 'Children with special needs in ordinary schools: Integration revisited', *Education Today*, **32**, 3, pp. 56–61.

WEINER, G. (1995) *Feminisms in Education — An Introduction*, Buckingham: Open University Press.

WHITTY, G. (1992) 'Education, economy and national culture', in BOCOCK, R. and THOMPSON, K. (eds) *Social and Cultural Forms of Modernity*, Oxford: Polity Press.

WHITTY, G. (1997) 'Social theory and education policy: The legacy of Karl Mannheim', *British Journal of Sociology of Education*, **18**, 2, pp. 149–63.

YATES, L. (1994) *The Education of Girls: Policy, Research and the Question of Gender*, Hawthorn: Australian Council for Educational Research.

Part Three

Experiencing the Impacts of School Effectiveness Research and the School Improvement Movement

Chapter 9

Realizing the Mission: Catholic Approaches to School Effectiveness

Gerald Grace

The field of school effectiveness research (SER) is currently marked by a lively debate and by conflicting evaluations of its own significance and effectiveness. For Reynolds (1995, p. 53) this 'infant discipline' has already achieved many positive results in that:

> ... it has helped to combat pessimism about the importance of the school system, to build professional self esteem and to provide a knowledge base that can act as a foundation for the development of improved practice ...

Reynolds emphasizes the important role which SER has played in overcoming earlier notions of structural and cultural determinism (the school as relatively ineffective against existing social divisions) and against feelings of powerlessness for educational practitioners which could arise from such an analysis. In short, against pessimistic forms of sociological pre-destination along the lines of 'abandon hope, all you who work in capitalist school systems', SER has offered a measure of hope and a form of empowerment for education professionals.

For Hamilton (1996, pp. 54–6), however, school effectiveness research is not an infant discipline but 'an international industry' engaged in 'peddling feel-good fictions' among educators by generating research and writing which is 'technically and morally problematic'. The problematic nature of its research and writing, according to Hamilton, is that it oversimplifies both the concept of 'effectiveness' and the comprehensive range of methodological approaches needed to appreciate it. Above all, it offers to New Right ideologues in education policy an apparently scientific legitimation for placing *all* of the blame for educational underachievement upon 'failing' schools and 'incompetent' teachers, while 'winning' schools and 'successful' teachers can celebrate the virtues of self-improvement. Such debates, as that represented here, are important for a field of research which has risen to prominence in only the last 20 years. For all his positive credo in praise of school effectiveness research, Reynolds (1995, pp. 54–9) does recognize that it is characterized by: 'many controversies concerning epistemological issues, methodological concerns and more theoretical matters'. He also recognizes that: 'we have been instrumental in creating a quite widespread popular view that schools do not just make *a* difference but that they make *all* the difference.' The value of these exchanges is that they draw the attention of all those working in the field of SER to some of its vulnerabilities as well as to some of its strengths.

This chapter is intended as a contribution to the debate. It will argue that despite the progressive origins of school effectiveness research in attempts to improve the schooling of the urban poor[1] and despite some positive and impressive achievement in the last 20 years (see Sammons, Hillman and Mortimore, 1995), the field remains vulnerable to the twin dangers of technical reductionism on the one hand and of ideological appropriation on the other. Most attention will be given to an examination of technical reductionism because arguments about ideological appropriation of research results are well known in the social sciences.

Technical Reductionism in School Effectiveness Research

As I have argued elsewhere, research in the social sciences runs the constant risk of becoming constituted as policy science rather than as policy scholarship (Grace, 1995). Policy science abstracts a given social phenomenon from its historical, cultural, ideological, socio-economic and political relations and then subjects it to close, technical analysis which has immediate policy consequences. Policy scholarship, on the other hand, recognizes that the social entity under investigation can only be understood and evaluated in the complexity of those social relations. Policy science marginalizes history, culture and economic and political relations — they are reduced to 'externalities'. Policy scholarship recognizes that a social institution, for instance, is crucially constituted by its history, its culture and its socio-political relations and that no in-depth or valid assessment of it can take place in abstraction from what are in fact 'centralities' for social science research. Part of current controversies about SER is related to a belief among its critics that it has not given sufficient attention to this distinction in research paradigms and that it has become largely the prisoner of policy science and of its conceptual and methodological limitations in technical reductionism.

A scrutiny of the available literature of SER (see Scheerens, 1992; Reynolds and Cuttance, 1992; and Creemers, 1994; among other studies) shows that technical reductionism in this sector of educational inquiry has two dimensions which may be called *Contextual reductionism* and *Mission reductionism*. Contextual reductionism involves a process of abstracting the scholarly and measurable performance indicators of a school from its own history and cultural formation, from its social and economic community setting and from its relation with the wider society.[2] Mission reductionism involves abstracting scholarly performance indicators per se from the whole integrated matrix of school outcomes and effects which constitute the educational mission of the school such that measures of academic performance are taken to be the 'real' measures of what a school is about.

There are many reasons why these forms of reductionism have become prevalent in school effectiveness research. Insofar as SER has become legitimated and funded by governments and state agencies looking for quick fire solutions and bullet point answers to complex educational situations, research contracts and pub-lication prescriptions may circumscribe the intellectual freedom and autonomy of scholars. Governments and state agencies in general are not prepared to pay for research which shows that their own social and economic policies have contributed significantly to crises in the schools. They would rather pay for research which shows that some schools have been able to overcome these created impediments more successfully and 'effectively' than other schools. Thus the ideological and political focus is shifted from analysis of the policies themselves to analysis of the differential ability of schools to cope with these policies.

This form of analytical reductionism arises wherever research is closely tied to policy prescription, wherever a 'bidding culture' for government controlled research funds is dominant and wherever relatively autonomous sources of research money for 'fundamental' research are limited. School effectiveness is one of a number of fields which now have to operate largely under these constraints.

Methodological issues are also implicated in what I have called mission reduc-tionism. In an early critique of the Effective Schools Movement (ESM), Lauder and Khan (1988, p. 53) argued that:

> Part of the responsibility . . . must rest with the quantitative research methodology employed by the ESM. For example, outcome measures like exam results or rates of truancy lend themselves to quantification and it may be for this reason that the ESM has placed such a heavy emphasis on exam results. In contrast, other edu-cational aims and processes whose outcomes may be no less important . . . are ignored.'[3]

The reduction of a school's educational mission to an assessment of its academic results and of its truancy and delinquent rates seemed not unreasonable in a research culture in which scientific objectivity was equated with certain kinds of measurement and in which assertions were made that this was the sort of information that most parents and citizens wanted to know. These two assumptions have shaped much of the work in school effectiveness research in the past. However both of these assump-tions are now subject to critical scrutiny. As qualitative inquiry matures and sophistic-ates itself as a research approach and with a growing recognition that a wider range of school outcomes must be evaluated, a more comprehensive and catholic paradigm for school effectiveness research can be established. Objectivity does not have to be the prisoner of a particular methodological approach.

The second assumption, that parents and citizens are concerned with school effectiveness only as measured by academic results, has been shown to be false by the research of Gewirtz, Ball and Bowe (1995) and by that of Vincent (1996). Parents show more interest in the social and affective outcomes of schooling, in its human and community faces, than many state agencies allow for. There is now an encouraging recognition in SER that mission reductionism must be overcome. Sammons, Hillman and Mortimore (1995, p. 4) in their review of research conclude that: 'studies which focus on only one or two outcomes may give only a partial picture of effectiveness' and they call for research which focuses on 'a broad range reflecting the aims of schooling'. Reynolds (1995, p. 65) concludes that: 'we are not at the moment tapping the school variables (climate? emotional tone? relationships?) necessary' and the implications here are that school effectiveness research must look more closely at the *cultural* features of schooling, e.g. the ethos and values climate of a school, the quality of interpersonal relations within it etc.

As other chapters in this book address in detail issues to do with contextual reductionism in SER, the remainder of this chapter will suggest some approaches to transcending mission reductionism in future research.

A Catholic Approach to School Effectiveness Research

The notion of a catholic approach to school effectiveness is used here in two senses. In the first place an argument is made that school effectiveness literature and research needs to be more catholic in the sense of being more comprehensive, universal and inclusive in the range of school outcomes which are taken seriously. While there can be general agreement with statements, such as that of Sammons, Hillman and Mortimore (1995, p. 3) that 'an effective school adds extra value to its students' outcomes in comparison with other schools serving similar intakes', a catholic approach to SER requires an elaboration of what these outcomes might be and of how 'extra value' assessment or appreciation[4] can be attempted in relation to those outcomes which do not have obvious performance indicators. Similarly, when Reynolds and Creemers (1990, p. 1) assert that: 'schools matter . . . schools do have major effects upon children's development . . . schools do make a difference', a catholic approach has to ask (in detail), 'difference to what?'

The difficult question which these considerations generate is how can school effectiveness research concentrate more systematically and seriously upon 'a broad range (of outcomes) reflecting the aims of schooling'?[5] The rhetoric of catholic assessment is relatively easy, its practical applications in research are much more challenging. One way forward would be to take school mission statements as the fundamental basis for school effectiveness research in the future.

Mission statements have many catholic virtues. They constitute a principled and comprehensive articulation of what a school claims to be its distinctive educational, social and moral purposes. They characteristically, therefore, specify a range of desired outcomes which are often the result of consultation exercises involving teachers, the pupils, parents and governors and sometimes members of the wider community. They are published to the community as a statement saying 'this is what this school is about' and (implicitly) saying 'this is the basis upon which you can judge us'. A research paradigm based upon school mission statements would therefore have the virtue of working with school and community generated 'desired outcomes agendas' rather than imposing only those generated by state agencies or by the formal research community. This could be the beginning, for English schooling culture at least, of a more democratic, more flexible, more sensitive and more humane practice of school effectiveness research. School effectiveness research could then become a report to the community on 'realizing the mission' and upon what aspects of the mission were being realized and what aspects were being impeded and why. This would be a catholic approach to SER in the sense of being inclusive of the range of school outcomes and inclusive of both school and community members in the processes of assessment and evaluation.

Catholic Schooling Culture as a Research Field

It is perhaps hardly surprising that the mission statements of Catholic schools provide a particularly rich source of material relevant to this argument, given that the Catholic school system has long claimed to have a distinctive educational culture and mission. There can be some value therefore in looking at a Catholic approach, in the second sense, i.e. that which is represented in the mission statements of the Catholic system and of Catholic primary and secondary schools.

The aspirations of Catholic education are constituted at two levels, i.e. that of formal ecclesiastical authority and that of individual school communities. At the formal level, the Sacred Congregation for Catholic Education, in publications such as *The Catholic School* (1988) defines 'the Catholic school's fundamental reasons for existing' (p. 8). These are stated at a high level of generality but nevertheless set the broad parameters for Catholic educational activity in the following way:

- 'Catholic schools [should] . . . provide a service which is truly civic and apostolic' (p. 9);
- 'This is the basis of a Catholic school's educational work. Education is not given for the purpose of gaining power but as an aid towards a fuller understanding of and communion with man (sic), events and things. Knowledge is not to be considered as a means of material prosperity and success but as a call to serve and be responsible for others' (p. 43);
- 'First and foremost the Church offers its educational service to "the poor or those who are deprived of family help and affection or those who are far from the faith"' (p. 45).

Such statements provide a broad and universal rationale for the Catholic educational system. Within these guidelines, individual Catholic primary and secondary schools are expected to formulate their own mission statements which relate these general principles to the particular circumstances of their own locations and sociocultural settings.

As part of a larger study of Catholic schools in deprived urban areas, I have recently undertaken an analysis of the mission statements of 25 secondary schools located in various parts of England.[6] The purpose of this analysis was to clarify the range of educational, spiritual, social and moral outcomes which such schools sought to achieve and how these related to the needs and challenges of their specific urban locations. I believe that the study of Catholic schools has much to offer to the general field of SER, in part because these schools characteristically link academic outcomes with wider spiritual, moral, personal, social and community outcomes, and their

notions of individual good with that of common good.[7] This is not to imply that
County schools and those of other religious faith communities are less significant
for SER — it is simply to assert that strong claims for Catholic school distinctiveness have resulted in rich and comprehensive mission statements as a basic data
source for SER.

The expectation that all schools will have produced formal mission statements
has been important for Catholic schools in urban poverty areas in a number of
ways. It has stimulated new thinking about the pastoral and educational mission of
Catholic schools in situations of high educational, social and economic challenge. It
has encouraged, in many cases, dialogue and participation involving school governors,
teachers, parents, community members and pupils in the process of formulating an
agreed statement of aims. It has caused people to think about the distinctiveness
of the Catholic educational mission in changing circumstances (see McLaughlin,
O'Keeffe and O'Keefe, 1996). While the emphasis of each mission statement reflected the 'desired outcomes agenda' of each specific educational community, it
was possible to discern across the 25 statements a fundamental set of aspirations
which extended well beyond academic performance indicators alone. The first of
these replicated the findings of Bryk, Lee and Holland (1993) in their major study
of Catholic schooling in the USA, that Catholic schools emphasize 'the primacy of
the spiritual and moral life as realised in Catholic religious culture' (p. 301). Effectiveness for Catholic schools has to be about:

- [developing] 'love for and commitment to Jesus Christ, the Catholic Church
  and the Gospel message of love, peace, truth and justice';[8]
- 'establishing a community based on love and care for the individual in
  which the Faith of the Church gives ultimate meaning to all the community's activities';
- 'developing the spiritual awareness of pupils';
- 'promoting the spiritual growth of all members of our community through
  prayer, the celebration of the Mass and the work of the Chaplaincy'.

These statements are important in placing spiritual and moral awareness on the
'desired outcomes agenda'. While there are those who would not wish to accept the
particular Catholic expression of these ends as desirable, it seems likely that a large
constituency would endorse the desirability of spiritual and moral awareness and
sensitivity, broadly conceived, as an aim for schooling. School effectiveness research
must then face the challenge of how such enhancement can be sensitively appreciated
and reported.[9] This will not be easy because such appreciation will require some
extended fieldwork participation in the life and culture of the school, in observations
of classrooms and teacher–pupil interactions, discussions with pupils on spiritual
and moral issues and some involvement with the wider community.

A second emphasis in the mission statements of the schools was focused upon
'the dignity of the person'. This fundamental aim can be interpreted in a variety of
ways. The dignity of a person is enhanced by the acquisition of knowledge and
skills and by the fulfilment of intellectual, physical, artistic and creative potential.[10]

All objectives relating to academic and personal achievement and attainment can be subsumed within this aim, which has the advantage also of relating achievement measures to issues to do with equal educational opportunities, to multicultural and anti-racist commitments, and to statements about respect for persons regardless of their social class, race, gender or ability status. In other words, 'dignity of the person', as an aim for schooling, includes measures of academic and personal achievement but places these in a more complex and sensitive matrix of respect and justice for all school members, i.e. a learning culture which is also a humane culture. From this perspective, effectiveness for Catholic schools has to be about:

- [creating] 'a place where children and staff feel valued — where children and staff are given individual support — where there is respect and trust for all';
- 'in addition to national curriculum and academic demands, [setting] out to create a happy atmosphere in which the dignity and worth of everyone is recognised, developed and safeguarded';
- 'encouraging, promoting, recognising and celebrating all aspects of achievement within the school';
- [creating] 'an environment which enables and encourages all members of the community to reach out for excellence in every sphere of academic, pastoral, social, moral, physical and spiritual activity';
- 'the distinctive Catholic ethos of our school which is distinguished by the quality of care extended to all its members regardless of race, gender, background or ability'. (CES, 1997, pp. 35–56)

Such statements are important because they encourage school effectiveness researchers to go beyond one dimensional 'value added' measures of pupil academic achievements, important though these are, to the more complex assessment of the culture of learning and the culture of pupil and teacher respect and dignity within each school.[11]

A third emphasis in the mission statements of the Catholic schools related to 'the importance of community' (Ibid). Almost every school claimed that the generation of community values, community support, community spirit and community commitment was an important educational aim. As statements relating to 'community' were also integral to spiritual and moral aims and to 'dignity of the person' aims, it can be said that Catholic schools have very strong aspirations for the educational realization of social bonding and solidarity and therefore that any evaluation of their effectiveness would have to engage seriously with these issues. These aspirations were expressed as:

- 'To create a multicultural community in which all the talents of both students and staff are recognized, valued and encouraged'; (Ibid)
- 'access for parents to counselling, advice and school facilities — the community is recognized as the world of the pupil, links are encouraged with the local community';
- 'the school aims to foster an active partnership between home, parishes and school which enhances our involvement in the wider community';

- 'to develop in members of the school community that sense of personal responsibility . . . which is essential as a preparation for active citizenship';
- 'We are proud of our reputation as a community caring for all children in a warm and friendly manner and seeking out ways of supporting the most vulnerable at any time. This will remain at the heart of our mission'.

The analysis of the nature of community has long been a challenge to the social sciences. The analysis of 'community effectiveness' therefore presents SER with many difficulties which it is tempting to ignore in favour of more individualistic and measurable performance indicators. However, to do so is to marginalize what many schools proclaim to be a major educational objective.

The fourth and final emphasis in the mission statements was closely related to the earlier aspirations of Catholic schooling but distinct from them in the discourse and imagery utilized. Some schools moved beyond a general discourse of 'community' to employ a more specific focus upon social justice, the common good[12] and notions of service. This was expressed as:

- 'To implant and foster in the pupils' minds an awareness of their duty to carry on their economic and social activities in a Christian manner';
- 'We recognise that our school has a special responsibility for meeting the needs of the poor . . . we offer our Catholic community as a radical alternative to a materialistic society';
- 'Our mission is to contribute . . . to the development of Christian women who are confident, can think for themselves, who understand the concepts of equality and justice and who can play a full and responsible part in a changing and multicultural society';
- 'The school aims to nurture an awareness of, and a response to, our brothers and sisters throughout the world'[13]

In general, it can be said that the aspirations of these Catholic school mission statements provided an integrated matrix of desired school outcomes and of pupil outcomes. Catholic schooling culture is, by its comprehensive and inclusive nature, resistant to policy science atomization and commodification. It continues to assert the interrelatedness of educational aims. This is powerfully expressed by one head-teacher in another context as:

> The total development of individuals to full potential — spiritual, intellectual, social, moral, and physical. It is *not* self-fulfilment but the development and use of our gifts to serve God through others. (Grace, 1995, p. 163)

While we cannot expect SER to bring God into the equation, we can expect that future research will be more sensitive to the complex and interrelated nature of school outcomes and therefore more innovative in its conceptual analysis and in its methodological approaches.[14] This could be achieved by extending the important concept of 'value-added' research to include the equally important concept of 'values-added' inquiry[15] — a more catholic paradigm.

Acknowledgment

I would like to thank Harvey Goldstein, Peter Mortimore, Kate Myers, Louise Stoll and Paddy Walsh for comments received on the draft version. They are not responsible for the final text but where I have taken their advice it has improved the analysis.

Notes

1 For a review of early school effectiveness studies in the USA, see Firestone (1991). Studies by Edmonds (1979) and Goodlad et al. (1979) are foundation texts in the field.

2 This tendency was classically referred to by C. Wright Mills (1973) as 'abstracted empiricism'. Angus, reviewing the field, (1993) notes:

> The school, the process of schooling, the culture of pupils, the nature of community, the society, the economy, are not seen in relation to each other. It is particular school practices and their direct connection with particular outcomes which is important. All else is 'simply' context and needs to be statistically controlled. (p. 341)

3 Harvey Goldstein and Kate Myers (1996, p. 15) have called for the use of a principle of multiple indicators in school effectiveness research: 'Multiple indicators should be presented rather than a single or summary one. This is intended to avoid over-concentration on one aspect of performance.' Goldstein also takes the view that a wide range of school outcomes are *potentially* quantifiable.

4 In less tangible categories of school and pupil outcomes, notions of critical appreciation or illuminative evaluation seem more appropriate than those of assessment and measurement. The use of triangulation of accounts may be helpful. For an example, see Grace, Bell and Browne (1996).

5 It should be noted that some studies have attempted this e.g. Mortimore et al. (1988). *School Matters* included in its outcome measures pupils' attitudes to schooling and issues to do with pupils' self-concept. In other words, serious attention was given to some of the social outcomes of schooling.

6 These schools are located in major urban centres such as London, Birmingham, Manchester, Liverpool and in smaller urban centres in Lancashire, Merseyside and Yorkshire.

7 For a discussion of the relation of Catholic schools to notions of the common good (in the USA) see Bryk et al. (1993).

8 All quotations are taken from the mission statements of the participating schools.

9 At present, the spiritual and moral culture of schools is commented on in reports of the Office for Standards in Education (OFSTED) and, additionally for Catholic schools, in Section 13 Reports by Diocesan inspectors. However, more needs to be known about the evidential basis of these reports and about the methodologies used in the collection of evidence.

10 There is evidence that Catholic schools are effective, in the main, in providing good standards of academic education. See Bryk et al. (1993) for the USA and CES (1995) for England and Wales.

11 Much more use could be made of accounts gathered from pupils and teachers about their experiences of the 'effectiveness' of cultures of learning and of personal respect in schools. Pupils, in particular, are well placed to comment upon the extent to which mission statement commitments are actually realized in practice.

12 A recent statement from the Catholic Bishops' Conference for England and Wales (1996) has given salience to discussions about the common good and its implications for the work of Catholic institutions.

13 This school (as with many other Catholic schools) had a serious and sustained commitment to fund-raising for the relief of poverty and famine in Africa and elsewhere. This was related to an educational programme which tried to clarify the causes of poverty and famine arising from colonialism and the current operation of the global economy. This raises the question, 'to what extent is world citizenship awareness a feature of the "effective" school?'

14 For a recent powerful argument in support of this view, see 'Evaluate what you value', Chapter 11 in Stoll and Fink (1996).

15 Such research would attempt to evaluate the relative effectiveness of a school's ethos and culture in contributing towards the social, moral and spiritual development of young people. This research would require an initial assessment and a final assessment. As Goldstein has pointed out (private communication, 1997) 'to judge whether a school has promoted "community values" you need to know where the students started from'.

References

ANGUS, L. (1993) 'The sociology of school effectiveness' in *British Journal of Sociology of Education*, **14**, 3, pp. 333–45.

BRYK, A., LEE, V. and HOLLAND, P. (1993) *Catholic Schools and the Common Good*, Cambridge, Mass.: Harvard University Press.

CATHOLIC BISHOPS' CONFERENCE (1996) *The Common Good and the Catholic Church's Social Teaching*, Manchester: Gabriel Communications.

CATHOLIC EDUCATION SERVICE (1995) *Quality of Education in Catholic Secondary Schools*, London: CES.

CATHOLIC EDUCATION SERVICE (1997) *A Struggle for Excellence: Catholic Secondary Schools in Urban Poverty*, London: CES.

CREEMERS, B. (1994) 'The history, value and purpose of school effectiveness studies', in REYNOLDS, D., CREEMERS, B., STRINGFIELD, S., TEDDLIE, C., SCHAFFER, E. and NESSELRODT, P. (eds) *Advances in School Effectiveness Research and Practice*, Oxford: Pergamon.

EDMONDS, R. (1979) 'Effective schools for the urban poor', *Educational Leadership*, **37**, 1, pp. 15–27.

FIRESTONE, W. (1991) Chapter 1 (Education, researchers & the effective schools movement) in BLISS, J. et al. (eds) *Rethinking Effective Schools*, New Jersey: Prentice Hall.

GEWIRTZ, S., BALL, S. and BOWE, R. (1995) *Markets, Choice and Equity in Education*, Buckingham: Open University Press.

GOLDSTEIN, H. and MYERS, K. (1996) 'Towards a code of ethics for performance indicators', *British Educational Research Association Newsletter*, No. 57.

GOODLAD, J. (1979) *A Study of Schooling*, Indiana: Phi Delta Kappa.

GRACE, G. (1995) *School Leadership: Beyond Education Management: An Essay in Policy Scholarship*, London: Falmer Press.

GRACE, G., BELL, D. and BROWNE, B. (1996) 'St Michael's Roman Catholic Comprehensive School', in NATIONAL COMMISSION ON EDUCATION (eds) *Success Against the Odds: Effective Schools in Disadvantaged Areas*, London: Routledge.

HAMILTON, D. (1996) 'Peddling feel-good fictions', *Forum*, **38**, 2, pp. 54–6.

LAUDER, H. and KHAN, G. (1988) 'Democracy and the effective schools movement', *International Journal of Qualitative Studies in Education*, 1, pp. 51–68.

MCLAUGHLIN, T., O'KEEFFE, B. and O'KEEFE, J. (eds) (1996) *The Contemporary Catholic School: Context, Identity and Diversity*, London: Falmer Press.

MORTIMORE, P., SAMMONS, P., STOLL, L., LEWIS, D. and ECOB, R. (1988) *School Matters: The Junior Years*, Wells: Open Books.

NATIONAL COMMISSION ON EDUCATION (1996) *Success Against the Odds: Effective Schools in Disadvantaged Areas*, London: Routledge.

REYNOLDS, D. (ed.) (1995) 'School effectiveness', *Evaluation and Research in Education*, **9**, 2, Special Issue.

REYNOLDS, D. and CREEMERS, B. (1990) 'School effectiveness and school improvement: A mission statement', *School Effectiveness and School Improvement*, **1**, 1, pp. 1–3.

REYNOLDS, D. and CUTTANCE, P. (eds) (1992) *School Effectiveness Research, Policy and Practice*, London: Cassell.

SACRED CONGREGATION FOR CATHOLIC EDUCATION (1988 version) *The Catholic School*, Homebush NSW: St Paul's Publications.

SAMMONS, P., HILLMAN, J. and MORTIMORE, P. (1995) *Key Characteristics of Effective Schools: A Review of School Effectiveness Research*, London: Institute of Education.

SCHEERENS, J. (1992) *Effective Schooling: Research, Theory and Practice*, London: Cassell.

STOLL, L. and FINK, D. (1996) *Changing Our Schools: Linking School Effectiveness and School Improvement*, Buckingham: Open University Press.

VINCENT, C. (1996) *Parents and Teachers: Power and Participation*, London: Falmer Press.

WRIGHT MILLS, C. (1973) *The Sociological Imagination*, Harmondsworth: Penguin Books.

Chapter 10

Effective Teachers for Effective Schools

Ian Hextall and Pat Mahony

The literature on 'effective' schooling and school improvement affords a prominent place to the development of effective teaching and school leadership in its accounts of the various factors which combine to make up an effective school. In this chapter we will explore the mechanisms through which the account of effective teaching and school leadership have been defined and shaped by the body responsible for teacher education in England — the Teacher Training Agency (TTA). Throughout our chapter we will draw on our recent ESRC funded research project, *The Policy Context and Impact of the Teacher Training Agency* (Mahony and Hextall, 1997a).

The TTA was established by the Conservative Government in 1994 with the officially designated purpose of improving the quality of teaching, raising standards of teacher education and training and promoting teaching as a profession. To grasp the significance of its interventions, it is important to note that its establishment was a part of a general move to construct 'agencies' within whole areas of the public sector including health, social security, child benefit, the prison service and housing where the concept 'effectiveness' plays a significant role.

There are a number of ways in which the concerns of this book and of this chapter are intermeshed with developments in 'new public management', managerialism, or the contract state. Even though we cannot explore them in detail here (Mahony and Hextall, 1997b), three points need to be noted. First, school effectiveness is anchored tightly into the broader issues of competitiveness and efficiency which frame and contextualize much current public policy and practice. There is a background story to these developments which runs as follows. UK plc must become more competitive in relation to the global economy:

> . . . smaller, medium sized enterprises in particular and the engineering companies all say we can't get the skills in the labour force that our competitors get in the rest of the world and that has an impact on UK competitiveness . . . [and that] . . . schools and universities have a particular responsibility to deliver the goods in relation to skills in the labour force. (TTA Board Member)

The quality of teaching is crucial in making some schools more effective than others, so the argument continues, therefore we need to produce more effective teachers. We can see this broader context of the 'competitive' state (Cerny, 1990) providing the legitimating framework for the TTA in the following quotation from the Chief Executive:

> ... everyone is now agreed that the top priority in education is the need to raise
> pupils' standards of learning. ... And there is a widespread awareness that, in a
> competitive world, constant progress is necessary just to maintain parity with other
> nations. (Millett, 1996b, p. 2)

It is a view which is unlikely to change substantially under the new Labour Government:

> Labour's vision is to boost the standards and the standing of the teaching profes-
> sion so that our education service can compete with the best in the world, as we
> enter the 21st century. (Labour Party, 1996, p. 1)

Second, within the domestic public policy arena, the concept of 'effectivity' occupies a central position in the justifications for the transformations in the wider field
of public management. For example the Next Steps Initiative is founded upon the
basis of delivering 'government services more efficiently and effectively within
available resources for the benefit of taxpayers, customers and staff' (Next Steps
Team, 1996, p. 1). Comparable formulations are subsequently found in the Framework Documents and Corporate Plans of bodies as diverse as the Prison Service,
the Child Benefit Agency and the Health Service, as well as those which pertain
more directly to the education sector, including the TTA. Any ambiguity and dispute
surrounding the whole concept of 'effectivity' is camouflaged by the mantra-like
incantation of what Chris Pollitt (1993) describes as the 'virtuous three Es: economy,
efficiency and effectiveness' (p. 59). Bartlett, Knight and Lingard (1992) remind us
of the ways in which political discourse uses such unproblematized repetition to
generate a version of 'common sense':

> ... each section of the text traverses the same terrain, but in increasing detail, so
> that by the end ... we are so familiar with its features that it assumes a necessary
> and material presence. (p. 24)

The most cursory glance at the literature on public policy reveals intense discussion
about the definitions and criteria which are being invoked, and more generally
about the imputed transference of private sector managerial, personnel and accountability models into the public sector (Hood, 1995).

Third, it is only possible to speak sensibly about the effectiveness of schools
in the light of criteria against which it can be judged and alongside procedures for
its recording and reporting. In other words, performance indicators and accountability mechanisms become critical. In addition, one way to achieve 'policy steering' to
enhance 'effectivity', is through tighter regulation. As Paul Hoggett (1996) says:

> In virtually all sectors operational decentralization has been accompanied by the
> extended development of performance management systems. Such systems seem
> designed to both monitor and shape organizational behaviour and encompass a range
> of techniques including performance review, staff appraisal systems, performance-
> related pay, scrutinies, so-called 'quality audits', customer feedback mechanisms,
> comparative tables of performance indicators including 'league tables', chartermarks,
> customer charters, quality standards and total quality management. (p. 20)

It is the translation of such seemingly neutral, technicist assertions into practice that reveals problems in the measures of effectiveness and improvement.

In education, including teacher education, league tables have been linked to the fostering of both competition and a market orientation. There has also been the introduction of a variety of alternative types of institutions to 'enhance' choice and diversity available to proxy consumers. In the light of such pressures, schools and other educational institutions have increasingly been driven to market themselves.

In this drive, school effectiveness is directly tied into the National Curriculum since the 'effectivity' of schools is predominantly judged in accordance with criteria derived from it, mediated through league tables of examination and assessment gradings and the performance indicators of OFSTED[1] inspection reports. Concomitantly, teacher education, professional development and quality teaching are to be interpreted vis a vis such 'effectivity'. Thus in announcing the proposals for the National Curriculum for Initial Teacher Training (NCITT), Gillian Shephard said that it will be:

> Based on the National Curriculum for pupils, will specify the essentials of what must be taught to trainee teachers in each core subject . . . (DfEE, 1996a, Annex p. 1)

In an accompanying letter to the TTA she also said that:

> You will also need to draw up national standards based on the curriculum content. . . . I should like you to set the detailed curriculum content and standards for the core subjects within a comprehensive set of new requirements for initial teacher training courses . . . They should set out much more clearly the standards of competence expected of all new teachers, whatever subjects they teach. (DfEE, 1996a, p. 2)

Finally, in spelling out the implications for teachers' whole careers she asserted that:

> I am not limiting this work to initial teacher training. It is equally important to focus on in-service training. (DfEE, 1996b, p. 3)[2]

An additional twist is provided by a dominantly managerial perception of what counts as an effective school. If learning outcomes constitute the super-ordinate criteria against which effectivity is to be judged, the management and leadership of the school provide the framing context for this learning. This intertwining of learning, teaching and leadership provides a basis upon which to address ourselves directly to the impact of the TTA.

Effective Schooling and the TTA

The TTA has time and again returned to its refrain that the underpinning rationale for all of its work and activities is the improvement of pupils' learning in schools and hence, by extension, to school improvement and effectiveness. In particular it commits itself to developing effective teachers and to generating a powerful model of school leadership.

Given that the TTA operates within this over-arching mission, what then constitute the elements of its work which are central to its fulfilment? The short answer is that everything that the Agency works on is intended to make some contribution. It is difficult to think of anything which is not couched in terms of 'improving pupils' learning' including: its origins and initial remit; the stated philosophy and values which underpin and justify its activities as embedded in Corporate Plans and Annual Reports; the forms of its own working practices; the agenda which it has generated as a framework for its activities; and the detail of the activities which it has undertaken. Some of these are: developing quality supply strategies; controlling the ITT process; formulating an NCITT; evaluating training via Standards for New Teachers; establishing Priorities for Continuing Professional Development; building a National Standards framework for stages of teaching; tightening appraisal procedures; rewarding quality teachers; defining pedagogy and sponsoring 'research-based professionalism'. All are geared towards the production of effective teachers for effective schools.

Who could possibly question such strategic vision? It surely makes no sense to have established an overall policy regarding school education without at the same time ensuring that the teaching force is capable of delivering the policy. In order for this to be accomplished, trained leaders are to be equipped with the managerial skills to ensure that the policies will be translated into effective practice. Similarly, it is necessary to know who is responsible for which aspects of the policy, what their responsibilities involve, and to be able to reward those who show the greatest capacity to undertake such work. In order for stasis in the system to be avoided, a tailored training and development programme will ensure a supply of fresh, appropriately skilled staff to step into levels of responsibility when needs and opportunities arise. The training and development model within which the TTA has been working appears to be superficially plausible and precisely tailored to deliver the necessary improvements in school effectiveness.

Why then might we want to raise questions about such an approach? Not because we are not committed to improving pupils', students' or teachers' educational experiences. Not because we are already well satisfied with the quality of learning experiences currently provided in schools, and certainly not because we are unconcerned about how current teaching and learning will best enable us to educate 'the citizens of the future'. The critical issues stem from disagreements with the value position upon which the TTA grounds its work and from differences as to the effectiveness of the policies being proposed by the Agency to achieve its own stated outcomes, even taken on their own terms. They stem from alternative perspectives on the effectiveness debate and from concern about the procedures through which the model has been established and is being put into place. Finally, the very images of schooling, education, society and the future with which the TTA is operating seem to us highly questionable.

A general concern about current definitions of school effectiveness is that there is no sense that any relevance is accorded to where students come from, the nature of their life experiences nor their prospective destinations. Laurie Angus (1993) has identified the assumptions underpinning such an approach:

> . . . educational practice is conceived of in a particularly mechanical way. . . . In keeping with economistic definitions of effectiveness, it is the bit that comes between 'input' and 'outputs'. It is seen largely as a set of techniques, the 'core technology', for managing 'throughput' rather than a complex and always unpredictable process of ongoing construction of educational practice. Practice is imposed rather than constructed, negotiated or asserted; it is a set of techniques to be employed by teacher technicians on malleable pupils. (p. 337)

This is highly relevant to the framework for National Professional Standards and Qualifications which the TTA is in the process of introducing.

The New Qualification Structure for Teachers

Central to the fundamental restructuring of teaching and recomposition of the teaching force is the development of a National Professional Standards and Qualification framework for the following designated stages within the teaching career: newly qualified teachers (NQTs); advanced skills teachers; subject leaders and school leaders. At the time of writing the National Professional Qualification for Head-teachers (NPQH) is being piloted and the standards for NQTs finalized. The other proposed standards, qualifications and implementation structures are currently moving through the consultation, development and application cycles. We shall focus our attention first upon 'leadership' and the NPQH.

Leadership

Many authorities in the school effectiveness field have identified 'leadership' as occupying a critical position in the development of effective schools. It is therefore no coincidence that of all the many places in which the TTA could have begun its work, one of its very first initiatives was directed towards headteachers. This constituency has remained centre-stage from that time, with the training, re-skilling, re-orientation, managerialization and certification of heads occupying a key place in the TTA's overall strategic vision:

> We also know that effective teaching must be supported by high quality management and leadership at middle and senior levels in the profession . . . We know from OFSTED evidence that the managers and leaders in our schools need: to offer leadership; to set tone, ethos, direction and purpose; to translate purpose into plans; to implement those plans; and to check, through monitoring and evaluation, that progress is taking place. Managers and leaders also need to be accountable for that progress, at whatever level they manage. (TTA, 1996a, para 10, p. 9)

How the role of the head is conceived within different conceptions of what constitutes an effective school are matters of considerable debate. In England such an account seems to embody a mixture of direct control ('old managerialism') and so called 'people-centred management' ('new managerialism') (Ball, 1997). A flavour of this can be detected from the first two 'Key Areas of Headship' as identified in the National Standards for Headteachers. In the section on 'Strategic Direction and Development of the School', heads 'lead', 'provide inspiration and motivation', 'create', 'implement', 'ensure', 'monitor', 'evaluate', 'review' and 'take action if necessary'. In relation to 'Teaching and Learning', they 'create and maintain', 'determine, organise and implement' and 'monitor and evaluate' (TTA, 1997, pp. 6–7).

As presented here this is a dominantly hierarchical, 'hands-on' management model which places other participants in the school community in a largely responsive relationship to the head's vision. As Angus (1994) says:

> Other organisational participants, such as teachers, parents and students, . . . are generally viewed as essentially passive recipients of the leader's vision. . . . the main skill required of most participants is for them merely to adopt the leader's vision and slot into the leader's definition of school culture. . . . The elitist implication of this view is that leaders are more visionary and trustworthy than anyone else. (p. 86)

We know from our experience of working with headteachers and from the growing literature on the subject that there are *other* recommended models of leadership for the UK and elsewhere. For example, writing about 'school cultures' in the Danish context, where policy is less centrally driven, Lejf Moos (1996), says:

> The Folkeskole is not the embodiment of the headteacher's beliefs or values. The vision or mission of the school is not disseminated from the top down. . . . where a discussion of goals and values takes place, it is a shared dialogue between teachers and 'management'. (p. 23)

This is an ideal which would be echoed and even extended to include other stake-holding members of the community. To that extent, Glatter's (1996) comments would resonate with many:

> . . . we in 'mainstream' educational management have become too preoccupied with what might be called the institutional side of leadership and management to the extent of disregarding or at least underemphasising policy and contextual factors. In doing so we may be playing into the hands of those who accuse educational management of being too technocratic and mechanistic and of paying insufficient regard to values. (p. 3)

This raises the problem of the social and political presumptions underpinning what it is that 'leaders' have to achieve:

> Insofar as managers in a managerialist system can be recreated as nodes receptive to direct central determinations, and can obviate the activities of the residue of a local democratic or state machinery, their recreation becomes as essential as substantive reform itself. (Fergusson, 1994, pp. 95–6)

Within the working body of the school, the TTA has also constituted a new teacher designation, namely, the subject leader. In identifying this as a national priority it is claimed that good leadership and management at subject level 'is essential if the quality of teaching and learning is to be systematically and effectively monitored, evaluated and improved' (Millett, 1995, p. 11).

School leadership and subject leadership are explicitly linked together and directly connected to the emergent career-long standards and the overall structure of the profession. Once again questions arise over the priority which is accorded to leadership per se and the model of 'leadership and management' which is entailed. Lurking behind the detail of the proposals are two general issues. One of these is education-specific, the other locates these education-related developments within a wider social frame.

The first issue is that schools are already differentiated organizations. The current proposals both reconstitute that differentiation within a finely grained, hierarchical model and provide much closer and more detailed specification of the positions within it, thus defining position holders in relation to others in terms of their 'line-management' responsibilities and accountabilities (TTA, 1996a, para. 10, p. 9). This has deep implications for the nature and texture of social relationships within schools and is predicated upon a particular version of 'leadership' which delegitimates the negotiating space accessible for other, competing styles of leadership.

The second issue is that such transformations in social relationships have been widely discussed in other sectors of the public service. This has often been covered with references to the professional/managerial split. In the health, criminal justice, housing and other social welfare sectors, it is being claimed that there is a growing divide between the orientations of those who see themselves as occupying client-related professional positions and the managers who administer the service as a whole. As a corollary to this the power of these areas is also being judged as shifting towards managerial 'leaders' (Taylor-Gooby and Lawson, 1993). At times the managers in this context have been imported from outside the service, often from outside the public sector altogether, but, in addition, 'professional' positions have been redefined as 'managerial' with attendant retraining and job respecification. Janet Newman (1994) amongst others has argued that such a reformulation of management and leadership has important implications in gender terms. We know that the TTA is treating as problematic what it sees as the 'feminization' of teaching. It remains to be seen over time whether the redefinition of leadership within schools will constitute an erosion of the limited opportunities available to women within middle and senior management structures. This has wide implications for the redefinition of 'professionalism' and for the social/occupational control of the teaching force (Ozga, 1993; Limerick and Lingard, 1995; Dominelli, 1996; Mahony, 1997).

Effective Teachers

In shifting our attention to the teaching force as a whole, we have seen that there has been a whole raft of activities which the Agency would claim are being directed towards the goal of increasing the 'effectiveness' of teachers. The following quotation from Anthea Millett (1995) provides an encapsulated view of how the Agency sees these initiatives:

> By seeking to raise teaching quality and teacher quality our proposals go to the heart of school improvement. They are designed to enhance teachers intellectual grasp of the materials that have to be taught and to promote the most effective ways of teaching them. By identifying expectations of NQTs, of expert teachers, of subject leaders and of headteachers, we shall tackle once and for all the issues of subject knowledge, pedagogy and organisation which lie at the heart of school improvement. (p. 14)

Individual papers could be written on each and every one of these elements detailing their origins, legitimating structures, procedures for construction, conceptual validity, consequences and implications. Taken together, this constellation constitutes a powerful intervention which both reshapes the nature of teaching and presages fundamental restructuring within the teaching profession of lines of power, responsibility and accountability. Even before career entry and then through all stages of professional development, the TTA can be seen as putting in place procedures for coordinating and regulating the occupational lives of teachers. Those bodies with responsibilities for these activities, will increasingly find themselves operating in accordance with priorities, regulations, criteria and indicators established at a distance, with limited scope for autonomous action at a local level. A major concern is that through this process definitions of 'good' teaching, 'relevant' professional development and career enhancement have all been removed from debate.

Underpinning these moves are mechanistic and technicist assumptions which reshape what may or may not be construed as 'professional'. Teachers' work is being calibrated to the extent that whole areas of their occupational lives are being pre-defined in accordance with requirements which circumscribe the degrees of choice and decision-making within which they operate. In constituting the indicators on the basis of which teachers' performance will be evaluated and rewarded,[3] such requirements represent the very antithesis of what is normally associated with the notion of 'professional'. Yet teachers will continue to have to make professional decisions, selected from the available range of practices, tailored to specific circumstances, within the realization that consequences will need to be sensitively evaluated and reflected upon. It is this which begins to meet the criteria for critical practice and to move us beyond the perception of teaching as 'technicist delivery'.

Whilst in no way wishing to disparage the value of 'teachers as researchers', a notion from which we ourselves have greatly benefited, it is interesting to note that the research bids funded by the TTA have concentrated predominantly on more effective mechanisms for delivery of already established 'best practice principles' rather than constituting a reflection on, extension of, redefinition or contextualization of these practices (TTA, 1996b). This links to the version of teaching and learning research which underlies David Hargreaves' proposals (1996) and also forms the backdrop against which Anthea Millett can presume an unproblematic version of the *most effective pedagogic practices*.

In a recent lecture Anthea Millett (1996a) made 'pedagogy' central to the issue of improvement/effectiveness. Having claimed that there exists 'a vow of silence on pedagogy' (which is as extraordinary as accusing the Catholic church of refusing to pay attention to the soul), she went on to propose a model composed of:

> . . . four soundly-based elements: the need for a secure command of the material to be taught; the need actively to teach; the need to have high expectations of pupils, and ensure appropriate pace and challenge; the need to have effective working relations with pupils. (p. 6)

Apart from rendering invisible the many people who have spent the majority of their professional lives working with beginning teachers to develop these areas of expertise, the real issue around pedagogy is how to unpack it in a manner appropriate for a changing world. The OECD report *Quality in Education* (1994) for example states that:

> Increasingly, teachers are diversifying their pedagogical strategies to incorporate pupil-centred and small group techniques, which are more consistent with contemporary theories of human learning and also more appealing to students who prefer more interactive learning. . . . The complex interactions of personalities and pedagogies make classroom dynamics increasingly unpredictable, and teachers must be adept at improvisation. As there is more to think about, reflection becomes an expected part of teachers' work, . . . Collaboration among teachers is also increasingly being required . . . (p. 70)

In contrast to this, stands the model of tight regulation and surveillance being moved into place in the English context.

Paradoxically, this restructuring is presumed to provide a sense of purpose, value and progression for the practising teacher, and a motivational inducement for people considering entry to the profession. In another recent lecture, Anthea Millett provided a very forthright statement of what the TTA sees as constituting the nature of the fundamental problems which currently bedevil teachers' professional status.

> My fourth question tonight — Which are the essential preconditions for creating a professional framework for teaching? — *takes us to the heart of what is currently amiss with teachers and teaching.* There is no clear direction, no structure of standards, no framework within which our teachers can progress . . . We must find ways of recognising high quality teachers and *rewarding them accordingly.* . . . That will inevitably be a major landmark in terms of recognition of teachers. And it provides *a framework of opportunity for the whole profession.* . . . I have already been told . . . that rewarding excellence with extra points is divisive and subjective. Is it beyond our wit to find a non-subjective and transparent means of doing so? *I believe that a framework of professional qualifications, to which all teachers can aspire, will provide the means and opportunity to provide a better, more responsive system of rewarding our teachers for their work.* (Millet, 1996c, pp. 11–12, our emphases)

Thus what many would see as the very essence of the deprofessionalization of teaching, namely, the increasingly dominant machinery of regulation, is being redefined as the 'solution' rather than as symptomatic of a problem.

It could be claimed that we have caricatured the TTA's position and that it has no intention of introducing such a mechanistic model of teaching. However, for a debate on this question to be possible there would need to be a context within which it could be conducted. As we argue below, it is just such contexts which are being progressively removed and undercut in schools, in HEIs and in training and development partnerships. For the moment let us briefly illustrate our point with reference to the National Curriculum (NC).

We have already seen that criteria for 'effectiveness' are increasingly being tied to the delivery of the NC. These criteria are also likely to form a key element in the NCITT and underpin the priorities for Continuing Professional Development (CPD). This raises questions about the critical space which remains for debating and contesting the NC framework itself. Where, if at all, is there to be an arena for such debate if it is intended to remove it from the contexts of initial training and CPD? Or are we to presume that the NC is beyond dispute, that it represents an end of ideology (which is, of course, itself an ideological position)?

This raises a more general problem. If teachers become so tightly controlled, where is the space within the system for difference of viewpoint on any professional matter? Built directly into these developments are silences which convey deep messages as to the models of teaching and learning within which the TTA is working. These are not simply models of how teachers should teach, although these are certainly present, but also implicit models of how the Agency sees teachers' learning and the theories of commitment and motivation with which they operate.

Centralization, Decentralization and Accountability

The issue of contestation binds together two concerns which have wide resonance throughout the whole area of public sector reorganization, namely, patterns of centralization/decentralization, and questions of accountability and representation. In a sense these can be combined into the one issue of 'ownership', or what in more contemporary terms has come to be called 'stakeholding'. As we shall see these find their expression in educational policy debate, not least in the context of school effectiveness/improvement.

Within the public policy literature there exists a vigorous debate about the uneasy tension between centralization/decentralization in which key parameters for policy are established at the centre, partly policed by the centre through surveillance and regulatory machinery, but, at one and the same time, subjected to internal, localized control. It is one of the 'paradoxical' features which many commentators pointed to in the Conservatives' 'long march' through the education system (Halpin, Power and Fitz, 1993). League tables, quality indicators, appraisal procedures, profiling and differentially rewarding quality teachers are all devices for individualizing institutional or personal judgments of effectiveness, whether of schools, HEIs or specific teachers. Such attributions of localized responsibility are seen as powerful methods for 'ratcheting up standards'. But as we have argued, such measures occur in a policy context within which room for manoeuvre is highly constrained. These elements, which have also been termed 'tight–loose coupling', can be discerned in the TTA's approach to the development of 'effective' teaching. Whilst on the one hand individual schools are attributed responsibility (and accorded blame), at the same time they are increasingly expected to operate within criteria and indicators over which they have little control and in which they have little say.

As we have seen, by emphasizing the centrality of the 'leadership' role, the Agency has accorded heads and subject leaders a critical location within the reformulation of teaching and the profession: while it imbues these 'leaders' with a degree of independence/autonomy in relation to policy setting which belies the highly centralized context in which they operate, it also ascribes high levels of accountability for performance to those leaders, 'at whatever level they manage'. This managerial/professional tension is one which has been picked up in the educational field but also more widely in the public sector (Bottery, 1996). Writing specifically about the redesignation of the heads' role in the context of the increasing impact of managerialism in education Fergusson (1994) says:

> In essence, the headteacher is ceasing to be a senior peer embedded within a professional group who has taken on additional responsibilities including a significant administrative function, and is becoming a distinctive and key actor in an essentially managerialist system, in which the pursuit of objectives and methods which are increasingly centrally determined is the responsibility of managers who must account for their achievement and ensure the compliance of teaching staff. (p. 94)

In each specific educational or public policy context the centre of gravity of this centralized/decentralized relationship will take on a different form and character. Certainly, to many, the actions and directions adopted by the TTA have taken a dominantly centralist form. The increasingly assertive role of the TTA in defining both ITT and professional development are taken as indices of this. At the same time there is the rhetoric of decentralization of responsibility, for example, in relation to appraisal or inspections, in which institutions and teachers are being required to adopt individualistic, quasi-competitive orientations.

Such issues of policy-making and attribution of responsibility begin to lose their abstract form when they are translated into the highly concrete contexts of, say, defining local continuing professional development priorities. At such points, questions of entitlement, local decision-making, responsibility and accountability, regulation, surveillance and social justice are unavoidable (Mahony and Hextall, 1997c). In any such local discussion it is unlikely to be 'effectiveness' or 'standards' per se which are in dispute. It would be a malicious or irresponsibly naive commentator who did not want schools or teacher education to be more effective, or standards of teaching, learning and behaviour to rise. The issues arise when we try to interpret what is meant by these terms and attempt to establish democratic and equitable procedures for the representation and reconciliation of differing viewpoints and value positions about the role of teachers, what counts as 'effective teaching' and how these are to be translated into practice.

Even more difficult issues of 'voice' arise when policy production pretends that there is no problem (Angus, 1994; Smyth, 1996). Margaret Simey has some telling points to make about the principles underpinning the concept of accountability which highlight the increasing 'democratic deficit' in the UK. She argues that there is an:

> . . . urgent need to grasp the fact that accountability is not a mechanism or a routine but a principle. More than that, it is a principle which serves a specific purpose. In a democracy, that purpose is to provide the basis for the relationship between the society and its members, between those who govern and those who consent to be governed. The word consent provides the significant clue. (Simey, 1985, p. 17)

We have become increasingly aware of the need to consider whether, like other government Agencies, the TTA is engaged in a political process involving the claiming and enforcement of consensus where none exists, leading to an evacuation of debate and the destruction of critical or contestational spaces (Mahony and Hextall, 1997b). Escaping from the shackles of political accountability was one major rationale for the whole movement towards 'agencification'. Much was made of the distinction between political and managerial accountability, and of the need to shift public policy and administration towards the latter. Not only do the two not necessarily map onto one another, they may indeed exist in tension or conflict. The criteria by which they are to be judged/evaluated are not identical. Transparency and 'Value for Money' are objectives which need to be reconciled through procedures which have to be constructed and vigorously sustained. In their 1994 report, *Quality in Education*, the OECD both recognize and stress the importance of establishing an appropriate balance:

> . . . between state controlled, profession controlled and consumerist accountability, which is adapted both to the extent of autonomy given to the school and to the resources and infrastructural support to use the autonomy constructively. Otherwise there is a danger that the power is kept where it is while the blame is being decentralised. (OECD, 1996, p. 12)

In considering what might constitute effective teachers for effective schools such negotiations would raise thorny questions as to whether it is teachers or teaching that make a difference, what kind of difference and how, whether it matters what kind of learners there are or how their needs (and those of society) are defined, whether it matters what form and impact 'leadership' has and how this is justified. We need to question the economic, cultural, social, historical, political and temporal parameters within which 'effectiveness' is being located; to question whether it is a public good that can be universally shared without being exhausted, or whether its achievement in one context can only be accomplished at someone else's cost.

These kinds of questions are inescapable if there is to be a robust and sustainable public debate about effective schools. Many teachers, parents, governing bodies, pupil councils, as well as academic researchers and policy professionals have engaged long and determinedly with such issues. It is therefore depressing to find little comparable awareness or reflection in the policy formulations of the TTA. Such questions require contexts in which they can be responsibly and seriously debated and where it does not feel as though 'dissensus will be identified with adolescent behaviour' (as one of our interviewees put it). Establishing structures and processes with adequate criteria of representation, responsibility and transparency through which proper debate can be conducted will be no easy task. There is, for example, no consensus even amongst its supporters as to what form a General Teaching Council should take (Mahony and Hextall, 1997b). But the dilemma cannot be resolved by either denial or the imposition of unrepresentative government Agencies.

Conclusion

The 'effectiveness' movement is located within specific geographical, temporal and material parameters. Failure to recognize these exposes any specific set of policy initiatives to the twin dangers of blinkered vision and short-termism. In drawing our chapter to a close we will briefly identify the shortcomings and risks which are embedded in the assertive stance adopted by the TTA in its commitment to produce effective teachers for effective schools.

The first of these raises education-specific issues which arose from a school effectiveness research project conducted by the Australian Council for Educational Research (ACER). They concluded that:

> School effectiveness is about a great deal more than maximising academic achievement. Learning and the love of learning; personal development and self-esteem; life skills, problem solving and learning how to learn; the development of independent thinkers and well rounded confident individuals; all rank as highly or more highly as the outcomes of effective schooling as success in a narrow range of academic disciplines. (McGraw et al., 1992, p. 174)

The orientation of this quotation from ACER can be directly compared with the following recent quotation from a public lecture delivered by Anthea Millett (1996a):

> In any specification of effective pedagogy we must ensure that teaching is talked about in terms of its effects on pupils' learning. Ensuring this, will make it easier to develop the culture we at the Teacher Training Agency are seeking — a culture where teaching is a truly evidence-based profession, where we learn about good practice from relevant research and inspection evidence and where that good practice is judged not on whether pupils are busier or happier or more forthcoming but whether the quality and standard of their learning improves. (p. 9)

Even within the school effectiveness 'movement', a major figure has argued that:

> In Britain and internationally, there is a sense in which the entire enterprise of
> school effectiveness appears in a 'time warp'. The studies that have been conducted
> are all ageing rapidly and are of less and less use in the educational world of the
> 1990s. This world has new needs at the level of pupil outcomes from schools —
> the skills to access information and to work collaboratively in groups, and the
> social outcomes of being able to cope in a highly complex world are just three new
> educational goals which are never used as outcomes in the school effectiveness
> literature. (Reynolds, 1994, p. 23)

As we have tried to show, such awareness appears to figure little on the agenda
within which a 'quality' teaching force is being prepared for the coming years.
Similarly, although 'The TTA will take action to stimulate and co-ordinate a con-
certed campaign to promote teaching as a high quality profession . . .' (TTA, 1996c,
p. 5), there seems to be little understanding of what might motivate or even inspire
teachers to enter or remain in teaching. Few currently labouring with the difficulties
of supply and recruitment would dispute the urgency of the TTA's task but many
are questioning the style and strategy being adopted to achieve it.

> Why, when other employers are valuing autonomy, talent, creativity, intrinsic
> motivation towards quality and improvement, active participation, high employee
> self-esteem, and investment in continuing professional development, would one
> enter the low-trust, tight control, centrally and seemingly ideologically defined
> environment of teaching? (ATL, 1996, p. 4)

There is no doubting that the TTA is thoroughly infused with a commitment to
school effectiveness and improvement, defined via learning outcomes and enhanced
by 'good leadership and effective teaching'. Through our argument we have identified
some of the areas in which we think that there needs to be a more widely drawn,
more open-textured debate than the Agency has been able to engage in so far. It is
to be hoped that a new political regime will recognize the necessity of promoting
such a debate and of establishing structures of governance which will foster it. Such
recognition could represent a beginning in creating an atmosphere of high-trust,
optimism and inclusivity, appropriate to an 'advanced' progressive democracy.

Notes

1   Office for Standards in Education is a regulatory agency responsible for the inspection of
schools and university departments undertaking initial teacher training.
2   As yet it is too early to judge what continuities or changes in policy will follow from the
Labour Party's 'Ten Point Plan for Teacher Training' (Labour Party, 1996) and the work
of the newly established Task Force on Standards. There also remains considerable
ambiguity as to how the remits and relationships between the TTA and the proposed
General Teaching Council will be drawn.

3   The implications of this bracketing of professional development with 'rewards' can be seen clearly in the TTA's recent submission to the School Teachers' Review Body on 'Better Pay for Better Teachers':

> The Agency is convinced that we need high calibre, well qualified teachers in all our schools. We have an extensive programme in development to recruit and retain quality candidates, and we want all teachers to benefit from continuous career development. Our ideas for rewarding teaching excellence and effectiveness are exciting and pave the way for the development of a profession that benefits teachers and pupils alike. (TTA, 1996d, p. 2)

References

ANGUS, L. (1993) 'The sociology of school effectiveness', *British Journal of Sociology of Education*, **14**, 3, pp. 333–45.

ANGUS, L. (1994) 'Sociological analysis and education management: The social context of the self-managing school', *British Journal of Sociology of Education*, **15**, 1, pp. 79–91.

ASSOCIATION OF TEACHERS AND LECTURERS (ATL) (1996) *Evidence to the Parliamentary Education and Employment Committee: Inquiry into the Professional Status Recruitment and Training of Teachers*, London: ATL.

BALL, S. (1997) 'Education policy and education policy research', *British Education Research Journal*, **23**, 3, pp. 257–74.

BARTLETT, L., KNIGHT, J. and LINGARD, B. (1992) 'Restructuring teacher education in Australia', *British Journal of Sociology of Education*, **13**, 1, pp. 19–36.

BOTTERY, M. (1996) 'The challenge to professionals from the new public management: Implications for the teaching profession', *Oxford Review of Education*, **22**, 2, pp. 179–97.

CERNY, P. (1990) *The Changing Architecture of Politics: Structure, Agency and the Future of the State*, London: Sage.

DfEE (1996a) 'National Curriculum for ITT', Letter to Geoffrey Parker, Chair of TTA.

DfEE (1996b) *Shake Up of Teacher Training and New Focus on Leadership Skills for Headteachers*, London: DfEE, 302/96.

DOMINELLI, L. (1996) 'Deprofessionalizing social work: Anti-oppressive practice, competencies and postmodernism', *British Journal of Social Work*, **26**, pp. 153–75.

FERGUSSON, R. (1994) 'Managerialism in education', in CLARKE, J., COCHRANE, A. and McLAUGHLIN, E. (eds) *Managing Social Policy*, London: Sage.

GLATTER, R. (1996) 'Context and capability in educational management', Paper presented at BEMAS Annual Conference, Coventry, September 1996.

HALPIN, D., POWER, S. and FITZ, J. (1993) 'Opting into state control? Headteachers and some paradoxes of grant-maintained status', *International Studies in Sociology of Education*, **3**, 1, pp. 3–23.

HARGREAVES, D. (1996) 'Teaching as a research-based profession: Possibilities and prospects', TTA Annual Lecture.

HOGGETT, P. (1996) 'New modes of control in the public service', *Public Administration*, **74**, Spring, pp. 9–32.

HOOD, C. (1995) 'Emerging issues in public administration', *Public Administration*, **73**, pp. 165–83.

LABOUR PARTY (1996) *Teacher 2000*, London: Labour Party.

LIMERICK, B. and LINGARD, B. (eds) (1995) *Gender and Changing Educational Management*, Rydalmere: Hodder Education.

MAHONY, P. (1997) 'Talking heads: Feminist perspectives on public sector reform in teacher education', *Discourse*, **18**, 1, pp. 87–102.

MAHONY, P. and HEXTALL, I. (1997a) *The Policy Context and Impact of the TTA: A Summary*, London: Roehampton Institute London.

MAHONY, P. and HEXTALL, I. (1997b) 'Problems of accountability in reinvented government: A case study of the Teacher Training Agency', *Journal of Education Policy*, **12**, 4, pp. 267–83.

MAHONY, P. and HEXTALL, I. (1997c) 'Sounds of silence: The social justice agenda of the Teacher Training Agency', *International Studies in the Sociology of Education*, **7**, 2, pp. 137–56.

MCGRAW, B., PIPER, K., BANKS, D. and EVANS, B. (1992) *Making Schools More Effective*, Hawthorn, Victoria: ACER.

MILLETT, A. (1995) 'Securing excellence in teaching', TTA Chief Executive's Annual Lecture, London: TTA.

MILLETT, A. (1996a) 'Pedagogy — Last corner of the secret garden', Invitation Lecture, Kings College.

MILLETT, A. (1996b) Chief Executive's Annual Lecture, London: TTA.

MOOS, L. (1996) 'Insights into school culture', *Managing Schools Today*, **5**, 8, pp. 22–4.

NEWMAN, J. (1994) 'The limits of management: Gender and the politics of change', in CLARKE, J., COCHRANE, A. and MCLAUGHLIN, E. (eds) *Managing Social Policy*, London: Sage, pp. 182–209.

NEXT STEPS TEAM (1996) *Next Steps: Briefing Note*, Cabinet Office.

OECD (1994) *Quality in Education*, Paris: OECD.

OECD (1996) 'Teachers and their professional development', Unpublished report, Paris: OECD.

OZGA, J. (ed.) (1993) *Women and Educational Management*, Milton Keynes: Open University Press.

POLLITT, C. (1993) *Managerialism and the Public Services* (second edn), Oxford: Blackwell Publishers.

REYNOLDS, D. (1994) 'School effectiveness and quality in education', in RIBNEW, P. and BURRIDGE, E. (eds) *Improving Education: Promoting Quality in Schools*, London: Cassell.

SIMEY, M. (1985) *Government by Consent: The Principles and Practice of Accountability in Local Government*, London: Bedford Square Press.

SMYTH, J. (1996) 'The socially just alternative to the "self-managing school" ', in LEITHWOOD, K. et al. (eds) *International Handbook of Educational Leadership and Administration*, The Netherlands: Kluwer.

TAYLOR-GOOBY, P. and LAWSON, R. (eds) (1993) *Markets and Managers: New Issues in the Delivery of Welfare*, Buckingham: Open University Press.

TTA (1996a) *Corporate Plan*, London: TTA.

TTA (1996b) *Teacher Training Agency Awards Research Funds to Teachers*, London: TTA 22/96.

TTA (1996c) *Better Pay for Better Teachers: Submission to the STRB*, London: TTA 29/96.

TTA (1996d) *A Strategic Plan for Teacher Supply and Recruitment: A Discussion Document*, London: TTA.

TTA (1997) *National Standards for Headteachers*, London: TTA.

Chapter 11

A Tale of Two Schools in One City: Foxwood and Cross Green

Bob Spooner

Introduction

The thrust of post-1988 education policy has been to mirror in schools the social divisions that increase all the time in our urban areas. Competition between schools inevitably results in winners and losers and those schools branded as failures see socially ambitious parents withdrawing their children and the average ability level of those who remain inevitably dropping. Measuring the success of schools by GCSE A–C predetermines which schools will come bottom of the tables. They will be deemed to be failing however well they are doing. To date the activity has been a self-defeating process. To be 'accused' of failure demoralizes staff and pupils. To go through the mockery of closing down, amalgamating and re-opening adds confusion and chaos to an already depressing scene. For a New Labour Government, elected in 1997, to embrace this policy, which hits hardest those pupils who are deprived and neglected, is difficult to comprehend. The following case study involving the closure of two schools in the north of England and their reopening as a 'Phoenix' school, which explores how it was handled and the cost involved in human terms, puts the New Labour policy into context.

Foxwood and Cross Green Schools

Foxwood was the first comprehensive school in the city. It was planned in the 1950s to serve the council estates, one of which had been designed as a purpose built ghetto, with a high proportion of four and five bedroom houses to meet the needs of so-called problem families. Foxwood was a 12-form entry school, for boys only. The Labour Group on the City Council was startled by its own courage in building a comprehensive school at all; to have made it co-educational as well would have been altogether too daring. All pupils then took the 11-plus, so the school had a 'selective' intake of 36 and a 'non-selective' intake of over 300, but amongst them were 76 boys with IQs over 110. They were 11+ borderline pupils who travelled a considerable distance to avoid secondary modern education.

The Labour Group set out to prove that comprehensive schools could compete with grammar schools, by building a boys' grammar school (Temple Moor) at some distance but designed to serve the same area. Ten years after opening, Foxwood's selective intake had shrunk to 6 and only 8 other pupils had IQs over 110, as other comprehensive schools had been opened just beyond the perimeter of its catchment area. Cross Green was one of them. It was the fourth comprehensive school opened in the city. Originally intended as a girls' school, it was at the last moment mixed and provided with a workshop annex for 'boys' skills'. It served two areas of substantial deprivation.

The two schools were not in direct competition, as they both had their own distinct hinterlands, but they were both 'creamed' of able pupils by Temple Moor, Roundhay, and the City of Leeds, which were all thriving selective schools, and Cross Green also lost pupils to Parklands, which was a girls' selective school in Seacroft.

Leeds 'went fully comprehensive' in 1974, and in preparation for this development Foxwood was mixed in 1971, though, because the former girls' selective school, Parklands, was retained as a girls' comprehensive school within its catchment area, boys' numbers were always well in excess of girls'. However, it had, for a time, a 15-form intake, which generated a sixth form of over 150 pupils. Cross Green also developed a successful sixth form, proportionate to its size. Both schools were proud of their academic records, which were based on what was then described as 'over-achievement' by their pupils. During the twenty years between 1965–85, over 500 pupils from the 2 schools became graduates. The schools specialized in developing many innovative and successful initiatives to meet the needs of pupils from deprived backgrounds. Historically Seacroft had an unemployment rate eight times higher than the national average and Osmondthorpe and Gipton were also unemployment blackspots.

The Leeds Tory Council undertook a massive reorganization in 1974, abolishing selective education and establishing a first, middle and high school pattern. Twelve years later Leeds started to plan another major upheaval. This was stimulated by a desire to replace all sixth forms with tertiary colleges, and in order to do this the middle schools, in spite of their success, were to be eliminated. Under this plan, Foxwood was to become a tertiary college, so after 1987 it suffered progressively from planning blight.

During the 1980s, falling rolls meant that all Leeds high schools developed surplus places, and as there was also a substantial population movement away from Seacroft, Osmondthorpe and Gipton, Foxwood and Cross Green suffered from this in an accentuated form. Empty spaces in the former grammar schools also meant that the intake of Foxwood and Cross Green became concentrated on their immediate catchment areas. As the socially aspiring parents moved out of these areas, their intakes increasingly consisted of pupils who came from impoverished, and in some cases, chaotic, backgrounds, many of whom had already fallen way behind academically before they entered the schools. At the depth of the depression in the 1980s, up to 80 per cent of their children came from families in which the main breadwinner was out of work. Over half had reading ages more than two years behind their chronological age at the time of entry and those exceeding it could be counted on one hand!

The DFE refused to sanction the Leeds 1989 development plan, so it had to be revised, omitting the provision of tertiary colleges. It was, however, still based on the original proposal to abolish the middle schools. In East Leeds, Foxwood was to remain open as a five-form entry, and Cross Green was planned the same size. However, a newly established school, Braim Wood High School, housed in the former Braim Wood Middle School, was also to be opened on the fringe of the East Leeds area, to cater only for boys.

One of the common criticisms of the reorganization plan which was designed to operate from 1992 was that too many places were provided in East Leeds. This was compounded when, on the argument that a six-form entry was necessary to make a comprehensive school viable, the intake at Foxwood and Cross Green was increased, on paper, to six-form entries. As between them, these schools had been built to cater for 22 forms of intake, this still left a combined surplus of 10 forms per year, or 1,500 surplus places, offset by the surrender by Foxwood of some space for adult education purposes. In defence of the proposals, the argument was deployed that by 2001 these extra places would be needed. Any East Leeds area calculation was artificial, as Roudhay and Braim Wood were sited in attractive residential areas on the border of East Leeds and would draw heavily from it. So Leeds deliberately planned to have for many years a vast number of surplus places in East Leeds schools most of which would be at Foxwood and Cross Green.

Fresh Image: Same Problems

Aware of the falling numbers, the governors of Foxwood on reorganization in 1992, decided to rename the school, and give it a fresh image. They would have liked to call it the Dennis Healey Secondary School but jibbed at the initials and finished up calling it 'East Leeds', on the ground that 'West Leeds' was the name of a successful school on the other side of the city. The publication of league tables accelerated the flight from the centre of Leeds to the perimeter and beyond, that had already followed the introduction of parental choice, and the desire of many parents that their offsprings should mix with 'socially more desirable' boys and girls. This widespread phenomenon still further reduced the numbers attending East Leeds and Cross Green. Whether the schools were good or bad, successful or failing, there were two in-built certainties: they would both have a massive number of surplus places and they would both feature at the bottom of the league tables, not because the teachers had an unduly low expectation of their pupils' academic potential — indeed both schools were demanding academically — but because it is absurd to expect pupils who have already fallen woefully behind academically, who have insecure and impoverished backgrounds and excessive out of school pressures, to get many GCSE grades A–C.

Political catch phrases rarely have any relationship to reality. It became the 'in' thing, even for those who condemned the league tables, to describe schools at the bottom of them as 'failing' schools. The same people will, in conversation, agree that failure is scattered over the whole spectrum, that all schools succeed in some ways and fail in others and that there is no reason to suppose that schools at the top of the league tables are not failing on a grand scale, but they forget reality when 'political' language is employed. It is also modish to claim that schools with surplus places have been 'rejected by the local community'. If this is a valid description, then the pupil 'drift' towards the perimeter of the city and beyond, means that almost all schools in Leeds have been 'rejected by their communities'. In the real world, parents value their children for qualities other than their academic ability. Indeed, only a narrow strata of society puts undue emphasis on academic skills. Parents want their children to be loving, trustworthy, generous and companionable. They hope they will live happy lives and form stable relationships. Of course they want them to 'do well at school' and get good jobs, but whereas the most valued qualities concern 'absolutes', doing well is always a relative thing. They mean doing as well as they can. Parents judge schools by their contribution to all these outcomes. Only politicians see success or failure in terms of GCSE A–Cs.

Even before the 1992 reorganization was complete, Leeds came under pressure over surplus places. A government which had depended on surplus places to operate a policy of parental choice, decided that LEA incompetence in preserving them must be eliminated. After the 1992 election, the Leader of the Leeds Labour Group, fearing widespread opting out, made it his prime objective to thwart it. He set up a non-political Schools' Council, composed mainly of middle-class, middle-aged, middle-intellect, middle-of-the-road males to examine the future of education in Leeds. One task was to look at surplus places in Leeds schools. It discovered, to no-one's surprise, the planned surplus places at East Leeds and Cross Green, and wanted them eliminated. The Labour Group charged three prominent Labour Councillors with the task of eliminating them. Presented with a paper that argued that the closure of East Leeds would save an estimated million pounds a year assuming that the displaced pupils went to Cross Green, they decided to bite the bullet and close this school. All three individuals no doubt made the decision reluctantly; all genuinely cared about the proper education of inner-city boys and girls, but the case seemed overwhelming. They believed pupils were not receiving a proper education at East Leeds and that the million pounds could be much better spent. The local MP was dismayed by the poverty he saw all around him and by the crime rate in the area.

School Reorganization

The experience of the two schools after reorganization in 1992 was very different. At East Leeds, though some senior staff had to go, most of those who were eligible to apply for their own jobs did so; the headteacher and the two deputies remained there. In effect, only the name was changed, though it was decided to spend lavishly to upgrade the school's image, and some policies were updated in consultation with parents. The school's PTA had owned two hostels in the Dales and before reorganization one of them had been sold for some £80,000 and the other had been considerably extended and improved. This was retained by East Leeds but has now been handed over to a trust, 'for the benefit of Seacroft Children'.

At Cross Green, the transition, in management terms, was more chequered. There the headteacher had intended to retire in the summer of 1991 to allow a new appointment to be made in good time, so that there would be a smooth handover. Under the Leeds assimilation agreement with the teachers' unions, only existing Leeds heads were eligible to apply for the newly established schools, and when the existing head realized that the only applicants for Cross Green had come from two middle school heads who had had, in her opinion, inappropriate experience, she applied for the post herself, and was duly appointed, being determined to stay until the vacancy could be nationally advertised. However the knowledge that she intended to retire led to a substantial number of staff seeking jobs in other Leeds schools. Fortunately, the deputies remained.

Early in the autumn term the two middle school heads were assimilated to posts in other Leeds schools, and the head was advised that she could now safely retire, as the post would be open to national advertisement, and she left at Christmas 1991. However, one of the middle school heads successfully argued that, under the assimilation rules, he was entitled to the headship, though he could not take it up until the following September, as he had his own school to close. So the senior deputy at Cross Green was made acting head for the spring and summer terms of 1992.

The new head took up his post in September 1992, but whether he had been maligned by the former head's lack of confidence was never put to the test. He suffered a series of illnesses, so that he spent very little time in the school, which was effectively managed by the former acting head. By June of 1993 the new head had retired. This was not the only management upheaval. During the 1993–94 academic year the acting deputy and the other permanent deputy retired.

OFSTED Inspections

Meanwhile, an OFSTED inspection was planned, which was wholly inappropriate bearing in mind the school's management problems. The LEA should not have allowed this to happen and it was left to the acting head to object. In the end, the inspection was not held until April 1994, but the school then lost out, as it was then inspected by a team of Leeds local advisers, who could not be expected to bring fresh minds to the job. East Leeds was also inspected by OFSTED but not until May 1994 and then by a team from Essex.

Before these inspections took place, both schools were warned that they might be classified as failing schools, which put their teachers under additional pressure. At East Leeds, some very able staff had been squeezed out during the 1992 re-organization, as the diminished roll did not allow their above scale allowances to continue at the same levels. But there was in the school a strong cadre of teachers who had progressively adjusted their teaching style to the needs of the area over the previous twenty years, there were some good new appointments and the management team remained intact. In the term before the inspection, however, the head of technology and of modern languages retired and on financial grounds were not replaced, so there were glaring weaknesses in these departments, but by and large the report reflected credit on the staff. The OFSTED inspectors went out of their way to insist that East Leeds was by no means a failing school. Over some crucial issues there was strong praise. As '5.3 per cent of the school population have statements' (in the top 10 per cent of all schools in the country) and as '68 per cent of pupils in the present Year 7 have reading ages that are two or more years behind their chronological age', the 'standards of achievement are below the national norms in all subjects', the report states. But 'the standards achieved by pupils with special educational needs are generally satisfactory or better.' Of the special needs department the report said, 'The department successfully raises pupil esteem and confidence'. On pupils' welfare and guidance it said that 'There is generally a high standard of pastoral care in the school and pupils are well supported by teachers, who have a sound knowledge of their abilities, as well as a detailed understanding of their personal and social development. Pupils feel confident and secure when at school'. It also says that a 'wide range of extra-curricular activities extends and enriches pupils' experiences'. Most of the teaching seen was more than satisfactory and there was some encouragement for most departments. Music is not an easy subject to teach to children from deprived backgrounds, but there was very warm praise for the music department. In general, the report revealed a school in which the pupils and teachers could feel proud and which contained a wealth of experience that would be lost were it to close.

At Cross Green the leader of the OFSTED team promised to let the staff know as early as possible his verdict. Halfway through the inspection he apparently told them that the school was likely to be declared a failing school, so the atmosphere in the staffroom became demoralized and angry. These moods make it difficult to teach sparkling lessons and it was no surprise when the report stated that 'special measures are required in relation to this school, since it is failing to give its pupils an acceptable standard of education'. A close and careful reading of the report reveals what I believe is a surprising level of hostility to the school; severe criticism is given with relish, and praise is consistently grudging, except for the provision for pupils with special educational needs, where it is said that 'the needs of individual pupils with learning difficulties are well provided for'. (OFSTED, 1994) As this covers a substantial percentage of the pupils in the school and should be a major part of the school's modus vivendi, surprisingly little is made of this success in the main summary. Having offered some grudging praise of the Senior Management Team's work in dealing with day-to-day issues and in short- and medium-term strategic planning, the report says, 'There is however an absence of long-term planning in the school'. This humourless comment is a gem in a report on a school under threat of imminent closure.

However, when due allowance is made for prejudice, no one reading the two reports would conclude other than that, if one of the schools had to close, it should be Cross Green. What happened next is of some public interest. The staff at Cross Green were indignant about the report and set about producing a detailed action plan. A team of HMIs was appointed to advise on its implementation and monitor it. The post of headteacher was advertised and the acting head was appointed. In applying for the post, he had sought assurances about the long-term future of the school and these were forthcoming. The governors also determined to advertise the two vacant deputy posts. Rumours were rife and the headteacher again sought specific assurances that the school had a long-term future, as obviously this was a question that applicants would ask. He was given them, and, indeed, applicants who sought reassurance from the appointing body of governors were told that the LEA plans for the area involved keeping the school open. This was, of course in line with the (still secret) recommendation of the three Labour Councillors entrusted with determining policy on the issue.

There was then some discussion as to how best to implement the policy and the greatest administrative problem was how to find jobs for the displaced East Leeds staff — over 30 of them — when the LEA had a 'no redundancy' policy. LMS had made this operation extremely difficult. A calculation would have shown that 10 East Leeds staff would be over 50-years-old, and they could be offered up to 10 years enhanced early retirement, but over 20 would need other jobs. If, on the other hand, both Cross Green and East Leeds were closed and 'merged' on the Cross Green site, then the number of staff over 50-years-old and so eligible for enhanced retirement, would be increased, and as the whole process of closing and re-opening and having to apply for one's own job is depressing, a strong fillip would be given to staff in both schools to apply for other jobs. In addition, if the two schools were merged, the pupils from East Leeds could be taken by bus to Cross Green, rather than attend their nearest school, which would happen if East Leeds alone closed.

These twin advantages must have appeared substantial to the individuals who made the decision, because they were bought at considerable expense and an extended period of disruption to twice as many pupils. In the last week of the Summer term, officers visited both schools and the staff were told that the schools were being merged and a 'new' school would be established on one of the sites. It was maintained that the site had still to be determined, but it seems improbable that there was ever the slightest intention to alter the original plan. As is now commonplace, the packaging was altered but, in the eyes of the Councillors, not the product, though of course the effect on staff and pupils in the short term was very different. Thus the solemn promises made to the new head and deputies at Cross Green were broken, within weeks of their being made, and the boost to the morale of the East Leeds staff from their favourable OFSTED report was dissipated. This behaviour would have been inconceivable before LMS, when Leeds was an LEA widely trusted by its employees. It is possibly a glaring example of how the powers and standards of an LEA can decline.

Horrific Scenarios

There was then sketched in an horrific scenario. The new school would not open for two years, to allow ample time to debate which site would be used, and time to allow appeals against the decision to be made. More time would then be needed for the redeployment of staff. During the two years, staff could be expected to leave and be replaced by temporary teachers and the schools would be expected to soldier on with constant staff changes and in an atmosphere of rumour and counter-rumour.

For the pupils involved, the decision was disastrous. Politicians often forget that each pupil has only one set of schooldays. To have these woefully disrupted can do them untold harm. Boys and girls from deprived backgrounds need to get a sense of security from their schools; those who struggle academically need to have the same teachers for Years 10 and 11. Above all else, they need to acquire self-respect and the chances of this are always enhanced when they have some confidence in the schools they attend. To be told that these schools are to be closed because they are failing, is the last thing they need. So over 700 pupils had their education threatened, twice as many as would have suffered had just one school closed. It seems that the needs of the pupils already in the schools were clearly a very low priority.

Once the closure of the two schools was made public, there was an outcry against it in the Leeds Labour Party, and a motion was moved in the District Labour Party, which theoretically determines the Party's local policies. This motion condemned the closure of both schools. The argument was deployed that children from deprived backgrounds needed a neighbourhood school and that the merger was a phoney device as, whichever school was closed, the children attending it had other nearer schools than the one that remained open. The financial argument that closing East Leeds would save a million pounds a year was shown to be ridiculous and indeed it was admitted that it would be less than half that figure. In reality, as pupils take their money with them and statemented pupils take their additional funding, the saving would be negligible, particularly as, in Leeds, 90 per cent of educational funding is distributed to schools, and most of this is based on pupil numbers.

In defending policies, councillors are often reduced to dredging up arguments that were never made when the original decision was taken. To her credit, the Labour Councillor who had been the prime mover in making the decision, was there to defend it. Her defence underlined the fact that the decision to house the new school in the existing Cross Green buildings had already been taken. She chose to argue that a higher proportion of children from feeder primary schools went to Cross Green than to East Leeds, so that school enjoyed more support from its community. To reach this conclusion, both the large primary school based on the same campus as Parklands High School and another which is close to Braim Wood High School had been described as East Leeds feeder schools! There was a rousing speech made by a councillor, who said it was negative to assume that the new school would not be different. One could not underestimate the contribution that a newly appointed headteacher would make. As Cross Green had had three newly appointed heads in three years and this was held by OFSTED to account, in part, for its supposed failure, it was not a compelling argument. The District Party condemned the closure of both schools by an overwhelming majority and supported the view that children from deprived areas need a neighbourhood school.

It did not make a scrap of difference. The OFSTED inspections which had been projected to the staffs of both schools as a guideline for the LEA, did not make a scrap of difference either. One wonders whether the Secretary of State for Education, Gillian Shephard, realized that, in effect, the 'successful' school was being closed and the one branded, however unfairly, a failure, would survive. In December 1994, the long-standing intention of the LEA to make Cross Green the site of the new school was publicly announced. Protest meetings were held in both schools, with a high percentage of parents attending. Speaker after speaker condemned the proposal and praised the caring ethos of the schools again. It did not make a scrap of difference. Just as staff disciplinary procedures are often a device to protect employers in industrial courts, and are unrelated to doing justice to employees, so the opportunities offered for public protest are designed to avoid the accusation of secrecy and allow those who suffer from the policies to let off steam. Only when schools are sited in politically sensitive areas do public protests ever affect decisions, and Seacroft is a safe Labour seat.

The motive behind the merger was to protect the interest of the staff in both schools and to ensure that one school achieved a 'viable intake' — as near as possible to a six-form entry. The choice of the Cross Green site, which is on the fringe of an industrial estate, and in the heart of nowhere, was to establish the merged school away from council estates and so 'out of the pupils' environment'. It is worth considering to what extent these three objectives were achieved.

For the staff in both schools, the result was an extended nightmare. Those over 50 were offered up to 10 years' enhancement, if they took early retirement in July 1995. At East Leeds, those who were eligible wanted, out of loyalty to the pupils, to stay for the last year of the school's life, particularly as most of them had started some work with Year 10. But the offer on the table was only available if they went in July 1995. With varying degrees of reluctance, all 10 of those eligible accepted. At East Leeds alone, the fruits of over 200 years of service from talented teachers, who had deliberately chosen to work there, were lost, and the LEA is contributing to their pensions, until they reach 60. This may cost more than closing one of the schools will save.

Councillors believe that these teachers were well treated, but being persuaded to go quietly is no way to end distinguished careers. Those teachers I have consulted all told me that they felt bitter about the decision. One highly successful teacher, who accepted 10 years' enhancement during the school reorganization of 1992, said to me:

> I was told on the Friday after my 50th birthday that the school no longer had any use for me, and I was offered enhancement, if I agreed to go by the following Monday. I felt unwanted and undervalued, so I went. I have lost nothing financially, as I make up my former salary on less than three days a week supply work in the same school, but I still feel very bitter about it. This from an LEA that runs courses to adjust people to the trauma of retirement!

Clearly, it was a very expensive way of saving money but, under LMS, as long as the money comes out of a different pocket, a saving is deemed to have been made.

Those who dreamed up the merger probably believed that the new school would start with the ablest teachers chosen from both schools, but there was no way to achieving this. The two years of stagnation gave some of those who were most marketable, time to get other jobs, and far from cutting out dead wood, early retirement involved the loss of some of the ablest and certainly the most experienced teachers. In practice the vagaries of LMS meant that there was no coherent assimilation policy. A new board of governors insisted on a new head being appointed. The two existing heads were not originally short-listed, but for the sake of decorum, this was remedied.

Although the new school was in the Cross Green building and would cater very largely for the same pupils, no coherent attempt was made to benefit from that school's experiences. The new head was appointed a term in advance, but was obliged to spend most of his time in forward planning and interviewing, augmented by a couple of training days for staff, held too late to allow their experiences to influence new strategies. A decent diffidence, and possibly a desire not to be identified with past 'failures', kept him, for most of the time, out of both schools. Some believe that knowledge is power, and that the best decisions are made in the light of all the evidence, but the governors wanted a clean break and seemed to think that knowledge of the past prejudices a fair judgment. This philosophy was dramatically demonstrated over interviews. No references were read until after a decision had been made. One candidate, whose work had been praised in the OFSTED report, asked governors whether they had read it. She was told that they deliberately ignored the report, lest it prejudice them.

This tactic may increase the chances of a wholly fresh start but there is a price to pay. It is not good for aggrieved staff, whose work has been undermined by school closure, to get the message loud and clear that none of the contributions they have made in the past count for anything. It so happened that at East Leeds there were two exceptional teachers. A senior HMI once told me that one of them was the best teacher he had ever come across. A Chief Adviser for Leeds remarked of the other that the two lessons she had just taught were the best he had ever witnessed in his life. Both had made exceptional — and original — contributions to out-of-school activities. They both had excellent administrative ability. Both were rejected as a result of this approach.

Some good appointments were made, but as after the interview procedure almost all of the teaching posts went to existing East Leeds and Cross Green staff, a less abrasive procedure might have spared a lot of anguish. In the last week of the Summer term, the two rejected teachers were being wooed to take up main scale posts on a temporary basis, with their above scale payments protected by the LEA. Over all, the intention of those making the merger to be sensitive to the needs of existing staff was not fulfilled: the process gave rise to a great deal of antagonism.

As for the pupils, it has already been noted that reorganizations are always disruptive. The pupils in Year 11 in both schools had already had their secondary education disrupted by the 1992 reorganization and this one meant that they had known no stability at all at secondary level. Working in a school in a deeply deprived area reveals to teachers how some children's education can be wrecked by instability and poverty; it also reveals how very resilient other children are. The boy at East Leeds who, in his last year, got eight 'As' at GCSE, four of which were starred, triumphed over this disadvantage, while reminding those who justify the closure of inner-city schools on the grounds that in them 'able children stand no chance', that this judgment should be qualified.

Talk of possible closure had reduced the 1993 intake at East Leeds to 65 in 1993, in 1994 it was 68 and in 1995, 21. By then the school's fate was public knowledge and those who had chosen it had done so, ignorant of its doom. The East Leeds management team argued that it was not in these pupils' best interest to start their secondary education in a school that had only one more year of life, but the parents' choice was held to be inviolate. Councillors and officers, who undeniably care about the future of children in general, often seem to show no evidence of this when considering children in particular circumstances. David Blunkett, the Labour Government's Secretary of State for Education, has used the term 'armchair intellectuals'. But the people responsible for these closures rarely sit in armchairs as they are very busy people; nor, I believe, do they show much evidence of intellect.

Conclusion: Lessons Learned?

There are lessons to be learned from this story. The decisions were no doubt made in good faith by men and women committed to the needs of deprived children and the democratic process. There was nothing sleazy about them; no one gained personally from them; there was no political hare to chase into a jug. Those taking the decisions were told several things, all of which were tenable. They were told that the two schools were failing, as they were at the bottom of the league table; they were told that a six-form entry was necessary in order to maintain a broad timetable; they were told that vast sums were being wasted on surplus places and the DFE would not tolerate it; they were told that money was being squandered on pupils in these schools to no effect. The belief that it does children in deprived areas good to be forced out of their environment no doubt played some part. Leeds has an excellent reputation as an employer and its record in supporting schools in areas of deprivation is very good. The intention no doubt was to protect the interests of staff and pupils as much as possible.

The main lesson is that the gap between intention and reality was very great. As the original decision to close East Leeds was opposed by parents and the ruling political party, the democratic process didn't work. For at least three years the education of the children involved was disrupted and the teachers demoralized. Very many very able teaches were lost to the profession prematurely; indeed, early retirement to suit the vagaries of LMS is a national scandal that needs exposing. And out of all the turmoil has emerged a school that is no other than the old Cross Green writ large, but not much larger, in the same buildings, with the same pupils and with staff who were expected to show extraordinary resilience and make a successful 'fresh start'. The school has inherited all the so-called endemic problems of the two closed schools and has been denied many of their most experienced staff. In addition, Seacroft has been left without a neighbourhood mixed comprehensive school.

In reality, the two schools were certainly not failing in the service they were giving to children most at risk. The OFSTED comments on their success in teaching pupils with learning problems bear witness to this fact. The special needs provision, arising from statements and from deprivation factors, was expensive, but the pupils carried this with them; it is part of their baggage. Those who have to travel five or more miles a day in addition to their other burdens will need some very startling provision to compensate for this handicap.

We should now recognize that the argument that a comprehensive school needs six-form intake to offer a sufficiently broad curriculum became less valid once the National Curriculum was introduced. Its purpose was to provide pupils, mainly in Years 10 and 11, with wide choices. The compulsory elements in the National Curriculum dramatically reduced choice and though it is creeping back with each modification of the curriculum, many schools thrive on smaller intakes than 180. Even so, the price of broadening the curriculum is that pupils have to take GCSE with ungenerous time allocations per subject. When one considers the needs of children brought up in poverty, often from unstable backgrounds or backgrounds where education is not greatly valued, who start secondary education with well-established records of educational failure, one has to accept that a generous time allocation devoted to their best subjects is the only solution, if they are to get A–Cs in GCSE, or indeed gain any sense of success from their school work. They don't want their noses rubbed in failure. They may well be better served in small schools by teachers who understand their needs, respect their environment and are able to respond to their emotional problems, rather than in a competitive ethos, where they are forever comparing their own academic achievement with that of other pupils in the schools, and where emphasis is placed on results rather than on personal achievement.

Those who argue that such pupils should be forced out of their backgrounds have, often without realizing it, a snobbish attitude to what used to be normal working-class values. One poisonous effect of the market economy is that it increasingly makes people see success in terms of house ownership and the accumulation of consumer goods. It is not much concerned with happiness or the quality of life.

Emotionally, and this is what matters most, Seacroft residents are as well balanced as those living in most communities. Rather more are in gaol and rather more misuse drugs, but most families, even many of the chaotic ones, offer their children warm love and care. When they don't, it is even more necessary that their school offers a secure refuge and that they attend one that is not out of sympathy with parental mores. Teachers who are forever seeking to project to children a lower middle-class morality that implicitly condemns their parents' way of life, are doing them no service. At best they fuel resentment; at worst despair. To be fair, in this case 'taking them out of their environment' involved taking them by bus to a school where the children come from a very similar background, white, deprived, insecure and decently unambitious. And, until the slow increase in the birth rate works its way through, it too will be a small school languishing at the bottom of the tables, though it may well be a good school in everything that matters most; indeed as good as East Leeds and Cross Green were. The biggest difference for some time will be the tiresome bus journey for up to a third of its pupils. As the truancy rate was an endemic problem in both schools, this must be seen as an inspired answer to it.

Footnotes

There are two ironic footnotes to this story. Because Cross Green was declared a failing school, a team of HMIs supervised the school's action plan. The OFSTED report had followed the normal pattern of setting targets for the school and the staff prepared an exhaustive response. The HMI linked with the school proved helpful and sympathetic and advised them to concentrate on finding some professionally realistic solutions to a limited range of problems involving attendance, truancy, the environment and, for the pupils, enhanced expectations. In spite of the way they had been treated, with the benefit of stable management, capable of stimulating staff commitment, the performance of the school clearly improved. Two HMIs carried out a mini-inspection in the autumn term of 1995 and made favourable comment. 'Despite the difficult circumstances, the staff and governors display a strong commitment to the pupils and parents of Cross Green School. Relationships between staff and pupils are very good', they said. The final monitoring inspection in May 1996 produced favourable comment, and accepted that the staff had 'creatively addressed many of the seemingly endemic problems.' Success was so marked and measurable that the HMIs offered to conduct a formal inspection in the last term with the expectation of declaring that it could no longer be considered a failing school. Although this might have soothed the *amour propre* of the staff, it would have been of no conceivable benefit to the pupils, and the offer was rejected. Since the OFSTED inspection, four teachers, described by the head as excellent, had left and two took early retirement. Another eleven obtained jobs in other schools (one as an acting headteacher). Fourteen obtained posts in the new school. They had the satisfaction of leaving a good legacy for the new school and in this lies the best hope for the future.

The determination of the governors to ensure a 'fresh start' resulted in their giving the school a new name, 'Copperfields College'. A mite pretentious one might think, but in a good tradition — when Foxwood opened in 1956, the head designed a short, royal blue gown, to be worn by prefects once a sixth form were established. New heads, in their euphoria, must be forgiven these flights of fancy. One must hope, for the sake of the pupils, that something good will turn up. The youth of Seacroft quickly re-christened it 'Chipperfields' and when this was criticized the pupils, ever compliant, substituted 'Billy Smart's'. There are worse fates than being named after such a successful ring master.

References

OFSTED (1994) *Report on Cross Green School, Leeds*, London: OFSTED.
OFSTED (1994) *Report on East Leeds School, Leeds*, London: OFSTED.

Chapter 12

A Tale of One School in One City: Hackney Downs

Sally Tomlinson

In the 1990s a new educational phenomenon appeared in Britain. This was the failing school, a demonized institution whose head, teachers and governors were deemed to be personally responsible for the educational underperformance of its pupils. Failing schools were castigated for failing whole communities, particularly in disadvantaged areas where 'pupils have only a slim chance of receiving challenging and rewarding teaching throughout their educational career' (OFSTED, 1993, p. 43), and for weakening the whole educational structure (Barber, 1996, p. 132). Failing schools were the subject of negative and derisory media coverage, with journalists competing to discover 'the worst school in Britain' (Brace, 1994) — an accolade seemingly handed out to a different school every few months in the mid-1990s. Politicians from major parties competed to demonstrate their 'zero tolerance of school underperformance' (Blair, 1996, p. 12), and a culture of shame and blame reached a high point in May 1997 when 18 out of some 300 underperforming schools were singled out for public naming (MacCleod, 1997).

This chapter describes the life and death of Hackney Downs School in East London, the first (and perhaps only) school to be designated as irretrievably failing and closed in December 1995 on the advice of an Educational Association.[1] The closure was long-drawn out and bitterly contested, and as O'Connor, Hales, Davies and Tomlinson have pointed out (1998), 'very many of those involved still feel a burning sense of injustice at what happened at Hackney Downs in 1995'. The story illustrates the nonsense of regarding individual schools as operating as though divorced from historical, social, economic and political contexts, from the consequences of national and local policies and decisions, and from personal agendas.

Effective Schools — Failing Schools

The failing school is the obverse of the effective school. School effectiveness researchers, in the 1970s and 1980s, were concerned to identify the characteristics of effective schools and made their findings available to practitioners to improve schools. The major school effectiveness studies in the UK (Rutter et al., 1979; Reynolds,

1982; Mortimore et al., 1988; Smith and Tomlinson, 1989) were undertaken from the initial hypothesis that schools with similar intakes of pupils in terms of prior attainment, social class and ethnic origin, might differ in the extent to which they helped pupils to progress. The intention was not to pillory and deride schools that did not appear to be as successful as others in helping all pupils to progress, but to identify factors which made for success. But by the 1990s the research had been hijacked politically to blame secondary schools which performed badly in the league tables of GCSE A–C passes. Schools which appeared to take in children with similar socio-economic backgrounds but 'did worse' than others nearby, were castigated as failing (Hofkins, 1993) and blamed for 'parading this (socio-economic background) as an excuse for low standards' (M. Tomlinson, 1997). Policy-makers and the inspectorate began to demand lists of factors which made for effective schools and assume that such lists would automatically identify ineffective schools.

The reality is that reliance on school effectiveness research to discover and isolate failing schools is simplistic and dangerous, as Goldstein (1996) has pointed out in a stringent critique of such a practice. In particular, it is *not* acceptable — educationally, methodologically, politically or morally — to ignore two major differences between the 1980s, when the major school effectiveness research was carried out, and the 1990s. A major difference is the effect of post-1988 market forces which must in the 1990s be taken into account when considering the intake of schools. Market forces have moved the more 'desirable' pupils out of particular schools, and ensured that other schools take in larger numbers of those children considered 'undesirable' in the market (Ball, Bowe and Gerwitz, 1996). Children with special educational needs, migrant and minority children, second language speakers, those excluded from other schools, are now concentrated more than ever in smaller numbers of urban schools. A second factor, not accounted for in earlier research, is the dramatic increase in poverty, unemployment and the effect of excess deprivation on families, which affect schools differentially, even those in the same neighbourhood.

Hackney Downs was a school experiencing these two effects. It had been included in a major school effectiveness study in the 1980s (Smith and Tomlinson, 1989). In 1986, the pupils achieved examination passes on a par with the other London schools studied. Yet already the school was experiencing staff, maintenance and resource problems and feeling the effects of an increasingly disadvantaged intake. By the early 1990s, two-thirds of the pupils had some form of special educational need, about 70 per cent being second language speakers. A high proportion of pupils had been taken in after exclusion from other schools. By 1995 the buildings the pupils were taught in were, almost literally, falling down. Yet this was a school in which the teachers in post were publicly blamed for 'short-changing' the pupils (North East London Education Association, 1995). The school was closed with precipitous haste in December 1995 while an appeal against its closure was still being heard, and has entered educational mythology as the prototype of a 'failing' school.

In 1970 Basil Bernstein wrote that 'education cannot compensate for society' (Bernstein, 1970). In 1995 the message to teachers seemed to be, 'If your school does not compensate for society it will close and you will be personally blamed'.

Origins

Hackney Downs Boys School, a foundation of the Worshipful Company of Grocers, was opened in 1876. Initially it offered a more practical curriculum than the classical grammar school education of the day, and was distinguished by the emphasis placed on English literature and on drama — subjects praised in a final inspection report over 120 years later. The school was handed over to control of the London County Council in 1906, and began to admit boys from Jewish immigrant families, providing an early example of successful multicultural education. The school continued its dramatic traditions, producing plays which in the later 1940s starred a young Michael Caine and a young Harold Pinter. Regrettably, a fire started accidentally in the theatre in 1963 caused the loss of much of the original school building. In 1969, despite its success as a grammar school, the school staff, supported by governors, parents and distinguished old boys in the 'Cloves Club', voted for comprehensive status under the Inner London Education Authority. The authority tried to ensure schools had truly comprehensive intakes through a system of ability 'banding'. However, throughout the 1970s the increasing impoverishment of the borough and the settlement of ethnic minority communities — Afro-Caribbean, Turkish, Indian, Pakistani, Bangladeshi, Kurdish and other groups — affected the banding system and the ability mix.

Hackney Downs — A Chronology

1876	Hackney Downs School founded by the Worshipful Company of Grocers to provide a practical education for local boys.
1906	The London County Council takes over the school, now a grammar school.
1969	The school becomes a comprehensive school under the Inner London Education Authority, but with pupils of all abilities.
1984–85	The school roll falls with fewer higher ability boys. An ILEA inspection worries that academic standards are low.
	Industrial action over teachers' pay disrupts classes.
1987	Removal of asbestos leads to partial closure of school temporarily.
1989	Black staff and parents form 'action groups'. Hackney prepares for abolition of the ILEA. Gus John is appointed as Director of Education. Michael Barber is Chair of Hackney Education Committee.
1990	The school is transferred from ILEA to Hackney as one of four Hackney secondary schools giving 'cause for concern'. The long serving head retires.
1991	The new head has to deal with intensified disputes over the role of the black teachers group.

1992	LEA inspectors put the school on an 'at risk' register — the head leaves for 'other duties'.
1993	A new acting head is appointed for two years, with help from a consultant head for two years.
1993	A Review of Secondary Schooling in Hackney proposes that Hackney becomes co-educational. The LEA recommends no Year 7 recruitment in 1994 to refurbish the school which is now unsafe in some areas.
1993 (Dec)	The acting head leaves.
1994 (Jan)	Another acting head appointed who leaves (sick) after two weeks.
1994 (Feb)	A third acting head (Betty Hales) is appointed. A dispute between the black teachers and the school results in the resignation/suspension of the head of the maths department and a campaign against the school.
1994 (Mar)	The DfE rejects the co-educational proposal, but the LEA still refuses to allow a Year 7 intake in September.
1994 (May)	OFSTED inspection.
1994 (July)	OFSTED reports that the school needs 'special measures'.
1994 (Aug–Oct)	School and LEA prepares action plans in response to OFSTED, the LEA refuses to allow a Year 7 entry — the school roll falls to 300.
	The LEA decides to consult on closure of the school.
1994 (Oct–Nov)	The governors oppose closure.
1994–95	A stormy consultation process ensues — parents and pupils are against closure.
1995 (Mar)	The Education Committee ratifies closures — boys are to be transferred to Homerton House School.
1995 (May)	Labour councillors have doubts about closure.
1995 (June)	The Education Committee refuses to endorse the closure proposal and rejects the Director's report recommending closure to the DfE. The school prepares to recruit and reorganize.
1995 (4 July)	The DfE confirms that the Secretary for State is no longer considering closure and has no further interest in the school.
1995 (13 July)	The Secretary of State decides to send an Education Association to the school.
1995 (27 July)	DfE announces the membership of the North East London Education Association.

1995 (28 July)	Michael Barber, now a member of the Association, writes in *The Independent* that the school is likely to be closed. The Old Boys 'Clove Club', and some distinguished old boys prepare to help the school.
1995 (Sept)	School opens with 200 boys and the EA in control. They appoint three independent inspectors to inspect the school.
1995	The EA publish their report on the school recommending closure.
1995 (14 Nov)	Closure is confirmed by the Secretary of State. Staff issued with redundancy notices on minimum terms.
1995 (17 Nov)	Michael Barber writes an article in the *Times Educational Supplement*, 'The school that had to die', alleging that the high costs of Hackney Downs were 'daylight robbery' from other Hackney pupils.
1995 (15 Nov)	Application for legal aid for a group of pupils and parents to seek a judicial review of the closure decision. Application refused and an appeal lodged.
1995 (15 Nov)	The school instructed to begin the transfer of boys to Homerton House. Year 11 boys' GCSE year is disrupted.
1995 (5 Dec)	Legal aid to pupils granted.
1995(8 Dec)	Leave granted to move for a judicial review.
1995 (11 Dec)	Mr Justice Popplewell hears the case and rejects it. Leave to appeal granted.
1995 (15 Dec)	Final school assembly at Hackney Downs. Staff told to leave premises by the evening.
1995 (18 Dec)	Appeal heard.
1995 (21 Dec)	Appeal rejected and school closes.
1996	GCSE examination results are no better at Homerton House than at Hackney Downs in 1995.

The 1980s

In the 1980s Hackney became and has remained, the poorest borough in London, with high levels of socio-economic deprivation and also the poorest record of child health in London. In 1980 six Hackney secondary schools (out of fifteen) were closed or merged, leaving Hackney Downs as one of the two boys schools. But the popularity of boys-only schools was waning. The Jewish population had moved elsewhere and in ability terms the school had become a secondary modern. However, a 1985 ILEA report, written by the then Chief Inspector Professor David Hargreaves, praised the school for its 'many individual and collective strengths', which included a 'most civilised and humane working environment'. But from this time, problems accrued. The school lost its sixth form when a sixth-form college opened locally. The mid-1980s teacher industrial action affected staff relations, with some militant teachers making themselves unpopular. In 1986 the school was closed temporarily while asbestos was removed from the buildings. In 1989 the headteacher, who had been in post for fifteen years, was faced with uncomfortable gender and race problems from which he retired in December. The issues centred around various staff discontents. A woman's staff group had met and complained about the attitudes of some pupils and male staff. This sparked an angry reaction from black male staff, who set up a black staff group and linked with a black parents' group. Although both black and white boys were regarded by staff as 'underachieving', the black group complained, in an unsigned letter to the head, about 'covert racism' in the school which affected black pupils' achievements. An ideological rift developed between staff which continued into the 1990s, even after a black Chief Education Officer had been appointed in the borough.

In 1988–89 the Inner London Education Authority prepared to hand over Hackney Schools to the new Hackney Local Education Authority, which had appointed the then local councillor, Michael Barber, as its Chair of the Education Committee. A final report of ILEA inspectors in November 1989 continued to praise the generally good relationships within Hackney Downs, but noted that improvements in teaching and learning were needed. This report also deplored a developing 'tough' sub-culture (a feature of boys schools not confined to Hackney Downs) and was openly critical of the physical state of the school. Their report noted that 'it is lamentable that the school has been allowed to fall into such a state of disrepair when staff and pupils were expected to have pride in their environment'.

The Early 1990s

Schools in London's poorest boroughs undoubtedly suffered from the break-up of the ILEA and the budget cuts forced on boroughs by the then Conservative Government. Labour-controlled Hackney was not in a good position to respond to cuts, being one of London's most politically turbulent authorities, with factions often vociferously opposed to each other and accusations of corruption in various services surfacing at times. HMI made a final visit to eight Hackney Schools and concluded that four, including Hackney Downs, were giving cause for concern. In response to HMI, Hackney drew up an action plan which promised the school extensive building improvements, staff stability and a 'secure and structured learning environment'. None of these were delivered. The newly appointed head attempted to obtain the promised resources for minor works, including the science labs, which a visiting teacher had described as 'dirty . . . many walls with peeling paint and rotting plaster . . . a shortage of gas taps and sinks'. A year later the head was still writing to the Director of Education asking for the promised maintenance. Nothing was forthcoming from the authority and the buildings continued to deteriorate until closure. Meanwhile the school continued to take in pupils excluded from other schools; over a third of the 'casual' intake between September 1991 and July 1992 being exclusions or truants from other schools, and also began to be affected by proximity to a local estate which was one of the first sites of domestic crack-cocaine transactions in London.

The head and staff were working hard with little outside help against a rising tide of socio-economic deprivation and taking in the 'problems of other schools'. In 1991 the head obtained a promise of funding from the Prince's Trust for a home-work and reading room, but this offer was then withdrawn with no explanation. A referral room for disruptive boys was set up and well used. The boys referred there had, without exception, deprived backgrounds, difficulties at previous schools and, in some cases, parents who admitted to inability to control their sons. However, there was little external help forthcoming. Hackney LEA had problems with its educational psychology service and its educational social work service.

In early 1991, after a promised report on a January inspection never appeared, irate correspondence between the governors and the Director of Education appeared to be hinting at the possible closure of the school. When this inspectors' report finally appeared it noted the 'neglect and disrepair' of the school's building with no acknowledgment of years of staff complaints about this, and subsequently no funding for buildings, resources or staff was offered to the school. The head began to suspect that the LEA had abandoned Hackney Downs and that this really would affect staff morale. Certainly, in 1993 staff reductions had to be made under LMS and the school lost experienced teachers.

HMI arrived in the school again in October 1992 and made a negative report on the school, noting the 'squalid' environment. The report sparked off more dis-agreements between the school governors and the Director who now suggested that there were three options for the school — closure, merger with a mixed local school, or becoming a mixed school. With nothing settled as regards the future of the school, the head left unexpectedly in December 1992, his job passing without discussion with the school governors or open advertisement, to the deputy head at Homerton House, the school to which the Hackney Downs boys were precipitously pushed in 1995. He was to be supported for two years by a retired head of a successful school in a neighbouring borough, and by two deputies. The new head found difficulty in managing the school — 'casual' entries of boys with disruptive behaviour being a particular problem — and he only stayed one year in post, leaving in December 1993. The consultant head, who battled unsuccessfully for improvements, stayed a further half year. She considered, for example, that the standard of free school meals supplied by the authority was the worst she had seen in 40 years' teaching, and in a borough that prided itself on multicultural achievements, took no account of dietary religious requirements. The head was replaced in January 1994 by one of the deputies, the appointment again being made without governor input. He stayed only two weeks in post, before going on sick leave, to be replaced as acting head, by Betty Hales, the other deputy.

1993–94

In 1993 Hackney LEA began a review of its secondary school provision and in May the Education Committee recommended that Hackney Downs should become a co-educational school and that the Year 7 intake should be 'frozen' in 1994 while refurbishments took place. The Secretary of State for Education rejected this proposal a year later, but the Year 7 intake was frozen, and the school role dropped, while the authority decided to keep the staff complement of 24. One of the most bizarre results of this decision was that in 1995 the Education Association accused the school of operating with an expensive high staff–pupil ratio and politicians of both major parties began to quote Hackney Downs as an example of schools which could not be improved by 'throwing money' at them.

By 1994 some 60 per cent of the pupils had been identified as having special educational needs and the National Union of Teachers was worried by the lack of specialist staff and permanent posts in the school. Betty Hales had agreed to take over as acting head on certain conditions — one of which was the appointment of permanent staff, a situation never rectified. By May 1994, when an OFSTED inspection of the school took place, two-thirds of the staff, including the whole of the senior management team and four departmental heads, were holding acting appointments. Despite all the difficulties, parental and community support for the school grew in 1994 and Betty Hales began to feel that there was a chance for the school to improve and develop. However, this feeling did not last long as the LEA did not provide the necessary support for the school or for her, as a new (acting) head. The consultant head, who had been an initial help, had her contract ended prematurely, and the OFSTED inspectors report, published in August 1994, although sympathetic to problems beyond the control of the school, was generally critical. The school was to be put under the 'special measures' laid down by the 1993 Education Act. The inspectors made 10 proposals for action by the LEA, governors and staff, including action on special needs, bilingual pupil support, health and safety and building refurbishment matters. They were scathing about the conditions of the school buildings. The school's only Conservative Party governor wrote to thank Betty Hales and her staff for the hard work they had put in over the year telling her that, 'What you and your staff have had to put up with has béen amazing and I have nothing but admiration for the way in which you have all managed to come through'. Meanwhile, the authority decided to advertise the headship, received 12 applications and drew up a short-list of 2 — Hales being 1 — for interview. The LEA then decided that Headship interviews could only go ahead with three interviews and no permanent appointment was made! Betty Hales was left in post to prepare an action plan in response to the OFSTED report, and to argue the detrimental effects on the school of a frozen Year 7 intake. Unreality appeared to take over the LEA at this point. It produced an action plan as required by authorities with schools under special measures, that would have cost over £2 million to implement, and simultaneously announced consultation on the possible closure of the school.

1995

Relations between the Director of Education, the school governors and the acting head were strained over the winter of 1994–95. The education committee confirmed the closure proposal in October 1994 and the aim then appeared to get the statutory closure consultation procedure over and prevent this school from organizing a campaign to save itself. However, a campaign was organized with petitions, a parental letter and a TV programme. One sympathetic journalist commented that 'A modern ritual of education politics appears to be in motion. From tabloid decryings to damning inspection report to shut-down, with the school sliding along rails to its end, greased by conservative education reforms. But there is an air of defiance and resentment against the Council, teachers say it's been neglecting Hackney Downs for years . . . and now wants to look tough by closing it down' (Beckett, 1994).

In March 1995, despite a stormy consultation process and a positive HMI report on the school progress the Education Committee ratified its decision to close the school, the boys were to be transferred to Homerton House in September 1995 and parents with children at feeder primary schools were immediately directed to send their sons elsewhere. In April 1995 the chair of governors wrote to the DfE complaining that the LEA had not met its commitment to treat Hackney Downs as a fully functioning school during the closure consultation period. In particular he noted lack of action on refurbishment, health and safety issues, removal of delegated powers, lack of support for the governors, and the denial of new pupil entries, the refusal to appoint a substantive head, the lack of advisory support and educational psychology support despite the high number of boys with special needs. In a response to the DfE, the Director claimed that improvements in the school had been due to a high level of LEA support, and that the school was no more disadvantaged than other Hackney schools. The Director also, with his deputy, visited the school in April 1995 to tell pupils in an assembly that they would receive 'better teaching' at Homerton House School.

In May 1995, Labour Councillors began to have doubts about the school closure and refused to endorse the closure procedures. On 8 June the Education Committee refused to ratify the closure decision or the Director's report to the DfE. On 28 June, the full Council rejected the closure proposals and informed the DfE. On 4 July the DfE replied that the Secretary of State's consideration of closure proposals had been terminated and she had no further interest in the school. Despite all this the LEA had obviously not given up. At a consultative meeting of heads, Betty Hales heard an official tell other heads that the survival of Hackney Downs would have a damaging effect on other schools in the borough.

On 13 July Betty Hales and the staff were astonished to learn via a fax from the press that the Secretary of State was 'minded' to set up an Education Association to take over the running of Hackney Downs from the LEA. What happened between 4 and 13 July to change her mind will probably never be known — although two DfEE officials who were in the school on 14 July let slip that they believed LEA officials had visited the DfEE after the Council vote which allowed the school to remain open. Many of the school's supporters began to believe that 'secret deals' had been done between central government and unelected education officials.

The Education Association: July–December 1995

On 27 July the school was told that it would come under the control of the North East London Education Association, established by Statutory Instrument under the

1993 Act. An education association, as a DfE White Paper of 1992 has explained, was to take over schools at risk of failure which had not been improved by their governing bodies or the LEA. It was to be in the position of a grant-maintained governing body and 'at the end of its stewardship, the normal expectation is that the school will become grant-maintained' (DfE, 1992, p. 50). Thus Hackney Downs, with evidence that it was now an improving rather than a failing school, and with nearly half of the two-year period allowed for in legislation concerning failing schools still to run, was to be taken over by a central government-appointed body. The school was again pilloried in the press as 'the worst school in Britain'. The editor of *Education* magazine, however, wondered why Hackney Downs school, when it was actually improving, had been selected as a sacrificial lamb out of some 80 'at risk' schools at the time.

The membership of the Education Association (EA) appeared to guarantee to deliver the decisions required by the government and the local education officials and to ignore the views of the elected local council, parents, pupils, teachers, the old boys 'Cloves Club' and many supporters in the local and wider community. The chair was a senior executive of an electronic security services conglomerate. The others were the former chair of Hackney Education Committee; a retired head-teacher of a selective independent school; an accountant; and the retired chief education officer of an Outer London borough.

The EA engaged three independent inspectors to visit the school in September 1995, and after only eight weeks of 'stewardship' sent a report to the Secretary of State on 26 October recommending closure. This was hardly surprising as Michael Barber (the former chair of Hackney Education Committee) had written an article the day after he was appointed to the EA 'New start for pupils sold short by council policies' (Barber, 1995) in which he had criticized the elected Council's decision to keep the school open. The Education Association's report, however, contained some surprising statements. It blamed the school for faulty financial management when its finances had, in fact, been under the control of the Hackney LEA since March 1994, and it suggested that the site could be sold when in fact this could not happen as the land on which it was built had been given by the Worshipful Company of Grocers on the abiding condition that it was to be used for educational purposes. The report also gave the impression that the school had long been functioning in favourable conditions without improvement but omitted to mention clear evidence of improvement not only from OFSTED but from two of the three inspectors appointed by the EA itself. The report also criticized staff 'who have forgotten what is possible in terms of standards in inner city education' — without bothering to point out that the average length of teaching experience of the staff was only three years, following the replacement of experienced, and therefore more expensive, staff in 1993 required as a result of LMS described above (North East London Education Association, 1995).

The school was closed with precipitate haste, the Secretary of State allowing only ten days for 'consultation' after the publication of the EA report. Two pupils and their parents took the decision to the High Court for judicial review on 8 and 12 December 1995, and subsequently to the Court of Appeal on 21 December, but both courts upheld the Secretary of State's decision. It is important to note that despite attempts by the plaintiffs' legal team to place all the facts before the courts, they were only able to review the *mechanisms* by which the Secretary of State made her decision and not the EA report itself or the evidence on which it was based. In his summing up of the Judicial Review, the High Court judge noted that there were no rules of conduct for this or any other Education Assocation and there was, for example, no bar to members publishing articles in the press *while* carrying out their duties and before reaching any decisions.

The boys were transferred to a neighbouring school, Homerton House, stated during the court hearings to be doing better than Hackney Downs although its 1995 examination results were no better and its 1996 results showed no improvement. The total cost of closing Hackney Downs was eventually estimated to be the same as keeping it open and putting it in reasonable repair.

Conclusion

By 1996, Hackney Downs had been superseded in the mythology of the 'worst school in Britain' by the Ridings School in Yorkshire (O'Connor, 1996), a school where staff refused to take in more students with learning and behavioural difficulties. Both schools, and most other schools which acquire the 'failing' label, illustrate the failure of simplistic, politically motivated education policies to get rid of 'bad' schools. It could have been foreseen or at least acknowledged that failing schools cannot, in the 1990s, be divorced from the results of market policies by which some schools now receive more than their fair share of troubled and deprived pupils. Politicians, locally and nationally, cannot continue to compete to be 'tough' on failing schools while ignoring the effects of their own policy and administrative decisions. Explanations as to why some schools suffer from uniquely difficult circumstances in a fierce market environment cannot be dismissed as special pleading. Children's education and teachers' careers cannot continue to be affected, through no fault of their own, by the lack of support illustrated by the Hackney Downs episode.

Between 1989 and 1995, Hackney Downs must have been the most inspected school in the country, yet despite a plethora of action plans, checklists and improvement criteria there was very little actual help with tackling the problems. Top of the 'Effective Schools' checklist is stable headship, yet Hackney Downs had four heads in five years and no permanent head for its final three years. Effective schools have experienced staff, yet during the final five years Hackney Downs had mainly young, inexperienced, or temporary staff. But most importantly, effective schools presumably have supportive LEAs whereas Hackney Downs appears to have been treated with a special kind of ineptitude by its LEA. Relations between schools and LEAs need clarification and a recent white paper produced by the new Labour Government has gone some way towards this (DfEE, 1997). The case of Hackney Downs offers an example of how *not* to develop a relationship and during its last years the LEA was part of the problem and not part of the solution.

The existence of poor schools which are a result of historical, social, and economic circumstances and political decisions is not unique to the UK. Many countries are attempting to improve school and pupil performance, particularly in deprived and poverty-stricken city areas. As a solution to these problems, none of them seems to have chosen the 'blame and shame' policy which characterizes the treatment of schools in this country in the 1990s, which results in school closure accompanied by public humiliation.

Note

1 The legislation on failing schools and education associations is set out in the Education Act 1993 (Part V, Chapters I and II) and DfE Circular 17/93 *Schools Requiring Special Measures*.

References

BALL, S.J., BOWE, R. and GEWITZ, S. (1996) 'School choice, social class and distinction: The realisation of social advantage in education', *Journal of Education Policy*, **11**, 1, pp. 89–112.

BARBER, M. (1995) 'New start for pupils sold short by Council policies', *The Independent*, 28 July.

BARBER, M. (1996) *The Learning Game*, London: Gollancz.

BECKETT, A. (1994) 'Scenes from the classroom war', *Independent on Sunday*, 27 November, pp. 48–50.

BERNSTEIN, B. (1970) 'Education cannot compensate for society', *New Society*, 26 February, p. 344.

BLAIR, T. (1996) 'Twentieth Anniversary Lecture', Ruskin College, Oxford, 16 December.

BRACE, A. (1994) 'Is this the worst school in Britain?' *Mail on Sunday*, 20 March.

DfE (1992) *Choice and Diversity: A New Framework for Schools*, London: Department for Education.

DfEE (1997) *Excellence for Everyone*, London: Department for Education and Employment.

GOLDSTEIN, H. (1996) *The Methodology of School Effectiveness Research*, London: Institute of Education.

HOFKINS, D. (1993) 'Branded as Failures', *Times Education Supplement*, 10 December, p. 8.

MACCLEOD, D. (1997) 'Schools "help squad" blitz', *The Guardian*, May.

MORTIMORE, P., SAMMONS, P., STOLL, L., LEWIS, D. and ECOB, R. (1988) *School Matters*, London: Open Books.

NORTH EAST LONDON EDUCATION ASSOCIATION (1995) 'The future of Hackney Downs School: A report to the Secretary of State for Education and Employment.'

O'CONNOR, M. (1996) 'Whose school is it anyway?', *The Independent*, 28 November, pp. 8–9.

O'CONNOR, M., HALES, E., DAVIES, J. and TOMLINSON, S. (1998) *Hackney Downs: The School That Dared to Fight*, London: Falmer Press.

OFSTED (1993) *Access and Achievement in Urban Education*, London: HMSO.

REYNOLDS, D. (1982) 'The search for effective schools', *School Organisation*, **2**, 3, pp. 215–37.

RUTTER, M., MAUGHAN, B., MORTIMORE, P., OUSTEN, J. and SMITH, A. (1979) *Fifteen Thousand Hours*, London: Open Books.

SMITH, D.J. and TOMLINSON, S. (1989) *The School Effect: A Study of Multi-Racial Comprehensives*, London: Policy Studies Institute.

TOMLINSON, M. (1997) 'The Devil is in the detail', *Education Guardian*, 7 January.

Chapter 13

The Utility of Qualitative Research for Influencing Policy and Practice on School Effectiveness

Sheila Riddell, Sally Brown and Jill Duffield

Introduction

A striking feature of research on school effectiveness and improvement is its popularity with policy-makers. Gray, Jesson and Sime (1991) have observed the 'vigour and enthusiasm' exhibited by many LEAs in England and Wales which have recently set up systems for monitoring and evaluating the quality of education on offer. In Scotland, the Scottish Office Education Industry Dept. (SOEID) has devoted a substantial part of its budget (£330,000) to commission research on school effectiveness. It has been suggested that enthusiasm among certain sections of the research community has assumed almost religious proportions. Describing Professor Peter Mortimore, one journalist commented:

> For just a second or two he looked and sounded like an evangelist bringing tidings
> of great joy. His aims were outstretched and his smile was blissful. 'In many ways
> I think our time is rapidly coming' he told his brethren. (Budge, 1994, p. 14)

The appeal of school effectiveness work undoubtedly lies, at least to some extent, in its promise of simple solutions to practical problems. In this chapter, our argument is that school effectiveness and improvement research does indeed have the potential to be useful to policy-makers and practitioners concerned with improving the quality of education. However, unless it is informed by an awareness of both the macro and micro contexts of schools, the research is likely to be intellectually bland and of little practical use. The key element in the macro context which school effectiveness and improvement work frequently ignores is social class. In the micro context, the problem is a neglect of how teachers themselves make sense of the world of the classroom and the importance of that in any strategy to bring about improvement.

We begin by commenting on the treatment of social class and teachers' thinking within school effectiveness and improvement work, and subsequently consider the way in which these occupied a central position within our own study.

The Popularity of School Effectiveness, Improvement and Some Problems with the Paradigm

Within education, as in other spheres of social welfare, policy-makers have a growing concern with making things work more effectively. The most powerful thrust of school effectiveness research has enabled **summative evaluation** of schools' performance to be carried out. Using multi-level modelling, which can control for social class and take children's prior attainment on entry to school as a base-line measure, it is possible to calculate valued-added measures, such that schools which are falling behind others in the task of helping pupils to make progress may be identified. The thinking underlying this strategy in at least some parts of the UK is that once schools have been identified as failing, they will take immediate remedial action, or be faced with the intervention of a 'hit squad'. If the actions of these rough and ready school improvers fail, then, it is suggested, more radical action will be called for and the school could face closure. (The difficulties inherent in such an approach are well illustrated, however, by the case of Hackney Downs School, see previous chapter, where not only did external intervention fail to produce the promised turn around in the school's fortunes, but closure also proved to be a far less straightforward option than anticipated.)

Quite apart from the problem of knowing what to do with ineffective schools once they have been identified, questions have been raised about the reliability of the value-added measures upon which such judgment and action might be based. For example, Lindsay Paterson (1992), has suggested that value-added measures are an unreliable basis on which to make comparisons between schools and that such judgments are likely to produce seriously flawed outcomes. In place of such measures, he suggests that teacher evaluation would represent a more reliable basis on which to judge and compare schools. A central argument of our work is that the use of value-added measures as a means of making comparisons between schools may, by controlling for social class of the school, obscure its role as a key variable in the identification of strategies for school improvement. Angus (1993), in a critical review of school effectiveness work, commented on the exclusion and marginalization of social class from most statistical analysis:

> Family background, social class, any notion of context are typically regarded as 'noise' as 'outside background factors' which must be controlled for and then stripped away so that the researcher can concentrate on the important domain of school factors. (p. 361)

Our argument is that social class has to be retained in other ways as a central element in the analysis if we are to understand the way in which schools operate within their given social contexts.

This concern with how schools operate, however, is largely the domain of the school improvers, whose aim is to work with teachers and schools in identifying their weaknesses and building on their strengths. Recently, school improvers like Louise Stoll (1993) have argued that by drawing on the findings of school effectiveness research, the process of school improvement may be assisted. The aspect of school effectiveness data used in this work is not so much concerned with the ranking of schools in value-added league tables, but rather in identifying process variables which appear to be associated with given outcomes.

In seeking to forge this link with school improvement, school effectiveness studies have identified a number of factors which, if put into practice, would be expected to produce better schools and could be seen as part of the process of **formative evaluation**. Mortimore et al. (1988), for instance, produced a list of 12 key variables:

- purposeful leadership of the staff by the headteacher;
- the involvement of the deputy head;
- the involvement of teachers;
- consistency among teachers;
- structured sessions;
- intellectually challenging teaching;
- work-centred environment;
- limited focus within sessions;
- maximum communication between teachers and pupils;
- record keeping;
- parental involvement;
- positive climate.

Such lists have an immediate appeal in that they hold out the promise of directing schools' attempts at self-improvement. However, as we also argue in this chapter, there is a danger that by focusing on variables which are predetermined by researchers, the salience of teachers' own constructs are ignored. Recognition of the complexity of the classroom context may be inconvenient for those looking for straightforward comparisons among schools, but, as we have suggested above, awareness of this context and the priorities of those working within it are essential in promoting change.

The essence of our argument is that invariably school effectiveness work assumes a top–down management model for education. Although reference is made to what happens in *classrooms*, it is at the *school* level that work always seems to start and often to finish. The effect of this has been to emphasize formal organizational variables with the assumption that matters of teaching, learning, socialization and curriculum will follow. Yet the classroom is where the crucial decision-making occurs and there is increasing evidence (e.g. Fitzgibbon, 1991), especially from studies using new statistical techniques, that the greater part of the variation among pupils' achievements can be accounted for by differences at classroom rather than school level. The recent study at the University of Bath of 'accelerating' subject departments (i.e. those adding significant value to pupil progress measures) concluded that these departments were characterized:

> ... as either working with or neutralising external influences. The schools they worked in were broadly supportive, but this was not a major factor in their success. They were largely successful because of their own efforts. (Harris et al., 1994)

Despite such findings, it is still the school on which the focus is invariably placed.

One purpose of this chapter is to suggest that these matters should be looked at the other way round. If the crux of school effectiveness is the quality of teaching and learning, then it is the classroom to which school improvers have to turn to achieve change. It has been argued elsewhere (Brown and McIntyre, 1993, pp. 15–16) that any serious attempt to innovate in classrooms has to start from where teachers are and how they construe their own teaching, their pupils and what they are trying to achieve. To bring about change it is necessary to mind-read teachers and start from the ways in which they make sense of their classroom world. It is no good *assuming* that the rational school effectiveness models of research and policy are reflected in teachers' thinking.

The Nature of the Present Study

The focus of the study reported here was to identify factors associated with pupil progress in more and less effective schools. Given the strong association between social background and pupils' educational attainment, the schools we selected varied in social class as well as effectiveness. Our primary interest was in *below-average* achieving pupils. There are three points to be made here. First, school improvements using traditional attainment measures are likely to be achieved by raising the performance of the lower achievers. Secondly, the proportion of low achievers is an important characteristic in distinguishing between high and low social class schools. Thirdly, schools with high proportions of low achievers rarely feature among the most effective schools (value-added).

The data used in identifying the sample of schools were gathered by the Centre for Educational Sociology at Edinburgh University. The socio-economic status SES information on the schools was the most recent available for pupils in their fourth year of secondary school (S4, age 16) from the region in which the schools were situated (1987–88). It was based on data about work (separately for mothers and fathers), parental education and household structure. The parents of pupils in the two schools identified as of lower SES had relatively low participation in paid work, their jobs were of relatively low status and they had left school at a relatively early age. In contrast in the two 'high SES' schools, parents had relatively high work participation, were in high status jobs and substantially more stayed on longer at school.

The statistical regression analysis of attainment in the schools was based on data from S4 in session 1990–91. Attainment on entry to secondary school was estimated by the performance in the Edinburgh Reading Test at the end of primary school. Estimates of attainment at S4 were carried out for eight measures: overall Scottish Certificate of Education Ordinary or Standard Grade awards at levels 1 to 3, and the average grade of award within each of seven curricular modes defined by the Scottish Consultative Committee on the Curriculum (science, English, mathematics, languages, social studies, aesthetic studies, and technology).

In comparison with the region as a whole, one each of the 'high SES' and 'low SES' schools had (i) at least three modes on which statistically significant figures suggested the average pupil would have higher attainment if he or she attended that school and (ii) no modes with statistically significant negative figures. The other two schools had no significant positive figures and at least three significantly negative ones. For the rest of this paper, they are referred to as follows:

School A   High SES, higher effectiveness
School B   High SES, lower effectiveness
School C   Low SES, higher effectiveness
School D   Low SES, lower effectiveness

We were particularly interested in the way in which the teachers construed progress and support and the actions they took to achieve their aims. Classroom observation and post-lesson interviews were used to gather data. We also interviewed pupils to gain insight into aspects of pupil culture. In order to develop a picture of school culture at a more general level, we drew upon interviews with members of the senior management team and school policy documents. The interviews with members of the senior management team in the school were semi-structured and included questions on the following: schools' recent history; pupil environment; school goals; school development planning; relationships with parents and pupils; the guidance system and support for pupils with behavioural and learning difficulties; teaching and assessment strategies; impact of recent innovation including the 5–14 programme, publication of league tables, parental choice of school and devolved management.

The Cultures of the Schools

At a general level, our findings suggested that SES distinctions among schools, rather than those of effectiveness, were most striking. While it appeared that the more effective were distinguished from the less effective by the opportunities they gave to their staff and pupils to make decisions influencing their own lives in school, the knowledge needed for improvement of the schools seemed to depend much more on the nature of the pupil and parent populations. The extensive learning difficulties, limited academic motivation and low self esteem of many of the pupils in the low SES schools, suggested that quite different strategies for improvement would be necessary from those in the high SES schools. Different levels of teacher morale and relationships with parents further exacerbated the distinction. The research did, however, have a reflexive dimension in that we were not simply interested in school culture in relation to measures of effectiveness and SES, but also in the way in which the school was evolving within a management and market-oriented climate. In this section, we offer a pen portrait of each of the four schools focusing on the salience of social class as a way of illustrating our general conclusions.

High SES, High Effectiveness (School A)

School A was a large, well-established, high-achieving former senior secondary school which was built in the nineteenth century in a university town. It was secure, therefore, in the privilege it was able to confer on its pupils and the variety of experiences it could offer them so they could fulfil their academic potential. Given its high levels of performance over most of its pupil population, it had the space to turn its attention to personal growth and the development of confidence among its pupils to enable them to cope with whatever they had to face in life.

Teaching time and homework hours were greater than those in the other three schools. The comparisons were particularly marked with the low SES schools where pupils had the equivalent of eight school days less of teaching time per year and about two thirds the hours of homework set by School A. Like the other schools, School A felt itself under pressure from the 5–14 Programme (Scotland's National Curriculum) with the requirement for greater differentiation in the early years of secondary. There was, therefore, a continuing acceptance of setting within subjects (especially mathematics) at this stage. However, this was of some concern in School A, as it was in School B the other high SES school, because it was seen as requiring predictive judgments that might be unrealistic and involve premature labelling of pupils. These views contrasted with those in the low SES schools which saw considerable advantages in setting in terms of improving the performance of the relatively small number of pupils likely to perform well in external examinations.

The content of the curriculum in this school was generally similar to that in the others. However, one interesting divergence was shared with School C, the other high effectiveness (but low SES) school: the opportunity of Latin or a second foreign language was offered to some pupils at the end of the first year in the school. This appeared to be a vestige of the senior secondary tradition which was still apparent in the more academic curriculum offered to higher achieving pupils. No such offer was available in the former junior secondaries which comprised our ineffective schools (B and D).

A striking feature of senior management in all the schools was their view that parents had a profound influence on the schools' culture. School A, like the other high SES school, was aware that most of its parents appreciated academic success and other spheres of the school's activities, were demanding and conscious of their children's rights, would be prepared to exert pressure elsewhere (e.g. with the regional authority) and expected the very best for their children. As such they were extremely supportive but could take up a great deal of staff time in the school and might even interfere with its smooth running. The influence of these middle-class parents was evident in the support for lower achieving pupils in both the high SES schools. Dyslexia (or specific learning difficulties) had a salience in parents' thinking about their children's learning difficulties that had no place in the low SES schools. School A, with the most extensive learning support staff of the four schools, had one half post above normal allocation which was designated to provide support for pupils with specific learning difficulties, although it had fewer pupils with learning difficulties than the other schools.

The pupil culture in School A reflected its high SES status and had clear similarities with School B. Positive attitudes to school, especially in the early years, enthusiasms and appreciation of the efforts made by the staff were apparent. The programme of extra-curricular activities in School A was very extensive and, unlike many schools in Scotland, revived immediately after the long period of teachers' industrial action in 1986. Even for second year pupils (14-year-olds), a council was established by the deputy headteacher and consulted on organizational matters, and several third year pupils acted as prefects, assisting in various ways with the running of the school. Problems, such as they were, seemed to arise mainly from parental pressure and high expectations, although pupils from working-class families might sometimes feel alienated. Low achievers appeared just as committed as high achievers and the interactions between the school and families had the effect of positive reinforcement of shared values.

An important focus of the research was schools' responses to educational changes such as the introduction of development planning, the publication of league tables, marketing of the school and parental choice of school. These are regarded by the government as central to the thrust for improvement in the effectiveness of schools. School A, together with the other high SES school and the other high effectiveness (low SES) school, although not antagonistic to development planning, was conscious of the constraints which might be put on schools' own wider creative ideas by the emphasis on priorities determined externally by the region or SOEID. The style of leadership cultivated by the headteacher, inherited from his predecessor, was described as 'listening', 'consensual' and 'discussion-based'. The reaction to league tables of raw results was, as in the other high SES school, relaxed — high SES ensures good examination results. Value-added measures were also regarded with satisfaction as evidence to counter any suggestion that this privileged school was less successful with lower achieving pupils. None of the other schools said anything in favour of value-added measures. The issue of parental choice had scant significance for School A: its geographical position made it relatively inaccessible from other areas and there were no other secondary schools in the same town to provide competition. Although the school was one of those piloting the region's scheme for devolved school management of resources, there was no sense in which this was construed as some great leap forward with possibilities for increased resources. Indeed, the decision to take part seemed to relate more to the prospect of an enhanced independence rather than to money.

School A had the self-confidence and familiarity with high levels of performance that enabled it to reflect on the wider goals of education and to focus a substantial part of its energies on lower achieving pupils. It did not have to strive as hard as other schools to improve the academic achievements of a large proportion of its pupils; they and their parents were already well motivated, accustomed to longer working hours and ambitious.

High SES, Low Effectiveness (School B)

The high SES status of this school suggested similarities with School A in such matters as parental influence on the school's culture, some aspects of support for low achievers, pupils' attitudes to school, opinions about development planning and reactions to raw results league tables. It also displayed similar attitudes to the other high SES school in its reservations on the value of setting. Indeed, of the four schools it appeared the most committed to mixed ability teaching and individualized learning and least likely to be observed using whole class teaching. It was only the incompatibility of this school's preferred practices with the differentiated Standard Grade (Scottish Certificate of Education) mathematics course at Credit level that resulted in some reorganization within mixed ability classes at the end of the second year to introduce some differential grouping. In almost all these respects it displayed differences from the two low SES schools (C and D), but it was similar to those schools in its increasing emphasis on academic achievement (even at the expense of social and personal goals). It was also closer to Schools C and D than to A in teaching time available and homework hours. Like the other low effectiveness (low SES) school, before comprehensivization its history was as a junior secondary although it opened as a purpose-built comprehensive.

School B had been involved in the region's pilot phase of school development planning, and was further advanced in this activity than the other three. Many committees relating to this had been set up within the school, although some teachers suggested there was sometimes a reluctance on the part of the headteacher to act on staff views and that the committee structure was over-elaborate. Another distinctive feature of School B was its particularly active marketing strategy in direct competition with other schools in the locality. Cultivation of the school's public image, an agenda driven by media concerns, operating the school as a business with the parents as customers, ensuring that school events were reported in local papers and planning to place leaflets advertising the school in banks and building societies were all part of the strategy. Gratification was apparent when preference over other schools, including the private sector, was displayed by parents. Considerable comfort was drawn from the school's relatively good showing on raw results league tables and sympathy was expressed for other local schools where such results looked like 'a disaster'. School B's relatively poor performance in value-added terms, however, seemed to generate little concern; the assumption seemed to have been made that negative value-added measures were unlikely to be understood or criticized by the general public. In contrast, high raw results seemed to be attracting more middle-class parents which, in turn, boosted those raw results. The school was quite clear that to sustain this it should not advertise itself as being good with low achievers, though it was pleased to be regarded as a caring institution.

This high SES but low effectiveness school, therefore, was the most market oriented of our case-study institutions. Its SES associated it in many respects with School A, but it was less assured of its academic standing and so put very great emphasis on academic goals in the light of what it saw as parents' demands. It could be described as the school which, more than our other case studies, had responded to the government's directives for educational innovations. That and its history as a junior secondary were the most obvious contrasts with the two more effective schools (A and C). Whether its market-oriented approach would pay off in improved value-added measures of effectiveness in the future remained to be seen.

Low SES, High Effectiveness (School C)

In common with the other high effectiveness school, School C was a former senior secondary school though in its establishment as a comprehensive it incorporated a nearby junior secondary with a progressive ethos. The school consciously nurtured its roots in the community by, for example, helping parents to organize a successful School Reunion leading to the foundation of a Friends of [School C] Association. Although the school occupied an open site, it was surrounded by local authority housing and the marks of the collapse of heavy industry, and the buildings had many of the disadvantages of early post-second world war construction. Like the two less effective schools, increasing emphasis was being placed on academic achievement, not least because an HMI report had stressed the need for this (whether HMI had access to the relatively high value-added measures we cannot say). Although there was a view in the school that academic awards were a crucial 'passport' for pupils to take on and that this must be the priority, the headteacher showed considerable concern for a greater focus on personal and social development and on dealing with problems like bullying.

Like the other low SES (low effectiveness) school, School C was conscious of the preponderance of low-achieving pupils in mixed ability classes who 'had a dragging' effect on the rest. Setting in mathematics was welcomed as providing opportunities for those who had the potential to achieve academic goals. In these circumstances, the need to target learning support on those with the greatest need was regarded as more important than the thin spread of learning support across mixed ability classes. In both low SES schools parents were less demanding, less supportive, less likely to attend parents' evenings, more inclined to leave decisions to the school and more likely to have values different from the school (e.g. with regard to physical violence) than in the high SES schools. Similar contrasts were apparent in the pupil cultures. The low SES schools' populations had significant numbers of disaffected, academically unmotivated pupils. School C placed considerable emphasis on trying to convince these young people that academic success was in their grasp, rewarding good behaviour, attendance and punctuality, and exploring ways of involving pupils in their own assessments to encourage more constructive thinking and activity. The headteacher bemoaned the demise of extra-curricular activities, particularly school sport, which had not been revived after the 1986 dispute over teachers' pay and conditions. The activities were seen as important in helping pupils develop self-discipline and a commitment to the school; their disappearance had had a negative effect on pupil morale. Such circumstances were also indicative of low teacher morale and the headteacher was well aware of the frustrations associated with working in an institution like School C. In the light of this, he endeavoured to support all teacher-led initiatives, even if they were costly, and urged the staff to seek support from their colleagues.

In considering school development planning the school was concerned, like the high SES schools, that the process was a mechanism for exerting too much external control and stifling the more creative and collegial system that was already operating in the school. Like the other low SES school, there was also anxiety about the unmanageable amount of paperwork and about the damaging effect of raw results league tables. School C saw such tables as essentially destructive with no constructive explanations of why things were the way they were or of action that might be taken to improve things. Despite the school's good showing on value-added measures, these were more or less discounted as incomprehensible to parents and likely to add to the confusion. Nor was there great rejoicing at the extra 200 pupils admitted as a result of parents' placement requests. This addition made little difference to the school's academic profile, and enlarged the school population in ways that have ensured even greater practical problems, especially of space and stress on teachers. Devolved school management was seen as providing opportunities to target extra resources on lower achieving pupils, especially those with learning difficulties, but there was an awareness that this might damage the school's public image in the current climate that puts so much emphasis on the performance of the more able. The fear of the re-emergence of 'fast-track' and 'sink' schools haunted the low SES institutions and made them wary of promoting too enthusiastically their work with lower achieving pupils.

School C's value-added measures identified it as a successful school that was working in difficult circumstances. Its senior secondary history was to its advantage and it might have benefited from an initial upheaval 20 years ago as it was incorporating a progressive junior secondary school. The major task of establishing shared understanding from two different traditions might, in the longer term, have established what seemed to be a reflective and creative tradition of collegial management and opportunities for staff to identify and develop their own priorities, opting into developments of their choice. Part of this tradition had included particular concerns for low achievers who formed a substantial proportion of pupils. More recently, the tradition seemed to be at some risk from central planning developments, concentration on the publication of performance measure and increases in the pupil population brought about by parental choice. As in the other high effectiveness (high SES) school, therefore, we had little evidence that these innovations were likely to have increased the school's effectiveness. Paradoxically, because that effectiveness might depend on the school's creative response to its role in a difficult environment, the innovations might have had a negative influence.

Low SES, Low Effectiveness (School D)

School D, the smallest of the four, served a socially disadvantaged area of villages/small towns with high unemployment and increasing crime and family breakdown. Its raw examination results were very low indeed. Despite admirable policies to fulfil the comprehensive school ideal, and a new, purpose-built and lavish building, the school had difficulties in attracting pupils. It had replaced a number of former junior secondaries and that replacement did not please all of the villages which lost their local schools.

As we have seen, it had many similarities with the other low SES school. It had a preponderance of low achieving pupils, somewhat alienated characteristics among the parent population, low motivation among many pupils, concern that a move away from mixed ability teaching towards setting and individual tuition was probably necessary to support both those with academic potential and those with the greatest problems, a belief that insufficient account was taken of social deprivation factors in the regional allocations of learning support staff and a concern that it should not present itself as a school for the less-able.

This school currently placed very heavy emphasis on academic goals. This was not necessarily of the school's own choosing, given its circumstances, but it was seen as the only performance measure that 'counts'. Within this, however, School D was committed to general improvement in its performance rather than what it saw as currently unattainable targets of excellence. It was frustrated that in a norm-referenced system (whether based on raw results or value-added measures) improvement on the school's own base-line measure of achievement seemed to count for little. Creative developments, such as the removal of barriers between a special needs unit attached to the school and the learning support department in order to provide opportunities for special unit pupils to integrate into mainstream classrooms and curricula (a beneficial spin-off from this allowed children in mainstream access to specialist teachers), got little recognition in a climate that lays so much stress on achievements that are relevant, for the most part, to the more able. Pipe bands and successful dramatic productions were probably of major importance in the achievements of a school of this kind, but were ignored by existing effectiveness measures. School D felt crucified by the local press and frustrated that some parents and associated primary schools continued to prefer to send their children to a neighbouring and former senior secondary (but less well appointed) school. The morale of enthusiastic young teachers recruited when the school opened was seen by some as having been sapped both by its poor academic performance and by the low expectations of older teachers who spent much of their earlier working lives in a junior secondary environment.

The Centrality of Social Class as an Influence on School Culture

Some contrasts between the schools were clearly based on measures of effectiveness. Both the high effectiveness schools were former senior secondaries and both placed considerable emphasis on the involvement of pupils and parents in the running of the school.

The most obvious contrast was their achievement profiles. While for the great majority of pupils in the high SES schools the goals of good certificate examination results seem entirely appropriate, in the low SES schools there is a substantial proportion of pupils for whom other goals would seem to have higher priority and who might well be seen as impeding the progress of the higher achievers. Although in all schools it could be argued that there is a continuum of achievement, in practice the high SES schools were able to take for granted the motivation of the great majority of the pupils and their parents towards awards for academic achievement; the minority for whom this is not the case (or have other reasons for differing from the majority) can then be given special attention. Because learning support staffing is based on the size of school rolls, and middle-class parents can make effective representations for special provision (e.g. for those deemed to be dyslexic), the high SES schools were able to provide effective help for those with learning difficulties. The task for the low SES schools appeared to be quite different. Here there was a tendency to see two populations of pupils; those for whom the pursuit of certificate awards is a priority and those for whom other kinds of goals are seen as having much greater urgency. Because the proportions of pupils with learning difficulties are substantial, and parents are less articulate in their demands for specific resources, learning support tends to be spread much more thinly than in the high SES schools. It seems very likely that the most effective structures and strategies for improving the effectiveness of schools in relation to low achievers would vary quite markedly among schools serving different SES populations.

Complementing the contrast of achievement profile in schools of different SES is one of motivation. A very great deal of effort in low SES schools has to be devoted to improving the morale of teachers, the attitudes of pupils towards learning and the level of involvement of parents in their children's education. High SES schools can to a far greater extent take these matters for granted and can expect an annual boost from the publication of raw certificate results which everyone understands; such results offer little comfort for the low SES schools. High SES schools may, of course, have problems such as excessive demands from parents, but these are *different* problems. While the low SES schools may put a priority on, say, the elimination of bullying and the persuasion of parents that physical violence cannot be condoned as 'standing up for yourself', the high SES schools may be more concerned about 'unreasonable' requests from parents for greater shares of resources for their children.

A third contrast relates to the marketing of schools. For both those serving low SES communities, this is a source of anxiety. A major responsibility which they must accept is to provide support for low achievers, yet they are clear that in the current culture of achievement they cannot advertise themselves as specializing in education for those with learning difficulties. Furthermore, the marketing game is very much one of competition on the basis of raw examination results, and low SES schools have little chance of winning. The school with high value-added effectiveness would welcome recognition of that measure, but it is convinced that the complexity of such information will not be grasped by many parents. In any case, it has no wish to increase the school population which is already of a size that produces considerable stresses and strains. For the other high SES school, with low effectiveness, market-ing appears irrelevant. For the other high SES school, with high effectiveness, it is a major thrust of policy. It could be seen as a satisfactory strategy, based as it is on good raw examination results and leading to more parents choosing to send their children to school. But this diverts attention from the less favourable value-added measures which, not surprisingly, are ignored in the marketing; this school, like the low SES schools, assumes that parents will be unaware of, or fail to understand, such measures.

To summarize, the social class context of the school is crucial in developing an understanding of why things turn out the way they do, and what interventions are likely to promote improvement. In regarding social class as merely a factor to be controlled for (and have rendered invisible) perhaps the key element contributing to a school's level of measured effectiveness is being ignored. Similarly, even when it is possible to identify two schools with broadly similar levels of measured effectiveness, their social context is likely to indicate very different strategies for bringing about improvement. That is the case whether they are identified as being of high or low effectiveness.

Let us now turn to aspects of the micro context of the school, that is, key elements of teachers' understanding and behaviour.

The Teachers' Eye View

The Scottish Office Education and Industry Department (SOEID) in its thinking about school improvement has endorsed the generalized 'five factor' model from school effectiveness research focusing on strong educational leadership, emphasis on basic skills, an orderly and secure environment and frequent assessment of pupil progress (Tibbitt, Spencer and Hutchinson, 1994). Our interest was to start from the classroom end rather than the policy-makers' formulation and to explore what in the teacher's eyes constituted *progress* and how they made sense of the *support* they provided for pupils.

To gain access to teachers' classroom thinking we observed lessons and then interviewed the teacher immediately afterwards. The data from these interviews related, therefore, to actual events observed with real pupils. Our interest was particularly focused on low achieving pupils and how teachers construed the low achiever. The expectation was that this would be more complex than straightforward test scores.

Our findings suggested that the teachers construed differences among pupils, and so low achievers, in terms of **enduring characteristics** and **behaviour on the day** (when discussing a given lesson). These features included ability, attainment, behaviour (e.g. quiet, disruptive), physical state (tired, hearing impaired), relationships with others (peers, teacher), preferences (grumbles, enjoyments), and approach to work (motivation, independence). The rich complexity of these constructs contrasted with the bluntness of the variables in large-scale work. Not unexpectedly we found a similar multi-dimensional picture in teachers' constructs of support.

The classroom support that teachers saw themselves (and were observed by us) as offering the pupils had dimensions that were unsurprising to anyone familiar with classrooms:

- informing
- directing
- explaining
- questioning
- encouraging
- giving feed back
- ensuring safety

- demonstrating
- disciplining
- helping
- monitoring/observing
- eliciting pupils' ideas

In looking at how the teachers thought about **students' progress**, six distinctive aspects emerged:

- Affective: confidence, sociability, responsibility
- Procedural/Organizational: task completion, catching up with other pupils, teacher's procedures
- Tangible Produce: production of homework, drawing, written work
- Cognitive 1: grasp or develop an idea or concept
- Cognitive 2: processes (can do, techniques, strategy)
- Cognitive 3: thinking beyond the lesson or task (e.g. 'thinking mathematically')

There are a number of tentative conclusions that might be drawn from this work. For example, the ways in which teachers conceptualize pupils' progress and the kind of classroom support that is needed to promote that progress, are much more complex and rich than the conceptions of progress and support implicit in school effectiveness research. The latter operationalizes progress very largely in terms of achievement and easily measurable non-cognitive criteria; support variables are for the most part management structures and practices, or broad-brush judgments about, for example, teaching methods. At the very least we have to think more carefully about whether the relatively crude and management-oriented variables can engage with teachers' thinking, and indeed, whether there is enough in common among teachers to be able to see such engagement as a possibility.

A difficulty with many approaches to change is that they are not based on the practitioners' implicit theories about what they are trying to do. Until these theories are taken into account the chances of real understanding of why things turn out the way they do (effective, not effective, improving, deteriorating) are negligible. It might be possible, of course, to change the ways practitioners think to bring them more in line with researchers, but to do that a start would have to be made from where the practitioners are now, not from policy-makers or researchers' ideas about 'what will work'.

Social Class and Teachers' Thinking — Classroom Strategies

Finally, it is worth briefly reporting the classroom outcomes which arose as a result of the wider social context of the school and the way in which teachers made sense of this reality. First, rather surprisingly, in the high SES schools at the end of S2 (age 14) teachers tended to be rather conservative in their assessment of pupils, placing very few pupils in the above average band for English and maths.

Although School D had by far the highest proportion of lower attaining pupils, it was very reluctant to place them in the lowest attainment band. This might well have been because teachers were loathe to suppress pupils' expectations. On the other hand, it might indicate that teachers were unrealistic and imprecise in their assessment of pupil progress, failing to give pupils and their parents an accurate view of the likely outcome of external examinations.

In terms of classroom organization, it was evident that in the high SES schools teachers tended to provide a varied range of activities within a lesson and to engage pupils in interactive work such as group discussion. More passive activities, such as silent reading, were used more extensively in the low SES schools. This might have been as a control device, since teachers in these schools were clearly anxious about pupil behaviour and felt overwhelmed by the number of pupils with learning difficulties. The greater use of interactive work in the higher SES schools might reflect the fact that teachers were able to assume certain levels of pupil motivation and commitment and had better resources available to assist less able pupils. Clearly, teachers' definition of the situation had very real consequences for pupils, since these understandings had effects on classroom practice.

Conclusion

We began this paper by noting the tendency of school effectiveness research to screen out what we consider to be key elements within the macro and micro context of the school and the classroom. At the macro level, social class is reduced to a variable to be controlled for and thereafter ignored, rather than recognized as a vital element in terms of accounting for the level of measured effectiveness and strategies for school improvement. Our discussion of the culture of four secondary schools illustrated the way in which those with similar levels of measured effectiveness, whether high or low, differed markedly in line with their SES. For example, the school with high SES but low effectiveness could count on the motivation of parents and pupils and placed considerable emphasis on the importance of marketing itself. The school with both low effectiveness and low SES suffered in comparison because it could certainly not count on a high degree of commitment from pupils and parents and had few marketable qualities other than its well-resourced and appointed buildings. Such differences indicate that the process of school improvement would have to start from very different points in the two schools.

At the micro level, the concern is with the mismatch between, on the one hand, the ways in which school effectiveness research and policy-makers' thinking have concentrated on management issues and broad generalizations and, on the other hand, the complexity of the ways in which those in the classroom (with the responsibility for effecting improvement) make sense of their work. Unless the former address the question of how classroom practitioners can be persuaded to reflect on and develop their own thinking (a bottom–up approach to balance the extraordinarily powerful top–down tendency), the search for improvements may well be pointless.

There is also an interaction between our two variables of concern: SES and teachers' constructs of teaching and learning. Our findings suggested, for example, that in low SES schools teachers tended to award relatively higher grades to pupils at the end of S2 than were warranted by their likely performance in external examinations. Injunctions to teachers to convey higher expectations to pupils in these circumstances would be unlikely to be helpful. Furthermore, the distinctly more restricted range of classroom activities in low SES schools (largely imposed through the problems associated with low achievement and disruptive behaviour) provides another dimension of differences between classrooms and teachers' thinking about their work.

Recognizing the Implications for Policy-makers

What are the implications for policy-makers such as HMI who seek to provide guidance for schools and teachers on how to improve? It might be tempting to argue that the entire project of identifying overarching factors associated with effectiveness is fundamentally flawed, but this would imply that each school would have to operate as a discrete entity, learning nothing from the experience of others. School self-evaluation may of course be a helpful means of moving schools forward, but there are dangers that bad practice will be reproduced uncritically. A more fruitful approach might be to sustain a commitment to identifying factors characterizing both effective and ineffective schools, but having done this to think more critically about how such knowledge might be interpreted. For example, as we have seen from the data presented earlier, over-optimistic judgments of pupils may result in low SES schools failing to assess accurately how well they are progressing and conveying artificially inflated expectations. Recognizing this as a danger may help low SES schools to avoid this trap. Similarly, the injunction to involve parents as much as possible in their children's education may have different significance for low and high SES schools. Whereas the goal for low SES schools was to get parents over the threshold and accepting rather than undermining the school's value system, for the high SES schools the aim was to place boundaries on the extent of parental involvement in order to avoid the challenging of every decision. In addition, the received wisdom from school effectiveness research that lessons should have a limited focus was called into question by our work. Pupils in the higher SES schools were presented with a wider range of tasks within lessons, since teachers had the confidence that the pupils would be able to cope with more rapid shifts in focus. In the lower SES schools, on the other hand, pupils' attention tended to be focused on a much narrower range of tasks.

Overall, perhaps the message to be conveyed to schools is that, like all research, the findings of school effectiveness and improvement work should not be regarded as representing absolute wisdom, but should always be subjected to critical scrutiny. Policy-makers should ensure that teachers are kept informed of large-scale research findings, but the key question for schools continues to be: Is this research relevant to my particular context, or are the circumstances within this particular school such that a different approach to change is required?

References

ANGUS, L. (1993) 'The sociology of school effectiveness', *British Journal of Sociology of Education*, **14**, 3, pp. 333–45.

BROWN, S. and MCINTYRE, D. (1993) *Making Sense of Teaching*, Buckingham: Open University Press.

BUDGE, D. (1994) 'Evangelism, sin, improving visions and demon drink', *Times Educational Supplement*, 25 March, p. 14.

FITZGIBBON, C.T. (1991) 'Multilevel modelling in an indicator system', in RAUDENBUSH, S.W. and WILLMS, J.D. (eds) *Schools, Classrooms and Pupils: International Studies of Schooling from a Multilevel Perspective*, San Diego: Academic Press.

GRAY, J., JESSON, D. and SIME, N. (1991) 'Developing LEA frameworks for monitoring and evaluation from research on school effectiveness: Problems, progress and possibilities', in RIDDELL, S. and BROWN, S. (eds) *School Effectiveness Research: Its Messages for School Improvement*, Edinburgh: HMSO.

MORTIMORE, P., SAMMONS, P., ECOB, R. and STOLL, L. (1988) *School Matters: The Junior Years*, Salisbury: Open Books.

PATERSON, L. (1992) 'Socio-economic status and educational attainment: a multi-dimensional and multi-level study', *Evaluation and Research in Education*, pp. 97–121.

STOLL, L. (1993) 'Linking school effectiveness and school improvement: Issues and possibilities', Paper presented to the ESRC Seminar on School Effectiveness and School Improvement, October 1993, Sheffield University.

TIBBITT, J.D., SPENCER, E. and HUTCHINSON, C. (1994) 'Improving school effectiveness: Policy and research in Scotland', *Scottish Educational Review*, **26**, 2, pp. 151–7.

Notes on Contributors

Stephen J. Ball is Professor of Sociology of Education and Director of the Centre for Public Policy Research at King's College London. He is the editor of the *Journal of Education Policy* and the author of several books on education policy, including *Politics and Policy Making in Education* (1990), *Education Reform* (1994) and, with Sharon Gerwitz and Richard Bowe, *Markets, Choice and Equity in Education* (1995). He is currently researching choice of Post-16 and Higher Education and the consumption behaviours of young children.

Margaret Brown is Professor of Mathematics Education. She has directed or co-directed 18 research projects in the area of the learning and assessment of mathematics across the 5–16 age group, including wide-scale surveys and small-scale case studies. She has assisted with both the development and evaluation of the national curriculum and national assessment. More recently she has been a member of the National Numeracy Task Force.

Sally Brown is Professor of Education and Deputy Principal of Stirling University. She was formerly Director of the Scottish Council for Research in Education. She has researched and written extensively in a number of areas including science education, assessment and special educational needs.

Jill Duffield is Research Fellow in the Department of Education, Stirling University. She has worked as a researcher on a range of projects including an evaluation of modern languages teaching in primary schools, policy and provision for children with specific learning difficulties and factors associated with school effectiveness. She has published in the areas of special educational needs and school effectiveness.

Gerald Grace has been Director of the Centre for Research and Development in Catholic Education since 1996 and a Professorial Research Fellow at the Institute of Education, University of London. His research interests include the nature of school leadership in England, with special reference to the changing position of the headteacher and of school governors. He also has a research interest in urban education, catholic education, and in the changing work conditions of teachers. His many publications include *School Leadership: Beyond Education Management* and *Teacher Supply and Teacher Quality: Issues for the 1990s*.

David Hamilton is Professor of Education at Umeå University, Sweden. Sensitivity towards recent school effectiveness research — as expressed in his chapter — arose from growing feelings of scepticism towards its irrationality. Worried by this trend in educational research, he plans to write a book on research as a rhetorical process rather than a search for truth.

Ian Hextall is a Senior Research Fellow at Roehampton Institute, London. He has written and researched in the area of education policy over a number of years, concentrating latterly on teacher education.

Ian Jamieson is currently Professor of Education and Dean of the Faculty of Humanities and Social Sciences at the University of Bath. He is the founder and editor of the *Journal of Education and Work* and a Fellow of the Royal Society of Arts. His major book publications include: *School Effectiveness and School Improvement* (1996); *Rethinking Work Experience* (1991); *Capitalism and Culture* (1990); *Mirrors of Work* (1988); and *Schools and Industry* (1982). He has contributed to numerous journals in the fields of education, management and sociology.

James G. Ladwig is a Senior Lecturer in the Faculty of Education at the University of Newcastle where he teaches in the areas of sociology of education, philosophy of education and educational policy. He is author of *Academic Distinctions* (1996) and his most recent research focuses on the sociology of school knowledge, reproduction of educational inequality and world systems. With Bob Lingard and Allan Luke he is conducting a three year longitudinal study of the restructuring of the Queensland public school system.

Hugh Lauder is Professor of Education and Director of the Centre for School Improvement at the University of Bath. His research interests are in the political economy of education. He is completing a book with David Hughes and the Smithfield team on the nature of educational markets, *Trading in Futures: Why Markets in Education don't Work*, to be published by the Open University Press and a book with Phil Brown entitled *The Paradox of Progress*. His recent publications include: *Education, Culture, Economy and Society* (1997, with A.H. Halsey, A. Stuart Wells and P. Brown) and 'Education, Globalisation and Economic Development' (1996, with P. Brown).

Bob Lingard is a Reader in the Graduate School of Education at The University of Queensland where he teaches and researches educational policy and the sociology of education. He is currently undertaking a three year Australian Research Council study of the OECD and the globalization of education policy production. His most recent book is *Education Policy and the Politics of Change* (with S. Taylor, F. Rizvi and M. Henry).

Allan Luke is Professor and Head of the Graduate School of Education at The University of Queensland where he teaches language and literacy education, sociology and discourse analysis. He is currently undertaking a three year Australian Research Council study (with C. Luke) of Asian/Australian inter-ethnic families. His most recent book is *Constructing Critical Literacies* (with P. Freebody and S. Muspratt).

Pat Mahony is Professor of Education at Roehampton Institute, London. She has worked for many years in the areas of social justice and teacher education and has published widely in these areas.

Joe Rea has taught in inner city schools throughout his career, spending fourteen years as Headteacher in four different schools. Under his headship, his most recent school gained a commendable OFSTED report and has consistently produced higher than average SATs results for its location.

Sheila Riddell is Professor of Social Policy (Disability Studies) at Glasgow University. Formerly, she worked as Research Fellow in the Department of Education, University of Edinburgh, on a project investigating the impact of the 1981 Education (Scotland) Act on children with special educational needs. From 1989 to 1996 she taught and researched at Stirling University and was promoted to a Personal Chair in 1995. In 1996–97 she was Dean of Arts and Social Science at Napier University, Edinburgh. She has researched and written extensively in the areas of special educational needs/disability and gender and education.

Roger Slee is Professor of Teaching and Learning and Dean of the Faculty of Education at the University of Western Australia. He is the founding editor of the *International Journal of Inclusive Education*.

Bob Spooner has been an active member of the Labour Party since 1946. He campaigned for comprehensive secondary education in the early fifties, was Chair of Governors of a pioneer comprehensive school, Churchfields in West Bromwich, and was for five years the Chair of an Education Committee and Leader of a Labour Group. He has been a governor of primary, secondary and special schools, FE colleges, a polytechnic and a university. He has long been a member of the Socialist Education Association. As a freelance education journalist he has contributed over 200 articles to various educational journals and over 60 book reviews. He has published six books on education, four satires, three novels and a book of short stories.

Sally Tomlinson is Professor of Educational Policy and Management at Goldsmiths College, University of London. She has written and researched extensively in the areas of educational policy, school effectiveness, the education of ethnic minorities and special education. Recent books include *Ethnic Relations and Schooling: Policy and Practice in the 1990s* (1995, with M. Craft) and *Education 14–19: Critical Perspectives* (1997). Soon to come is *Hackney Downs: The School that Dared to Fight* (forthcoming, with M. O'Connor, B. Hales and J. Davies).

Gaby Weiner is Professor of Educational Research at South Bank University, London. Involved with social justice issues since the 1970s, she has published widely on a range of topics, in particular relating to equal opportunities and gender. She also is involved in research on the processes of academic writing and publication.

Felicity Wikeley was until recently a Research Fellow in the Centre for School Improvement, University of Bath and is currently an Associate Director of the International School Effectiveness and Improvement Centre at the Institute of Education, University of London. She has researched and worked with schools on a variety of school effectiveness issues and has published in the areas of parental involvement with schools, teacher appraisal and school improvement.

Index